PHILIP'S

GU

FLAGS

OF THE WORLD

COMMISSIONING EDITOR Christian Humphries

EDITOR Jo Potts

EXECUTIVE ART EDITOR Mike Brown

DESIGNER Alison Todd

PRODUCTION Sally Banner

First published in 2003 by Philip's,
a division of Octopus Publishing Group,
2–4 Heron Quays, London E14 4JP

Copyright © 2003 Philip's

ISBN 0–540–08375–5

A CIP catalogue record for this book is available
from the British Library.

Printed in China

Details of other Philip's titles and services can be
found on our website at:
www.philips-maps.co.uk

All national flags copyright
The Flag Institute

All sub-national flags and flags of
international organizations copyright
Raymond Turvey

Signal flags copyright Philip's

All mapping copyright Philip's

All stamps supplied by Stanley Gibbons

CONTENTS

WORLD FLAGS *ANATOMY*

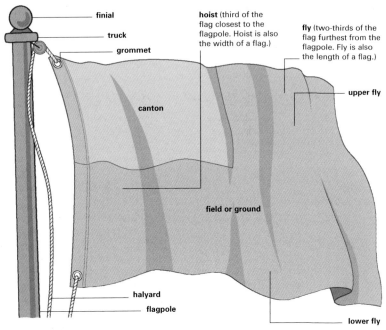

finial

truck

grommet

hoist (third of the flag closest to the flagpole. Hoist is also the width of a flag.)

fly (two-thirds of the flag furthest from the flagpole. Fly is also the length of a flag.)

upper fly

canton

field or ground

halyard

flagpole

lower fly

Proportion of flag (width:length)

National = flag of a country / Civil = public flag / State = government flag

FLAG RATIO: 1:2 **USE:** National/Civil **DATE ADOPTED:** 1992 **LAST MODIFIED:** 1992

Official year of flag's adoption

Year of last modification to existing flag design

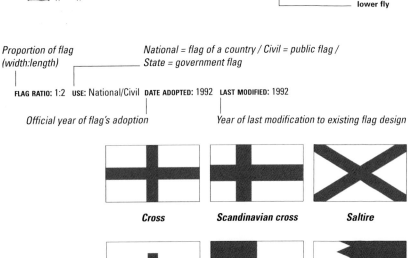

Cross

Scandinavian cross

Saltire

Crouped or Greek cross

Canton

Serration

Triangle

Triband (or tricolour if three colours used)

Bicolour

Fimbriation

A BRIEF HISTORY OF FLAGS

The ancient kingdoms of **Egypt** and **Assyria** had metal staffs topped with sacred symbols. The ancient **Romans** carried *vexilloids* – staffs ornamented with discs, surmounted (from 100 BC) by an eagle. Ancient **China** probably flew the first cloth flags. It is said that Wen the Martial, founder of the Zhou dynasty (1030 BC–221 BC), carried a white flag before him. Early flags were emblems of leadership in battle, serving as rallying points and distinguishing friend from foe.

Flags are frequently mentioned in the early history of **Islam**. With the religious stricture on the representation of nature, Islamic flags usually had a monotone field. According to tradition, Muhammad's banner was black. In AD 661, the Khawarij adopted a red flag of revolt against the Caliph Ali. The Umayyad dynasty (661–750) from Damascus adopted a plain white flag, while the Abbasid dynasty (750–1258) from Baghdad reverted to the black flag. Green was the colour of the Fatimid dynasty from Morocco, and became the colour of Islam. In the 20th century, red, white, black and green became **Pan-Arab** colours and many Arab nations use them in national flags.

In the 12th century, **Crusaders** from Europe adopted the **cross** as an emblem of Christendom united in battle against Islam in the Holy Land. Upon their return from the Middle East, many leaders of European 'nations' adopted a flag with their country's patron saint. England, for example, flew the cross of Saint George in the 13th century. After the advent of **heraldry** in Europe in the 12th and 13th centuries, European royalty created coats of arms that soon became the basis of

their flags. The flags of modern European nations such as Spain and Luxembourg recall the colours of these medieval coats of arms. According to heraldic tradition, European flag usage normally discourages the juxtaposition of yellow and white ('metals'), and of colour and colour without yellow or white interposed. As the cross became a common symbol of Christian nations, the **crescent** emerged as a popular motif for Muslim countries after Ottoman Turkey adopted it around 1250.

Prince William of Orange, leader of the Revolt of the Netherlands (1567–79) against Spain, adopted a **tricolour** flag. This *Prinsenvlag* became an emblem of liberty. This association strengthened when the French *tricolore* emerged during the French Revolution of 1789, and other nations have since chosen the tricolour flag as a symbol of liberty.

The **South American** nations of Colombia, Ecuador and Venezuela have a yellow, blue and red tricolour, reflecting their common history as part of Greater Colombia. Likewise, Argentina, El Salvador, Honduras, Nicaragua and Uruguay retain the blue-white-blue flag of the **Central American Federation**.

The flags of **Asian** nations are remarkably diverse. One general pattern is the use of a circle against a monotone or bicolour field (Bangladesh, India, Japan, Kakazstan, Kyrgyzstan, Laos, South Korea). Many **African** nations' flags use the red, gold and green of the **Pan-African** movement.

Many national flags reflect former colonial ties. The red, white, and blue of the United States' 'Stars and Stripes' recalls its links with Britain, as do the flags of Australia, New Zealand, Fiji, and Tuvalu.

WORLD FLAGS *STYLES*

CROSS

 Dominica Dominican Republic United Kingdom Switzerland

CROSS
SALTIRE

 Burundi Jamaica

CROSS
SCANDINAVIAN

 Denmark Finland Iceland Norway

 Sweden

TRIANGLE AT HOIST

 East Timor Bahamas Comoros Cuba

 Czech Republic Djibouti Equatorial Guinea Eritrea

 Guyana Jordan Mozambique Philippines

 São Tomé & Príncipe South Africa Sudan Vanuatu

 Zimbabwe

SERRATION

 Bahrain Qatar

6

VERTICAL STRIPE AT HOIST WITH HORIZONTAL STRIPES

Benin

Guinea-Bissau

Madagascar

Oman

United Arab Emirates

CENTRAL DIAGONAL STRIPE(S)

Congo

Brunei

Lesotho

Namibia

Solomon Islands

St Kitts & Nevis

Tanzania

Trinidad & Tobago

SINGLE-COLOUR FIELD *WITH OR WITHOUT DEVICE*

Albania

Brazil

Congo (Dem. Rep.)

Cyprus

Kazakstan

Kyrgyzstan

Libya

Maldives

Mauritania

Micronesia

Morocco

Saudi Arabia

Somalia

St Lucia

Tunisia

Turkey

Turkmenistan

Vietnam

Zambia

TWO STRIPES VERTICAL
HOIST STRIPE GREEN

Algeria

Portugal

TWO STRIPES VERTICAL
HOIST STRIPE YELLOW

Vatican City

7

WORLD FLAGS *STYLES*

TWO STRIPES VERTICAL
HOIST STRIPE WHITE

Malta

Pakistan

TWO STRIPES HORIZONTAL
TOP STRIPE RED

Angola

Belarus

Burkina Faso

Indonesia

Monaco

Singapore

TWO STRIPES HORIZONTAL
TOP STRIPE BLUE

Haiti

Liechtenstein

Ukraine

TWO STRIPES HORIZONTAL
TOP STRIPE WHITE

Poland

San Marino

THREE STRIPES VERTICAL
HOIST STRIPE RED

Canada

Guinea

Mongolia

Peru

THREE STRIPES VERTICAL
HOIST STRIPE ORANGE

Ivory Coast

THREE STRIPES VERTICAL
HOIST STRIPE GREEN

Cameroon

Ireland

Italy

Mali

Mexico

Nigeria

Senegal

THREE STRIPES VERTICAL
HOIST STRIPE BLUE

Andorra

Barbados

Chad

France

Guatemala

Moldova

Romania

St Vincent

**THREE STRIPES
VERTICAL**
HOIST STRIPE BLACK

Afghanistan

Belgium

**THREE STRIPES
HORIZONTAL**
TOP STRIPE RED

Armenia

Austria

Belize

Bolivia

Croatia

Egypt

Ghana

Hungary

Iraq

Laos

Latvia

Lebanon

Luxembourg

Netherlands

Paraguay

Spain

Syria

Tajikistan

Yemen

**THREE STRIPES
HORIZONTAL**
TOP STRIPE ORANGE

India

Niger

**THREE STRIPES
HORIZONTAL**
TOP STRIPE YELLOW

Colombia

Ecuador

Lithuania

Venezuela

WORLD FLAGS *STYLES*

THREE STRIPES HORIZONTAL
TOP STRIPE GREEN

| Ethiopia | Gabon | Iran | Sierra Leone |

THREE STRIPES HORIZONTAL
TOP STRIPE BLUE

| Argentina | Azerbaijan | Cambodia | El Salvador |

| Estonia | Honduras | Nauru | Nicaragua |

| Rwanda | Uzbekistan | Yugoslavia |

THREE STRIPES HORIZONTAL
TOP STRIPE BLACK

| Germany | Malawi |

THREE STRIPES HORIZONTAL
TOP STRIPE WHITE

| Bulgaria | Russia | Slovak Republic | Slovenia |

MORE THAN THREE HORIZONTAL STRIPES
WITH CANTON

| Central African Rep. | Greece | Liberia | Malaysia |

| United States | Uruguay |

MORE THAN THREE HORIZONTAL STRIPES
WITHOUT CANTON

| Botswana | Cape Verde | Costa Rica | Gambia |

| Israel | Kenya | Korea, North | Mauritius |

Suriname

Swaziland

Thailand

Uganda

CANTON
UNION JACK

Australia

Fiji

New Zealand

Tuvalu

CANTON
WITH SINGLE COLOUR FIELD

Burma (Myanmar)

China

Georgia

Samoa

Taiwan

Tonga

CANTON
WITH BICOLOUR FIELD

Chile

Togo

CENTRAL DISC *WITH SINGLE COLOUR FIELD*

Bangladesh

Japan

Palau

Korea, South

UNUSUAL

Antigua & Barbuda

Bhutan

Bosnia-Herzegovina

Grenada

Kiribati

Kuwait

Macedonia (FYROM)

Marshall Islands

Nepal

Panama

Papua New Guinea

Seychelles

Sri Lanka

11

WORLD FLAGS *MAPPING*

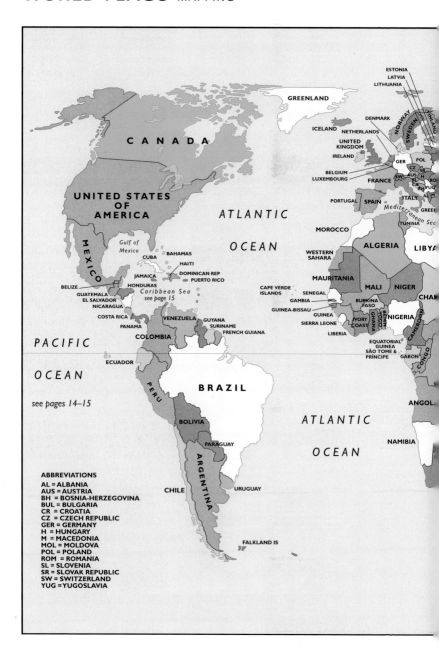

ABBREVIATIONS
AL = ALBANIA
AUS = AUSTRIA
BH = BOSNIA-HERZEGOVINA
BUL = BULGARIA
CR = CROATIA
CZ = CZECH REPUBLIC
GER = GERMANY
H = HUNGARY
M = MACEDONIA
MOL = MOLDOVA
POL = POLAND
ROM = ROMANIA
SL = SLOVENIA
SR = SLOVAK REPUBLIC
SW = SWITZERLAND
YUG = YUGOSLAVIA

see page 15

see pages 14–15

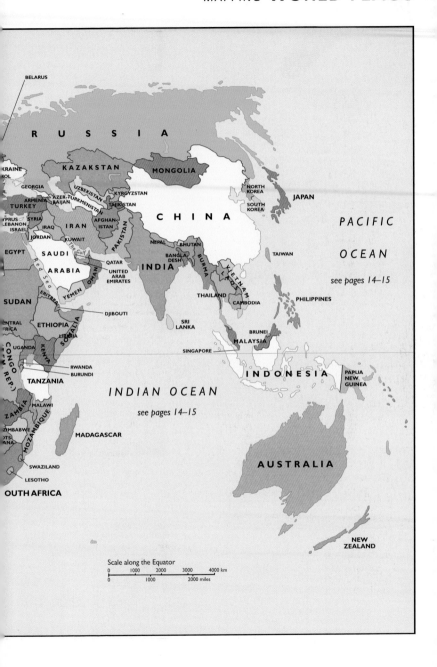

BELARUS

R U S S I A

KRAINE
VOL
GEORGIA
KAZAKSTAN
MONGOLIA
UZBEKISTAN
KYRGYZSTAN
ARMENIA AZER- TURKMENISTAN
TURKEY BAIJAN TAJIKISTAN
YPRUS SYRIA AFGHAN-
LEBANON IRAQ IRAN ISTAN
ISRAEL JORDAN PAKISTAN
EGYPT KUWAIT
SAUDI QATAR
Red Sea ARABIA OMAN UNITED
ARAB
EMIRATES
SUDAN ERITREA YEMEN
ENTRAL
RICA DJIBOUTI
ETHIOPIA SOMALIA
LIBERIA
CONGO UGANDA KENYA
M REP.) RWANDA
BURUNDI
TANZANIA
ZAMBIA MALAWI
ZIMBABWE MOZAMBIQUE
TS
ANA SWAZILAND
LESOTHO
OUTH AFRICA

NORTH
KOREA JAPAN
SOUTH
KOREA

C H I N A

NEPAL BHUTAN
BANGLA-
DESH BURMA
INDIA LAOS
VIETNAM
THAILAND
CAMBODIA
SRI
LANKA
BRUNEI
MALAYSIA
SINGAPORE

TAIWAN

PHILIPPINES

PACIFIC

OCEAN

see pages 14–15

I N D O N E S I A

PAPUA
NEW
GUINEA

INDIAN OCEAN

see pages 14–15

MADAGASCAR

AUSTRALIA

NEW
ZEALAND

Scale along the Equator
0   1000   2000   3000   4000 km
0   1000   2000 miles

13

WORLD FLAGS *MAPPING*

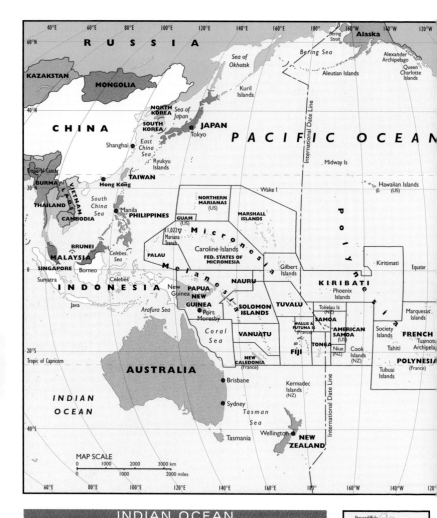

R U S S I A **Alaska**
Bering Strait

KAZAKSTAN MONGOLIA

Sea of Okhotsk *Bering Sea* Alexander Archipelago

Aleutian Islands Queen Charlotte Islands

NORTH KOREA *Sea of Japan*

C H I N A SOUTH KOREA **JAPAN**

Shanghai *East China Sea* Tokyo P A C I F I C   O C E A N

Ryukyu Islands Midway Is

Tropic of Cancer Wake I

BURMA **TAIWAN** Hawaiian Islands (US)

THAILAND VIETNAM Hong Kong

CAMBODIA *South China Sea* Manila NORTHERN MARIANAS (US) **P**

BRUNEI **PHILIPPINES** GUAM (US) MARSHALL ISLANDS **o**

MALAYSIA *11,022* Mariana Trench M i c r o n e s i a **l**

SINGAPORE *Celebes Sea* PALAU **y**

Borneo Caroline Islands Gilbert Islands KIRIBATI Kiritimati Equator

Sumatra I N D O N E S I A New Guinea FED. STATES OF MICRONESIA **n**

Java PAPUA NEW GUINEA NAURU Phoenix Islands **e**

Arafura Sea Port Moresby SOLOMON ISLANDS TUVALU Tokelau Is (NZ) Marquesas Islands **s**

Coral Sea VANUATU SAMOA AMERICAN SAMOA (US) Society Islands **FRENCH** **i**

WALLIS & FUTUNA Is (France) Tahiti Tuamotu Archipela **a**

FIJI TONGA Niue (NZ) Cook Islands (NZ) **POLYNESIA** (France)

Tropic of Capricorn NEW CALEDONIA (France)

AUSTRALIA Brisbane Kermadec Islands (NZ) Tubuai Islands

INDIAN OCEAN Sydney

Tasman Sea Wellington **NEW ZEALAND**

Tasmania

MAP SCALE
0 1000 2000 3000 km
0 1000 2000 miles

INDIAN OCEAN

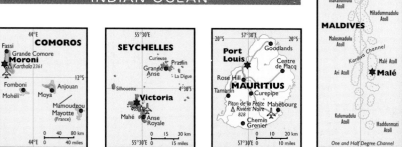

44°E **COMOROS**
Fassi
Grande Comore
Moroni
△ Karthala 2361
Fomboni Anjouan
Mohéli Moya
Mamoudzou
Mayotte (France)
0 40 80 km
44°E 0 40 miles

55°30'E
SEYCHELLES
Curieuse
Grande Praslin
Anse La Digue
Silhouette 4°30'S
Victoria
Mahé Anse Royale
0 15 30 km
55°30'E 0 15 miles

20°S 57°30'E 20°S
Port Louis Goodlands
Centre de Flacq
Rose Hill **MAURITIUS**
Tamarin Curepipe
Piton de la Petite Mahébourg
△ Rivière Noire
828 Chemin
Grenier
0 10 20 km
57°30'E 0 10 miles

Ihavandiffulu Atoll
MALDIVES Miladummadulu Atoll
Malosmadulu Atoll
Ari Atoll Malé Atoll
Malé
Kolumadulu Atoll
Haddunmati Atoll
One and Half Degree Channel

14

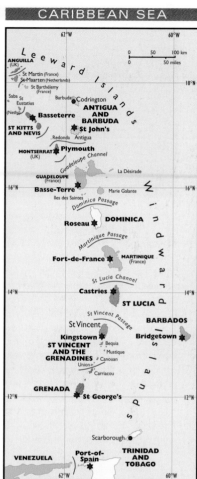

AFGHANISTAN

FLAG RATIO: 1:2 **USE:** National **DATE ADOPTED:** 1992 **LAST MODIFIED:** 1992

The **tricolour** of **black**, **red** and **green** **vertical stripes** returned as the flag of Afghanistan after the defeat of the Taliban regime in 2001. First adopted in 1992, the flag uses the colours of the *Mujaheddin* ('holy warriors') who fought against the Marxist regime and Soviet forces in the Afghanistan War (1979–89). Green represents **Islam**, **red** stands for the blood shed in war, and **black** denotes the country's dark past. The **coat of arms** consists of a **mosque** and a wreath of **wheat ears**. The wheat recalls the crowning of Afghan monarchs with wreaths of wheat. Above the coat of arms is the *shahada*, the declaration of Muslim faith, and '*Allah-u Aqbar*' ('God is Great').

AREA: 652,090sq km (251,773sq mi)
POPULATION: 24,405,000
CAPITAL (POPULATION): Kabul (2,454,000)
GOVERNMENT: Interim administration
ETHNIC GROUPS: Pashtun (Pashtu) 52%, Tajik 20%, Uzbek 9%, Hazara 9%, Chahar 3%, Turkmen 2%, Baluchi 1%
LANGUAGES: Pashtu, Dari (Persian) both official
RELIGIONS: Sunni Muslim 85%, Shi'a Muslim 15%
NATIONAL ANTHEM (DATE):
"*Sououd-e-melli*" (1978)

HISTORY

Buddhism arrived in the 2nd century BC, while Arab armies brought **Islam** in the 7th century. **Shah Nadir** extended Persian rule to most of Afghanistan. His successor, **Ahmad Durrani** established the first unified state in 1747. **Britain** fought three wars for control of the region. In 1919 Afghanistan regained its **independence**. In 1933 **Muhammad Zahir** became Shah. In 1964 Zahir proclaimed a constitutional monarchy. In 1996 the fundamentalist **Taliban** seized Kabul. In 2001 the **United States** launched airstrikes after the Taliban refused to hand over **Osama Bin Laden**, accused of masterminding the terrorist attacks on the United States of America on September 11, 2001. In December 2001, Afghan opposition forces, led by **Hamid Karzai**, overthrew the Taliban.

***Afghan stamp** from 1987, showing a dove of peace over the outline of Afghanistan.*

16

Albania's flag is a striking **red field** with a **black, double-headed eagle**. The two-headed eagle was the seal of Albanian national hero Gjergj Kastrioti. Taken hostage by the Turks, Kastrioti converted to Islam, was renamed Iskander, and given the title of bey (hence his byname Skanderbeg). In 1444, after embracing Christianity, Kastrioti successfully organized Albanian resistance against the Turks.

HISTORY

The **Balkan** republic of Albania is mountainous and prone to earthquakes. It formed part of ancient **Illyria**. In 167 BC, Albania was subsumed into the **Roman Empire**. Between 1469 and 1912, Albania was part of the **Ottoman Empire**. In 1939 Italy invaded and **King** Zog fled into exile. In 1943 **Germany** occupied Albania. In 1944 Albanian Communists, led by **Enver Hoxha**, took power. Hoxha, who remained in office until his death in 1985, built a **Stalinist**, isolationist state. In 1967 Albania became the world's first **atheist** nation. In 1992 Democratic Party leader **Sali Berisha** became Albania's first non-communist president. In 1997, the collapse of nationwide **pyramid finance schemes** sparked a large-scale rebellion in southern Albania. The government resigned and **Fatos Nano** became prime minister. In 1999, nearly 500,000 ethnic **Albanian refugees** fled to Albania from the Serbian province of **Kosovo**.

AREA: 28,750sq km (11,100sq mi)
POPULATION: 3,510,484
CAPITAL (POPULATION): Tirana (288,217)
GOVERNMENT: Multi-party republic
ETHNIC GROUPS: Albanian 96%, Greek 3%, Macedonian, Montenegrin, Roma
LANGUAGES: Albanian (official)
RELIGIONS: Shi'a (Bektashi) Muslim 45%, Sunni Muslim 20%, Albanian Orthodox Christian 25%, Roman Catholic 10%
NATIONAL ANTHEM (DATE): "*Himni i Flamurit*" "Hymn to Our Flag" (1912)

Shqiperia, the Albanian name for the country, means 'Land of the eagle'.

17

ALGERIA

FLAG RATIO: 2:3 **USE:** National/Civil **DATE ADOPTED:** 1962 **LAST MODIFIED:** 1962

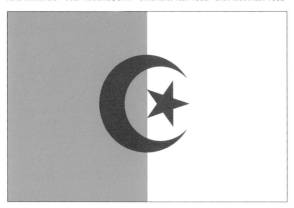

The **red star** and **crescent** at the centre of Algeria's flag are common symbols of Islam. **Green** is also traditionally associated with Islam. **White** stands for purity and also recalls the banner of Abd al-Kadir, an early hero of the liberation movement. The National Liberation Front (FLN), which led the struggle for independence from France, adopted the present flag in 1954. From 1958 to 1962 it was the flag of the government in exile. On July 3, 1962, it was hoisted as the national flag of an independent Algeria.

HISTORY

Algeria is the second largest country in **Africa**. In the 9th century BC, coastal Algeria (**Numidia**) formed part of the empire of **Carthage**'s. **Berbers** controlled Algeria until the arrival of the Arabs in the late 7th century AD. The Arabs converted Algeria to Islam. In the early 10th century, the **Fatimids** built an empire from their base in north-east Algeria. In 1830 **France** invaded. **Abd al-Kadir** led resistance to French colonization. In 1954 the **National Liberation Front (FLN)** launched a war of liberation that claimed more than 350,000 lives. In 1962 Algeria gained **independence**. In 1965 **Houari Boumédienne** overthrew **Ahmed Ben Bella** in an army coup. **Chadli Benjedid** served as president from 1978 to 1991. In 1999 a civil concord promised an end to a **civil war** between government forces and Islamic militants that claimed more than 100,000 lives. The Berber language gained official recognition in 2001.

AREA: 2,381,700sq km (919,590sq mi)
POPULATION: 31,193,000
CAPITAL (POPULATION): Algiers (2,562,428)
GOVERNMENT: Socialist republic
ETHNIC GROUPS: Arab 83%, Berber 17%
LANGUAGES: Arabic, Berber (both official), French
RELIGIONS: Sunni Muslim 99%, Christian (mainly Roman Catholic)
NATIONAL ANTHEM (DATE): "*Qassaman*" "The Pledge" (1963)

This stamp celebrates elections to Algeria's parliament, the Conseil de la Nation.

ANDORRA

FLAG RATIO: 2:3 USE: National DATE ADOPTED: 1866 LAST MODIFIED: 1866

Andorra's (French, *Andorre*) **tricolour** flag of **vertical stripes** links with its neighbouring countries. The **blue** and **red** stripes associate it with France, the **red** and **yellow** with Spain. At the centre of the yellow stripe is the **coat of arms**. The **shield** divides into four quarters. The first quarter stands for the bishopric, depicted by a **golden mitre** and **crozier**. The **three red stripes** symbolize the Counts of Foix. The **four stripes** signify Catalonia, while the **cows** are a symbol of the French province of Béarn. The **civil flag** omits the arms.

HISTORY

Andorra is a small state situated high in the eastern **Pyrenees** between France and Spain. In 803 **Charlemagne** regained Andorra from its Moorish rulers. In 843 Charlemagne's grandson, **Charles II (the Bald)**, granted Andorra to the Count of Urgell. In 1278 and 1288, the **Bishop of Urgell** and the **Count of Foix** signed two *Pariatges* agreeing to share sovereignty of Andorra in return for an annual tribute (*quèstia*) from Andorra. This feudal arrangement between the Spanish Bishops of Urgell and the French Counts of Foix persisted almost unchanged for 715 years. In 1589 Henry II of Foix became **Henry IV of France** and the title of joint ruler passed to the French head of state. In 1993 Andorrans approved a **democratic constitution** and the creation of a 'parliamentary co-principality'.

Stamp honouring the 25th anniversary of Andorra's Society of Arts and Letters in 1993.

AREA: 453sq km (175sq mi)
POPULATION: 65,971
CAPITAL (POPULATION): Andorra la Vella (21,189)
GOVERNMENT: Parliamentary co-principality
ETHNIC GROUPS: Spanish 43%, Andorran 33%, Portugese 11%, French 7%, other 6%
LANGUAGES: Catalan (official), French, Castilian
RELIGIONS: Roman Catholic 90%
NATIONAL MOTTO: "*Virtus Unita Fortior*" "Virtue United in Strength"
NATIONAL ANTHEM (DATE): "*El Gran Carlemany*" "The Great Charlemagne" (1914)

19

ANGOLA

FLAG RATIO: 2:3 USE: National/Civil DATE ADOPTED: 1975 LAST MODIFIED: 1992

A ngola's flag derives from the flag of the MPLA (*Movimento Popular de Libertacão de Angola*), leaders of the struggle for liberation from Portugal. The flag has **two horizontal stripes**. The **red** stripe symbolizes the blood shed in Angola's fight for independence. The **black stripe** represents Africa. The central motif, a **cogwheel**, **machete** and **star**, is reminiscent of communist symbolism. The cogwheel stands for industrial workers, and the machete represents the peasants. The star signifies socialism and progress. The **gold** colour of the symbol represents Angola's mineral wealth.

HISTORY

Bantu-speaking people settled in Angola *c*.2000 years ago. In the early 1600s, Angola became an important source of **slaves** for the Portuguese colony of Brazil. After the decline in the slave trade, Portuguese settlers began to develop the land. Portuguese immigration increased dramatically in the early 20th century. In 1961 the **MPLA** led a revolt in Luanda, the capital. In 1966 southern peoples, including many Ovimbundu, formed the National Union for the Total Independence of Angola (**UNITA**). In **1975** Portugal granted **independence**, and **civil war** ensued between the MPLA government, led by **Agostinho Neto**, and UNITA forces led by **Jonas Savimbi**. In 1979 **José dos Santos** succeeded Neto as president. The **Lusaka Protocol** (1994) led to a lull in the civil war. In 2002 government troops killed Savimbi and UNITA declared a ceasefire.

AREA: 1,246,700sq km (481,351sq mi)
POPULATION: 12,781,000
CAPITAL (POPULATION): Luanda (2,080,000)
GOVERNMENT: Multi-party republic
ETHNIC GROUPS: Ovimbundu 37%, Mbundu 22%, Kongo 13%, Luimbe-Nganguela 5%, Nyaneka-Humbe 5%
LANGUAGES: Portuguese (official)
RELIGIONS: Roman Catholic 69%, Protestant 20%, African traditional beliefs 10%
NATIONAL ANTHEM (DATE): "*Angola, avante!*"
"Angola, advance!" (1975)

Angola *stamp celebrating the 50th anniversary of the United Nations in 1995.*

20

ANTIGUA AND BARBUDA

FLAG RATIO: 2:3 **USE:** National/Civil **DATE ADOPTED:** 1967 **LAST MODIFIED:** 1967

In 1967 Antigua and Barbuda became self-governing and held a competition to design the national flag. The 16-pointed **golden star** at the centre of the flag represents the rising sun, symbolising the dawning of a new era in Antigua and Barbuda's history. The red **triangles** mark a 'V' for victory. **Red** stands for the energy of its people, **blue** signifies hope, and **black** recalls the African heritage of its people. The sun rising above the blue band and **white** triangle is a stylized representation of the sun, sea and sand that attracts visitors to Antigua and Barbuda.

HISTORY

In 1493 **Christopher Columbus** landed on Antigua, naming it after Santa Maria Antigua, Saint of Seville. The indigenous **Caribs** resisted European settlement. England colonized Antigua in 1632, and the smaller island of Barbuda in 1666. In 1684 **Sir Christopher Codrington** established the first **sugar plantation**. The English brought in **slaves** from Africa to work on the plantations. In 1784 **Horatio Nelson** built a naval base on Antigua. In 1834 Britain abolished slavery. From 1871 to 1956 the islands formed part of the British colony of the **Leeward Islands**. **Vere Bird**, of the Antiguan Labor Party (ALP), led the nation to **independence** in 1981. His son, **Lester Bird**, succeeded him as Prime Minister in 1994.

Antigua and Barbuda is 2100 kilometres (1300 miles) from the coast of Florida.

AREA: 440sq km (170sq mi)
POPULATION: 65,000
CAPITAL (POPULATION): St John's (41,700)
GOVERNMENT: Constitutional monarchy
ETHNIC GROUPS: Black 91%, Mixed race 4%, White 2%
LANGUAGES: English (official), Creole
RELIGIONS: Anglican 40%, Methodist 33%, other Protestant 12%, Roman Catholic 5%
MOTTO: "Each Endeavouring, All Achieving"
NATIONAL ANTHEM (DATE): "Fair Antigua, We Salute Thee" (1967)

21

ARGENTINA

FLAG RATIO: 1:2 USE: National/Civil DATE ADOPTED: 1818 LAST MODIFIED: 1818

General Manuel Belgrano, leader of Argentina's independence struggle against the Spanish, designed the **triband** flag shortly before the Battle of Rosario (1812). He based the design on the celeste (**sky-blue**) and **white** colours worn by the patriotic forces. In 1818 Congress approved the addition of a **32-rayed golden sun** on the centre of the white band. It is called the '**Sun of May**' in honour of the sun shining through the clouds above Buenos Aires on May 25, 1810, when rebels overthrew the Spanish Viceroy. The sun, an Inca symbol, has **alternate straight** and **flaming rays** and a **human face** on its disc.

HISTORY

Argentina is the second-largest country in South America and the eighth-largest in the world. In 1516 **Spanish** explorers reached the coast, and settlers followed in search of silver and gold. Spanish rule continued until 1810. In 1816 Argentina declared **independence**. After General **Juan Manuel de Rosas**' dictatorship (1835–52), Argentina adopted a federal constitution in 1853. In 1944 **Juan Perón** toppled the pro-Axis government of Ramón Castillo. With the aid of his wife, **Eva**, Perón established a popular dictatorship. In 1955 a military junta ousted Perón. In 1973 Perón returned from exile to head a civilian government. Torture, 'disappearances' and arbitrary imprisonment characterized the military 'rule of the Generals' (1976–83). **Carlos Menem** was president from 1989 to 1999.

AREA: 2,766,890sq km (1,068,296sq mi)
POPULATION: 36,027,041
CAPITAL (POPULATION): Buenos Aires (13,755,993)
GOVERNMENT: Federal multi-party republic
ETHNIC GROUPS: European 85%, Mestizo 10%, Native American 4%
LANGUAGES: Spanish (official)
RELIGIONS: Roman Catholic 80%, Evangelical Protestant (mainly Pentecostal) 8%
NATIONAL ANTHEM (DATE): "*Himno Nacional Argentino*" (1813)

Stamp *celebrating the 50th anniversary of the Universal Declaration of Human Rights.*

22

A rmenia's flag is **tricolour**, comprised of **horizontal stripes** of **red**, **blue**, and **orange**. Red stands for the blood spilled by Armenians fighting for independence and religious freedom. **Blue** symbolizes the sky and hope for the future, and orange represents Armenia's fertile lands.

HISTORY

Armenia lies in the southern **Caucasus** Mountains. In 303 it became the first country to adopt **Christianity** as a state religion. From the 11th to the 15th century, the **Mongols** were the greatest power in the region. By the 16th century the **Ottoman Empire** controlled Armenia. In 1828 **Russia** gained Persian Armenia. During **World War I**, Armenia was a battleground for the Turkish and Russian armies. Turkish troops killed more than 600,000 Armenians, and deported 1.75 million

people. In 1918 Russian Armenia became the **Armenian Autonomous Republic**, the western part remained part of Turkey, and the north-western region became part of Iran. In 1922 Armenia, Azerbaijan, and Georgia federated to form the **Transcaucasian Soviet Socialist Republic**, one of the four original republics of the Soviet Union. In 1936 Armenia became a separate **republic**. **Earthquakes** in 1984 and 1988 killed more than 80,000 people. Armenia gained **independence** from the Soviet Union in 1990. In 1999 gunmen assassinated the prime minister. In 1992 war broke out between Armenia and **Azerbaijan** over **Nagorno-Karabakh**, an Armenian enclave within Azerbaijan.

AREA: 29,800sq km (11,506sq mi)
POPULATION: 3,336,100
CAPITAL (POPULATION): Yerevan (1,247,200)
GOVERNMENT: Multi-party republic
ETHNIC GROUPS: Armenian 95%, Azerbaijani 3%, Russian, Kurd
LANGUAGES: Armenian (official)
RELIGIONS: Armenian Apostolic (Eastern Orthodox Christian) 90%
NATIONAL ANTHEM (DATE): "*Mer Hayrenik*" "Our Fatherland" (1991)

Stamp *marking the millennium of Grigor Narekatsi's* "A Record of Lamentations".

23

AUSTRALIA

FLAG RATIO: 1:2 **USE:** National/Civil **DATE ADOPTED:** 1909 **LAST MODIFIED:** 1912

In 1901 the new nation of Australia held a competition to design a national flag. The **British 'Union Jack'** flag in the top left corner reflects Australia's historic ties with Britain. The **'Star of Federation'** on the lower hoist has seven points, one point for each of the six Australian States and one for its territories. On the right half of the flag is the kite-shaped constellation of the **'Southern Cross'** or Crux, which can be seen in the night sky above all States and territories. In 1995 the government gave legal recognition to the **Native Australian flag** and the **Torres Strait Islander flag**.

AREA: 7,686,850sq km (2,967,893sq mi)
POPULATION: 19,169,083
CAPITAL (POPULATION): Canberra (315,400)
GOVERNMENT: Federal constitutional monarchy
ETHNIC GROUPS: European 93%, Asian 4%, Native Australian/Torres Strait Islander 2%
LANGUAGES: English (official)
RELIGIONS: Roman Catholic 27%, Anglican 22%, Uniting Church 7%, Presbyterian 4%, Baptist 2%, Lutheran 1%, Muslim 1%, Buddhist 1%
NATIONAL MOTTO: "Advance Australia"
NATIONAL ANTHEM (DATE): "Advance Australia Fair" (1984)

HISTORY

Native Australians (**Aborigines**) arrived from south-east Asia more than 50,000 years ago. They remained isolated from the world until the arrival of the first European explorers. In 1770 British explorer **Captain James Cook** reached Botany Bay and claimed the east coast for Great Britain. In 1788 Britain built its first settlement (for convicts), on the site of present-day **Sydney**. In 1901 the States of Queensland, Victoria, Tasmania, New South Wales, South Australia and Western Australia united to form the **Commonwealth of Australia**. In 1911 Northern Territory joined the federation. **Sir Robert Menzies** served as Prime Minister from 1939 to 1941 and from 1949 to 1966. In 1999 Australians narrowly voted against becoming a republic in a national **referendum**.

Stamp *marking the opening of the National Museum of Australia in 2001.*

24

FLAG RATIO: 2:3 **USE:** National **DATE ADOPTED:** 1919 **LAST MODIFIED:** 1984

Austria's flag dates to 1230. It derives from the seal of **Duke Frederick II**, the last **Babenberg** ruler of Austria (1230–46). According to legend, the first Babenberg ruler **Duke Leopold V** (r.1177–1194) received the **red-white-red** colours at the Battle of Ptolemais (1191), when his tunic became so blood-stained that the only white remaining was the band covered by his sword belt. At the centre of the **state flag** is a **coat of arms**, derived from the **double-headed eagle** of the Habsburg Empire. The crowned, one-headed eagle grasps a **hammer** and **sickle** in its talons. In 1945 the Second Republic added **broken chains** to the eagle's legs, symbolizing liberation from the shackles of Nazism.

HISTORY

Once part of the **Holy Roman Empire**, Austria united with Bohemia and Hungary in 1526. Under Habsburg rule it was the greatest state in the Empire. The succession of **Maria Theresa** led to the **War of the Austrian Succession** (1740–48). Austrian power declined after defeat in the **Austro-Prussian War** (1866). The Austro-Hungarian Empire collapsed after defeat in World War I (1914–18) and the **First Republic** was born. In 1938 **Adolf Hitler unified** Germany and Austria. Defeat in World War II (1939–45) led to the creation of the Second Republic. In 1955 Austria became a **neutral** republic. In 1995 it joined the **European Union (EU)**.

***Austria** celebrated the 150th anniversary of its stamps in 2000.*

AREA: 83,850sq km (32,347sq mi)
POPULATION: 8,065,166
CAPITAL (POPULATION): Vienna (1,562,676)
GOVERNMENT: Federal multi-party republic
ETHNIC GROUPS: Austrian 98%
LANGUAGES: German (official)
RELIGIONS: Roman Catholic 78%, Lutheran 5%, Muslim 2%
NATIONAL ANTHEM (DATE): "*Land der Berge, Land am Strome*" "Land of Mountains, Land on the River" (1947)

AZERBAIJAN

FLAG RATIO: 1:2 **USE:** National/Civil **DATE ADOPTED:** 1991 **LAST MODIFIED:** 1991

A zerbaijan's **tricolour** flag dates to 1918, the start of a brief period of independence before Russian occupation in 1920. In 1991 Azerbaijan regained independence and readopted the flag. The flag reflects the Azerbaijani motto "Turkify, Islamize, and Europeanize". **Light blue** is a traditional Turkic colour. At the centre of the middle, red stripe is a **white crescent and star**, traditional symbols of **Islam**. The star has **eight points** to represent each of Azerbaijan's Turkic peoples. **Red** stands for modernity and progress. **Green** is a traditional colour of Islam.

AREA: 86,600sq km (33,436sq mi)
POPULATION: 7,771,092
CAPITAL (POPULATION): Baku (1,725,500)
GOVERNMENT: Federal multi-party republic
ETHNIC GROUPS: Azerbaijani 90%, Dagestani 3%, Russian 3%, Armenian 2%
LANGUAGES: Azeri (official)
RELIGIONS: Shi'a Muslim 60%, Sunni Muslim 40%, Christian 3%
NATIONAL MOTTO: "Turkify, Islamize, and Europeanize"
NATIONAL ANTHEM (DATE): "*Azärbaycan Respublikasinin Dövlət Himni*" "Azerbaijani National Hymn" (1992)

HISTORY

Azerbaijan is the world's oldest centre of **oil** production. In the late 7th century Arabs conquered the region, and Islam became the main religion. In the mid-11th century **Seljuk Turks** occupied present-day Azerbaijan. The **Mongols** ruled the region in the 13th century. In the 16th century the **Iranian Safavid dynasty** assumed control. By the early 19th century Azerbaijan formed part of the **Russian Empire**. In 1920 the Bolsheviks invaded the fledgling nation and, in 1922, Azerbaijan became part of the **Soviet Union**. In 1991, the Soviet Union collapsed and Azerbaijan gained **independence**. In 1992 war broke out between Azerbaijan and **Armenia** over **Nagorno-Karabakh**, an Armenian enclave within Azerbaijan.

***Azerbaijan** stamp from 1992, showing a view of the Caspian Sea.*

FLAG RATIO: 1:2 **USE:** National **DATE ADOPTED:** 1973 **LAST MODIFIED:** 1973

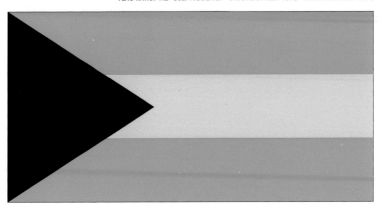

The Bahamian flag emerged from a combination of winning entries to a national competition in 1973. The central **gold stripe** recalls Bahama's sandy beaches, while the **aquamarine** bands represent the clear Atlantic waters that surround the Bahamas. The **black triangle** on the hoist side stands for the strength and pride of the Bahamians.

HISTORY

A popular tourist destination, the Bahamas consists of 700 islands in the **West Indies**, off the coast of south-east Florida. In 1492 **Christopher Columbus** landed on San Salvador island. He called the Atlantic waters "*baja mar*" (Spanish, 'low sea'). The 40,000 native **Lucayan** **Indians** died within 25 years of Spain's arrival. In 1648 the English Puritan **Eleutherian Adventurers** built the first European settlement. In the 17th century, the islands became notorious for **piracy**. By 1783 **Britain** had full control of the Bahamas. The islands prospered on trade with the **Confederacy** during the American Civil War and smuggling alcohol during **Prohibition**. In 1964 the Bahamas gained self-government as a prelude to full **independence** in 1973. **Lynden Pindling** served as Prime Minister from 1967 to 1992.

AREA: 13,860sq km (5350sq mi)
POPULATION: 295,000
CAPITAL (POPULATION): Nassau (179,300)
GOVERNMENT: Constitutional monarchy
ETHNIC GROUPS: Black 85%, White 12%, Asian and Hispanic 3%
LANGUAGES: English, Creole (among Haitian immigrants)
RELIGIONS: Baptist 32%, Anglican 20%, Roman Catholic 19%, Methodist 6%, Church of God 6%, other Protestant 12%
MOTTO: "Forward, Upward, Onward, Together"
NATIONAL ANTHEM (DATE): "March on, Bahamaland" (1973)

The flamingo is the national bird of the Bahamas.

27

BAHRAIN

FLAG RATIO: 3:5 **USE:** National/Civil **DATE ADOPTED:** 1933 **LAST MODIFIED:** 2002

Bahrain's flag is **red** with a vertical, **serrated white** border on the hoist side. Red and white are traditional colours of the **Gulf States**. The **vertical white** stripe dates from the General Maritime Treaty with the British East India Company in 1820. The treaty sought to prevent piracy in the Persian (Arabian) Gulf, and the white stripe identified the friendly Arab States. In 1932 the stripe acquired a serrated edge to distinguish it from the flag of **Dubai**. The flag is identical to **Qatar**'s flag, except for the shade of red and the number of steps in the serration. Bahrain's flag has **five steps**, signifying the five Pillars of **Islam**.

HISTORY

Bahrain is an Emirate archipelago in the Persian Gulf. Bahrain has been **Arab** and Muslim since the Arab conquest in the 7th century. The **Khalifa** dynasty, a branch of the Bani Utbah tribe, has ruled the islands since 1783. In 1861 Bahrain became a **British Protectorate**. In 1932 Standard Oil made the first discovery of **oil** on the Arabian Peninsula in Bahrain. In **1971** Bahrain declared **independence** and **Sheikh Isa** became Emir. In 1999 Sheikh **Hamad bin Isa al-Khalifa** succeeded Isa, his father, as Emir. Tensions exist between the Sunni and the majority Shi'a populations. In 2002 Bahrain became a **constitutional monarchy** and held its first elections for 27 years. Bahrain's aluminium smelting plant is the largest non-oil industrial complex in the Gulf.

AREA: 678sq km (262sq mi)
POPULATION: 683,000
CAPITAL (POPULATION): Manama (148,000)
GOVERNMENT: Constitutional monarchy
ETHNIC GROUPS: Bahraini 63%, Asian 19%, other Arab 10%, Iranian 8%
LANGUAGES: Arabic, English, Farsi, Urdu
RELIGIONS: Shi'a Muslim 70%, Sunni Muslim 30%
NATIONAL ANTHEM (DATE): "*Bahrainona*"
"Our Bahrain" (1971)

Bahrain *stamp marking the 21st Supreme Council of the Gulf Cooperation Council.*

FLAG RATIO: 3:5 USE: National/Civil DATE ADOPTED: 1972 LAST MODIFIED: 1972

Bangladesh's flag is a simple **red disc** on a **green field**. Adopted following independence in 1971, the red disc represents the dawn of independence and commemorates the blood shed in the struggle for freedom. Green stands for the lush landscape of Bangladesh and is also traditionally associated with **Islam**, the country's principal religion. The red disc is set slightly towards the hoist of the flag so that when the flag is flying it appears central.

HISTORY

Bangladesh is the most densely populated country in the world (834 people per square kilometre). It is prone to **flooding**. Its early history is synonymous with that of **Bengal**. In 1576 Bengal became part of the vast **Mogul Empire** under Akbar I (the Great). In the late-18th century, the **British East India Company** assumed control of Bengal. In 1947 British India was partitioned between the mainly Hindu India and Muslim **Pakistan**. Present-day Bangladesh became the Pakistan province of East Bengal. In March 1971, the **Awami League**, led by **Sheikh Mujibur Rahman**, declared **independence**. More than 1 million East Bengalis died in the ensuing nine months of civil war. With Indian military aid, East Bengal defeated Pakistan and gained independence as Bangladesh. **Hasina Wazed**, Sheikh Rahman's daughter, became prime minister in 1996 elections. In 2001 **Khaleda Zia**, Sheikh Rahman's wife, succeeded Hasina as prime minister.

Nearly two-thirds of Bangladeshis work in the agricultural sector.

AREA: 144,000sq km (55,598sq mi)
POPULATION: 129,247,233
CAPITAL (POPULATION): Dhaka (5,378,032)
GOVERNMENT: Multi-party republic
ETHNIC GROUPS: Bengali 98%, tribal groups
LANGUAGES: Bengali (official)
RELIGIONS: Sunni Muslim 88%,
Hindu 10%, Buddhist, Christian
NATIONAL ANTHEM (DATE): "Amar Sonar Bangla"
"My Golden Bengal" (1972)

29

BARBADOS

FLAG RATIO: 2:3 **USE:** National/Civil **DATE ADOPTED:** 1966 **LAST MODIFIED:** 1966

arbados held a competition to design a national flag upon gaining independence in 1966. The flag has **three vertical stripes** (ultramarine-gold-ultramarine) and a **black trident** in the centre of the middle gold band. The **two ultramarine** bands stand for the sky and the sea, the **gold** band represents the sun. Barbados' colonial flag, which featured the sea-god Neptune wielding a trident, inspired the symbol at the centre of the new national flag. On the new flag the shaft of the trident is broken, symbolising the break with Britain at independence.

HISTORY

The **Windward Island** of Barbados is the easternmost island of the **West Indies**. The first European explorer, Portuguese navigator **Pedro Campos**, landed in 1536. Campos named the island *Los Barbados* (Portuguese, 'bearded ones'), after its bearded fig trees. The Spanish enslaved the island's **Carib** population, which quickly died out. In 1627 **Britain** settled the island. The British used **slaves** from West Africa to work on the **sugar plantations**. In 1816 Bussa inspired a **slave revolt**. Britain finally abolished slavery in 1834. From 1958 to 1962 Barbados formed part of the Federation of the West Indies, led by Barbadian politician **Grantley Adams**. In 1961 Barbados gained **self-government**. In 1966 **Errol Barrow** led the nation to independence. **Owen Arthur** became prime minister in 1994 elections. The great cricketer **Sir Garfield Sobers** was born on Barbados.

AREA: 430sq km (166sq mi)
POPULATION: 265,000
CAPITAL (POPULATION): Bridgetown (97,500)
GOVERNMENT: Parliamentary democracy
ETHNIC GROUPS: African descent 96%, white 4%
LANGUAGES: English
RELIGIONS: Anglican 40%, Pentecostal 8%, Methodist 7%, other Protestant 12%, Roman Catholic 4%
NATIONAL ANTHEM (DATE): "National Anthem of Barbados" (1966)

In 1627 the William and John, *captained by William Powell, landed on Barbados.*

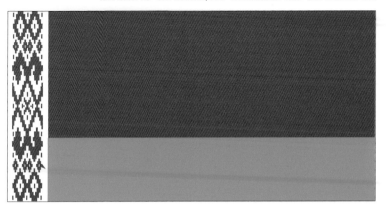

The current Belarus flag is almost identical to the flag flown from 1951 to 1991, when Belarus was a republic of the Soviet Union. From 1991 to 1995 Belarus had a white-red-white striped flag. In 1995 Belarus readopted the **red** and **green horizontal stripes** of the Soviet-era flag, omitting the communist symbols and adding a **decorative white band** on the hoist to represent Belarus' rich cultural heritage. Red was the colour of the standards of the Belarussian regiments that defeated the Teutonic Knights at the Battle of Tannenberg (1410) and of the Soviet Red Army and the Belarusian guerrilla forces that fought against fascism. Green symbolizes hope for the future and the fields and forests.

HISTORY

In 1529 the Grand Duchy of **Lithuania** recognized Belarus. Russia acquired Belarus in the **Partitions of Poland** (1772, 1793, 1795). In 1919 the Bolsheviks established the Belorussian Soviet Republic. **Poland** gained western Belorussia in the Treaty of Riga (1921). A quarter of Belarusians died under Nazi German occupation during World War II. Belarus achieved **independence** after the collapse of the Soviet Union in 1990. President **Alexsandr Lukashenka** committed Belarus to **integration** with Russia in 1997.

Golden cross of Saint Euphrosyne of Polotsk crafted in the 12th century.

AREA: 207,600sq km (80,154sq mi)
POPULATION: 10,045,000
CAPITAL (POPULATION): Minsk (1,680,000)
GOVERNMENT: Multi-party republic
ETHNIC GROUPS: Belarusian 81%, Russian 11%, Polish, Ukrainian, Jewish
LANGUAGES: Belarusian, Russian (both official)
RELIGIONS: Belarusian Orthodox 80%, Roman Catholic 15%, Jewish 1%
NATIONAL ANTHEM (DATE): "*Maladaya Belarus*" "Young Belarus" (1955)

BELGIUM

FLAG RATIO: 13:15   **USE:** National/Civil   **DATE ADOPTED:** 1831   **LAST MODIFIED:** 1831

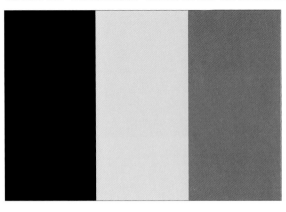

The colours of Belgium's flag date back to the 13th-century seal of Count Philip of Flanders, which featured a **black** lion on a **gold** field. In 1234 the Duchy of Brabant's flag consisted of a gold lion with **red** tongue and claws set against a black background. Rebels displayed the colours in the failed Brabant Revolt (1787–89) against Austrian rule. In 1830 revolutionaries raised the colours in a successful rebellion against the rule of William I of the Netherlands. In 1831 Belgium adopted its present flag, with the arrangement of the colours based on the French *tricolore*.

AREA: 30,510sq km (11,780sq mi)
POPULATION: 10,239,085
CAPITAL (POPULATION): Brussels (959,318)
GOVERNMENT: Federal constitutional monarchy
ETHNIC GROUPS: Fleming 58%, Walloon 31%, German, Italian, French, Dutch, Turkish, Moroccan
LANGUAGES: Flemish (Dutch), French, German (all official)
RELIGIONS: Roman Catholic 75%, Muslim 3%
NATIONAL MOTTO: "*L'Union fait la force*" or "*Eendracht maakt*" "Strength Lies In Unity"
NATIONAL ANTHEM (DATE): "*La Brabançonne*" "The Brabant Song" (1938)

HISTORY

From 1363 to 1467 the **Dukes of Burgundy** ruled the Low Countries. In 1585 the southern **Spanish Netherlands** (now Belgium) separated from the northern United Provinces of the **Netherlands**. After the War of the Spanish Succession (1701–14) the Spanish Netherlands became the **Austrian Netherlands**. Captured by France in 1795, the French Revolutionary Wars resulted in the united **Kingdom of the Netherlands** in 1815. Dutch discrimination led to rebellion and Belgium declared **independence** in 1830. In August 1914, **Germany** invaded Belgium, prompting British entry into World War I. Germany captured Belgium in World War II. **Brussels** is the administrative headquarters of the European Union (EU). In 1989 Walloonia, Flanders and Brussels gained regional autonomy.

Belgium has been famous for producing luxury chocolate since the 17th century.

At the centre of Belize's flag is a white disc featuring the coat of arms. The tripartite shield contains tools and products of the timber trade. Above the shield grows a mahogany tree. Beside the shield stand two wood-cutters, representing the nation's two main ethnic groups. A ring of 50 laurel leaves surrounds the disc, marking the year 1950, the start of the liberation struggle. Belize's motto appears below the shield. The motto refers to Belize's former dependence on Britain. In 1981 a national committee chose a design that added red stripes to the top and bottom of the royal blue field.

HISTORY

Between c.300 BC and AD 1000, Belize was part of the Maya Empire. In c.1638 shipwrecked British sailors founded the first European settlement. Although subject to regular Spanish incursions, Britain gradually took control of what became known as British Honduras. The British used slave labour for logging and on the sugar plantations. In 1871 British Honduras became a British Crown Colony. In 1950 currency devaluation prompted the birth of the People's United Party (PUP). Renamed Belize in 1973, it gained independence in 1981. George Price was the first prime minister.

AREA: 22,960sq km (8865sq mi)
POPULATION: 241,204
CAPITAL (POPULATION): Belmopan (8130)
GOVERNMENT: Constitutional monarchy
ETHNIC GROUPS: Mestizo 46%, Creole 28%, Mayan 10%, Garifuna 6%, European 4%, East Indian 3%
LANGUAGES: English (official), Creole
RELIGIONS: Roman Catholic 58%, Anglican 7%, Pentecostal 6%, Methodist 4%, Seventh-Day Adventist 4%, Mennonite 4%
NATIONAL MOTTO: "Sub Umbra Florero" "I Flourish in the Shadow"
NATIONAL ANTHEM (DATE):
"Land of the Free" (1981)

Belize has 300 species of orchid, including this Maxillaria elatior.

33

BENIN

FLAG RATIO: 2:3 **USE:** National/Civil **DATE ADOPTED:** 1959 **REINTRODUCED:** 1990

B enin, then called Dahomey, adopted its current flag in 1959. In 1975 Dahomey became the People's Republic of Benin and acquired a new flag, consisting of a green star against a red field. In 1990 Benin introduced a new constitution and reverted to the previous flag. Red, yellow and green are colours of the **Pan-African** movement and thus symbolize African unity. In addition, **green** stands for the palm groves in southern Benin. The **yellow** represents the savannahs in the north, while **red** signifies the blood shed in the struggle for independence.

HISTORY

Benin is one of Africa's smallest nations.

AREA: 112,620sq km (43,483sq mi)
POPULATION: 6,395,919
CAPITAL (POPULATION): Porto-Novo (179,938)
GOVERNMENT: Multi-party republic
ETHNIC GROUPS: Fon, Adja, Bariba, Yoruba, Fulani, Somba
LANGUAGES: French (official)
RELIGIONS: African traditional beliefs 60%, Christian (mainly Catholic) 23%, Muslim 15%
NATIONAL MOTTO: "*Fraternité, Justice, Travail*" "Brotherhood, Justice, Work"
NATIONAL ANTHEM (DATE): "*L'Aube Nouvelle*" "The Dawn of a New Day" (1960)

The ancient Kingdom of **Dahomey** had its capital at **Abomey**, in what is now southern Benin. In the 17th century, the Kings of Dahomey became involved in the lucrative **slave trade**, and by 1700 more than 200,000 slaves were transported annually from the 'Slave Coast'. Despite British abolition in 1834, slavery persisted well into the 19th century. By 1894 France had conquered Dahomey. In 1904 it became part of the huge Federation of **French West Africa**. In 1958 Dahomey achieved self-government as a prelude to full **independence** in 1960. In 1972 General **Mathieu Kérékou** seized power in a military coup. In 1975 Dahomey became the **People's Republic of Benin** and adopted Marxism-Leninism as the state ideology. In 1990 Benin abandoned communism in favour of multiparty democracy.

Dugout canoes *deliver mail to some rural areas of Benin.*

34

FLAG RATIO: 2:3 USE: National/Civil DATE ADOPTED: 1969 LAST MODIFIED: 1969

The Bhutanese often call their country *Druk Yul* ('Land of the Thunder Dragon'). The **dragon** used on the national flag dates to the 17th-century introduction of the Drukpa Kagyu school of Tantric Mahayana Buddhism. The **jewels** in the dragon's claws represent Bhutan's wealth. The **white** colour of the dragon symbolizes purity. The rest of the flag is divided horizontally into **gold** and **orange triangles**. The gold triangle represents the secular power of the *Druk Gyalpo* ('Dragon King'), while **orange** signifies the spiritual power of Buddhism.

HISTORY

In 1616 the Buddhist monk **Ngawang Namgyal** unified Bhutan and established Drukpa Kagyu as the state religion. He also founded a dual system of government (temporal and theocratic), which lasted until 1907. Villages developed around the *dzong* (castle-monastery). The *Tashichho Dzong* ('Monastery of Auspicious Religion') in Thimphu is the seat of government. War with Britain led to the British annexation of southern Bhutan in 1865. In 1907, with British support, **Ugyen Wangchuck** became the first **hereditary monarch** of Bhutan. In 1968 King **Jigme Dorji Wangchuk** (r.1952–72) abolished slavery. Bhutan joined the United Nations (UN) in 1971. **Jigme Singye Wangchuk** succeeded his father as king in 1972. In the 1990s racial tension forced nearly 100,000 ethnic **Nepalese** into refugee camps in Nepal.

AREA: 47,000sq km (18,000sq mi)
POPULATION: 657,548
CAPITAL (POPULATION): Thimphu (53,600)
GOVERNMENT: Hereditary monarchy
ETHNIC GROUPS: Bhote 50%, ethnic Nepalese 35%, indigenous or migrant tribes 15%
LANGUAGES: Dzongkha (official), Bhotes speak various Tibetan dialects, Nepalese speak various Nepalese dialects
RELIGIONS: Buddhist (mainly Drukpa Kagyu) 70%, Hindu 25%, Muslim 5%
NATIONAL ANTHEM (DATE): "Druk Tsendhen" "Thunder-Dragon Kingdom" (1953)

'Four Friends' (elephant, monkey, rabbit, bird) is a popular Bhutanese folk tale.

35

BOLIVIA

FLAG RATIO: 2:3 **USE:** National **DATE ADOPTED:** 1851 **CODIFIED:** 1888

The colours on the Bolivian flag are traditional colours of the Aymará and Quechua peoples. In 1826, after gaining independence from Spain, Bolivia adopted a **tricolour** flag with **horizontal stripes** of (from the top) **yellow, red** and **green**. In 1851 Bolivia reversed the positions of the yellow and red stripes. Red represents the blood shed in the liberation struggle. Yellow symbolizes its mineral wealth. **Green** stands for the fertile land and agricultural wealth. The **state flag** has the coat of arms at the centre.

HISTORY

Bolivia was home to one of the great **pre-Colombian** civilizations. Before the

AREA: 1,098,580sq km (424,162sq mi)
POPULATION: 8,784,000
CAPITAL (POPULATION): La Paz (804,600),
Sucre (202,700)
GOVERNMENT: Multi-party republic
ETHNIC GROUPS: Quechua 30%, Aymara 25%,
Mestizo 30%, White 15%
LANGUAGES: Spanish, Aymará, Quechua
(all official)
RELIGIONS: Roman Catholic 80%,
Protestant 15%, indigenous beliefs 5%
NATIONAL ANTHEM (DATE): *"Himno Nacional"*
"National Hymn" (1842)

Spanish invasion in 1532, the **Quechua** had subsumed the **Aymará** into the **Inca Empire**. Spain exploited the Andean silver mines with native forced-labour. In 1824 **Antonio José de Sucre, Simon Bolívar's** general, liberated the country. **War** with Paraguay (1932–35) cost *c.*100,000 lives. **Victor Paz Estenssoro** of the National Revolutionary Movement (MNR) was president for much of the late 20th century (1952–56, 1960–64, 1985–89, 2001). In 1952 he nationalized the **mines**. In 1964 a military coup toppled Paz's government. From 1964 to 1982, military dictators, most notably Colonel **Hugo Banzer Suárez** (1971–78), ruled Bolivia. Banzer led a civilian government from 1997 to 2001.

Centennial stamp featuring the Andean condor, Bolivia's national symbol.

BOSNIA-HERZEGOVINA

FLAG RATIO: 1:2 USE: National/Civil DATE ADOPTED: 1998 LAST MODIFIED: 1998

In 1998 Bosnia-Herzegovina adopted a new flag because Croats and Serbs argued that the previous flag was synonymous with the wartime Muslim regime. The **blue background** and **white stars** derive from the flag of the **European Union (EU)**, while the **yellow triangle** stands for equality between the three main ethnic groups within Bosnia.

HISTORY

Bosnia-Herzegovina is one of five republics that emerged from the break-up of the former **Yugoslavia**. In 1946 Bosnia-Herzegovina became a constituent republic of **Tito**'s socialist federal republic. In 1991 the republic disintegrated with the secession of Croatia, Slovenia, and Macedonia. Fearing the creation of a Greater Serbia, Croats and Muslims pushed for independence. In March 1992 a referendum, boycotted by Serbian parties, voted for **independence**. **Alija Izetbegović** became president of the new nation. **War** broke out between Bosnian government forces and the Serb-dominated **Federal Yugoslav Army (JNA)**. Bosnian Serbs established a separate Serb republic led by **Radovan Karadžić** (1992). Serbs forced Muslims from their villages in a deliberate act of 'ethnic cleansing'. The three-year conflict claimed more than 200,000 lives. The **Dayton Peace Accord** (1995) preserved Bosnia-Herzegovina as a single state, but partitioned it between the Muslim-Croat Federation and Bosnian Serbs (**Republika Srpska**). Bosnia has a **tripartite**, ethnically based presidency.

Bosnian stamp *featuring Croat folk attire from the region of Kraljeva Sutjeska.*

AREA: 51,129sq km (19,745 sq mi)
POPULATION: 3,835,777
CAPITAL (POPULATION): Sarajevo (434,000)
GOVERNMENT: Transitional
ETHNIC GROUPS: Bosniac 46%, Serb 31%, Croat 14%
LANGUAGES: Bosnian, Serbian, Croatian
RELIGIONS: Sunni Muslim 43%, Serbian Orthodox 30%, Roman Catholic 18%
NATIONAL ANTHEM (DATE): (1999)

37

BOTSWANA

FLAG RATIO: 2:3 USE: National DATE ADOPTED: 1966 LAST MODIFIED: 1966

Botswana adopted its present national flag upon independence in 1966. The **white-black-white stripes** at the centre of the flag signify racial harmony. The colours are also symbolic of the zebra, Botswana's national animal. The **blue bands** symbolize water, vitally important to the arid land of Botswana.

HISTORY

The cattle-owning **Tswana**, modern Botswana's majority population, first settled in eastern Botswana more than 1000 years ago. The Tswana gradually forced the native **San** (Bushmen) into the **Kalahari Desert**. In 1885 Britain made the **Bechuanaland Protectorate** to prevent incursions by Afrikaners and discourage German colonialism. In 1966 Bechuanaland achieved **independence** as **Botswana**. Sir **Seretse Khama** served as president from 1966 to 1980. One of the 'front-line states', Botswana provided a haven for refugees from South Africa's **apartheid** government. Botswana is a stable multi-party democracy. It is the world's largest exporter of gem-quality diamonds. Botswana has the world's highest rate of **HIV** infection: more than 38% of adults have HIV.

AREA: 581,730sq km (224,606sq mi)
POPULATION: 1,695,482
CAPITAL (POPULATION): Gaborone (213,017)
GOVERNMENT: Multi-party republic
ETHNIC GROUPS: Tswana (or Setswana) 70%, Kalanga 10%, San 5%, Basarwa 3%, other (including Kgalagadi and White) 7%
LANGUAGES: English (official), Setswana
RELIGIONS: African traditional beliefs 34%, Protestant 26%, African churches 5%, Roman Catholic 7%, Muslim 3%
NATIONAL MOTTO: "*Pula*" "Let there be rain"
NATIONAL ANTHEM (DATE): "*Fatshe la Rona*" "Our Country" (1966)

North-west Botswana *is famous for its basket weaving, using the Mokola palm tree.*

In the 19th century, Brazil adopted green and yellow as national colours to symbolize the union of the House of Bragança with the House of Habsburg. The **yellow diamond** on a **green field** became the national flag upon independence from Portugal in 1882. In 1889 the government added the **blue disc** and **motto**. The blue disc represents the sky over Rio de Janeiro on the night of independence and includes the constellation of the **Southern Cross**. There are **27 stars**, one for the capital and one for each State. The **green** of the modern flag represents Brazil's rainforests, while **yellow** stands for Brazil's gold and mineral wealth.

HISTORY

In 1500 Portuguese explorer **Pedro Alvarez Cabral** claimed Brazil for **Portugal**. Portugal employed Native Americans and *c*.4 million African **slaves** to work on the sugar plantations and in the mines. In 1807 **Napoleon**'s invasion of Portugal led King John VI to flee to Brazil. In 1822 he returned to Portugal, and his son **Pedro I** declared Brazil an **independent Empire**. In a bloodless revolution (1889), Brazil became a **republic** and Marshal **Manuel Deodoro da Fonseca** became the first president. **Getúlio Vargas** used the army to maintain his autocratic regime (1930–45, 1950–54). In 1964 the military seized power, maintaining control through the use of torture and death squads. Civilian government finally returned in 1985.

AREA: 8,511,970sq km (3,286,472sq mi)
POPULATION: 169,543,612
CAPITAL (POPULATION): Brasília (2,043,169)
GOVERNMENT: Federal multi-party republic
ETHNIC GROUPS: White 53%, Mulatto 22%, Mestizo 12%, African American 11%, Japanese 1%, Native American 0.1%
LANGUAGES: Portuguese (official)
RELIGIONS: Roman Catholic 75%, Protestant 20%, African/syncretist 4%
MOTTO: "*Ordem e Progresso*" "Order and Progress"
NATIONAL ANTHEM (DATE): "*Hino Nacional do Brasil*" "National Anthem of Brazil" (1922)

The azure jay (gralha azul) is the State bird of Paraná, southern Brazil.

39

BRUNEI DARUSSALAM

FLAG RATIO: 1:2 **USE:** National/Civil **DATE ADOPTED:** 1906 **LAST MODIFIED:** 1959

In 1906 Brunei became a British dependency and added two **diagonal stripes** to the previously all-yellow flag. The **yellow** represents the Sultan of Brunei, while the **white** and **black** stripes denote his two chief ministers. The constitution of 1959 added the **red coat of arms** to the flag. The crest has a parasol, wings, hands, and crescent. The **parasol** is a national symbol for royalty. The **wing** has four feathers, symbolizing the protection of justice, tranquillity, prosperity and peace. The **hands** signify the government's pledge to promote welfare, peace and prosperity. The **crescent** is a traditional symbol of **Islam**. Written in **yellow Arabic script** on the crescent is the national motto, "Always Render Service by God's Guidance". The **scroll** beneath the crest reads "*Brunei Darussalam*" ("Brunei, the abode of peace").

HISTORY

During the 16th century, Brunei was the seat of a powerful **Sultanate** that ruled over the whole of **Borneo** and parts of the Philippines. In 1888 Brunei became a **British Protectorate. Hassanal Bolikiah** succeeded his father **Omar Ali Saifuddin** as Sultan in 1967. In 1984 Brunei gained **independence**.

AREA: 5765sq km (2225sq mi)
POPULATION: 333,000
CAPITAL (POPULATION): Bandar Seri Begawan (46,000)
GOVERNMENT: Multi-party republic
ETHNIC GROUPS: Malay 67%, Chinese 20%, indigenous 6%
LANGUAGES: Malay (official), English, Chinese
RELIGIONS: Shafeite Sunni Muslim (official) 67%, Buddhist 13%, Christian 10%, indigenous beliefs and other 10%
NATIONAL MOTTO: "Always Render Service by God's Guidance"
NATIONAL ANTHEM (DATE): "*Allah Peliharakan Sultan*" "God Bless the Sultan" (1951)

Brunei *stamp celebrating the opening of the Malay Technology Museum in 1988.*

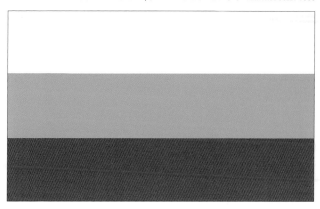

Bulgaria is the only Slavic nation to have **white**, **green** and **red** as its national colours rather than the Pan-Slavic colours of blue, white and red. Bulgaria adopted the **tricolour** flag of **horizontal stripes** in 1879. In 1947 Bulgaria's communist government added socialist symbols such as a red star to the coat of arms (a rampant golden lion), which it placed on the upper hoist of the flag. In 1990, after the collapse of the communist regime, the old flag returned. White stands for peace, love and freedom. Green represents agriculture. Red symbolizes the fight for independence.

HISTORY

The first Bulgarian Empire (681–1018) was a major power in the **Balkans**. In 1018 Basil II annexed it to the **Byzantine Empire**. A second Bulgarian Empire (1186–1396) encompassed the whole of the Balkans before it fell to the **Ottoman Empire**. The crushing of a Bulgar rebellion (1876) brought **Russian** assistance, and Bulgaria gained **autonomy** in 1879. In 1908 Tsar Ferdinand declared Bulgaria an **independent monarchy**. It allied with Nazi Germany in **World War II**. In 1944 the **Soviet** army overran Bulgaria. From 1954 to 1989 **Todor Zhivkov** led a communist government. In 2001 former King **Simeon II** became premier.

Stamp featuring a painting by the Bulgarian modern artist Tzanko Lavrenov.

AREA: 110,910sq km (42,822sq mi)
POPULATION: 7,973,671
CAPITAL (POPULATION): Sofia (1,096,389)
GOVERNMENT: Multi-party republic
ETHNIC GROUPS: Bulgarian 86%, Turkish 9%, Romany 4%, Macedonian, Armenian,
LANGUAGES: Bulgarian (official)
RELIGIONS: Eastern Orthodox Christian 86%, Muslim 10%, Roman Catholic 1%
NATIONAL MOTTO: "*Obedinenieto Pravi Silno*" "Unity is Strength"
NATIONAL ANTHEM (DATE): "*Mila Rodino*" "Dear Native Land" (1964)

41

BURKINA FASO

FLAG RATIO: 2:3 **USE:** National/Civil **ADOPTED:** 1984 **ESTABLISHED BY LAW:** 1997

In 1984 **Upper Volta** was renamed Burkina Faso ('Land of the Incorruptible'). It adopted a new flag with **Pan-African** colours to celebrate the break from its colonial past and to champion unity among African nations. The upper, **red horizontal band** represents the blood shed in the liberation struggle. The **green horizontal band** symbolizes Burkina Faso's fertile agricultural land. The central **yellow five-pointed star** represents the nation's revolutionary ideals.

HISTORY

From *c.*1100 the **Mossi** migrated north to what is now Burkina Faso. They established small, highly complex kingdoms.

The Moro Naba, an absolute monarch, ruled the state of **Ougadougou**, which defeated invasions by the mighty **Songhai Empire**. By 1897 **France** had conquered virtually the whole of Burkina Faso. In 1919 it became the French **colony** of Upper Volta. In 1958 Upper Volta became an autonomous republic – a prelude to full **independence** in 1960. In 1966 General **Sengoulé Lamizana** led a successful military coup against the elected government. Lamizana dominated the politics of Upper Volta until his overthrow in 1980. In 1983 **Thomas Sankara** seized office. **Blaise Campaoré** captured power after Sankara's assassination in 1987. Campaoré won elections in 1992 and 1998. **AIDS** is a major problem.

AREA: 274,200sq km (105,869 sq mi)
POPULATION: 12,083,700
CAPITAL (POPULATION): Ouagadougou (839,800)
GOVERNMENT: Multi-party republic
ETHNIC GROUPS: Mossi 48%, Mande 9%, Fulani 8%, Bobo 7%
LANGUAGES: French (official)
RELIGIONS: Muslim (mainly Sunni) 50%, indigenous beliefs 25%, Roman Catholic 20%
NATIONAL MOTTO: "*Unité, Progrès, Justice*" "Unity, Progress, Justice"
NATIONAL ANTHEM (DATE): "*Ditanyé*" "Hymn of Victory" (1984)

Burkinabe *stamp celebrating International Women's Day.*

Burma's flag is **red** with a dark **blue canton** containing the national emblem in the top left corner. The emblem, added in 1974, consists of a **cogwheel** and **rice plant**, symbolizing industry and agriculture respectively. The circle of **14 stars** around the emblem represent the seven States and seven Divisions of Burma. Red stands for bravery, unity and determinism. Blue represents peace and stability, while the **white** of the emblem symbolizes purity.

HISTORY

Conflict between the **Burmans** and **Mons** dominated Burma's early history. Wars with **British India** dominated the 19th century. The first war (1824) saw Britain gain the coastal regions of Tenasserim and Arakan. Britain acquired the **Irrawaddy** delta in the second war (1852), and annexed Burma in the third war (1885). In 1942 Japan conquered Burma. **Aung San** led resistance to Japanese control. In 1947 Aung San was murdered. Burma achieved **independence** in 1948. **U Nu** was the first prime minister. The military dictatorship of General **Ne Win** ruled Burma from 1962 to 1988. In 1989 Burma changed its name to the **Union of Myanmar**. The National League for Democracy (NLD), led by **Aung San Suu Kyi**, daughter of Aung San, won elections in 1990, but the military annulled the result. Aung San Suu Kyi was under house arrest until 2002.

Golden lions flank the human pyramid set against the outline of Burma.

AREA: 676,577 sq km (261,228 sq mi)
POPULATION: 50,913,600
CAPITAL (POPULATION): Rangoon (4,101,000)
GOVERNMENT: Military regime
ETHNIC GROUPS: Burman 68%, Shan 9%, Karen 7%, Rakhine 4%, Chinese 3%, Mon 2%
LANGUAGES: Burmese (official)
RELIGIONS: Theravada Buddhist 89%, Christian 5%, Muslim 4%
NATIONAL ANTHEM (DATE): "*Gby majay Bma pyay*" "We shall always love Burma" (1948)

43

BURUNDI

FLAG RATIO: 3:5 USE: National/Civil DATE ADOPTED: 1967 LAST MODIFIED: 1982

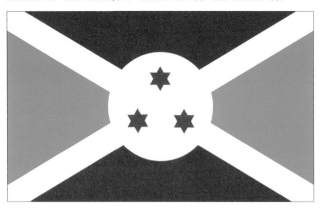

Burundi adoped its present flag after becoming a republic in 1967. In 1982 it altered the **ratio** from 2:3 to 3:5. A **white diagonal cross** divides the flag. A central **disc** contains **three red stars**, each representing an element of the national motto '*Unité, Travail, Progrès*', and also each of the three main ethnic groups in Burundi. The **red** symbolizes the blood shed in the fight for independence. **Green** stands for hope, while the **white** cross and disk signify peace.

HISTORY

About 1000 years ago, Bantu-speaking **Hutus** began to settle in the area. From the 15th century the **Tutsi**, a tall, cattle-owning people, gradually gained control. The Tutsi forced the Hutu majority into serfdom. In the 1890s **Germany** conquered the region. In 1916 **Belgium** occupied what was known as **Ruanda-Urundi**. In 1962 Burundi gained **independence**, ruled by a Tutsi king. In 1966 the monarchy was overthrown and a **republic** established. Another attempted coup led to the creation of a **one-party state** in 1969. A Hutu president, **Melchior Ndadaye**, became president in 1993 multi-party elections. Ndadaye was assassinated in a military coup and two months of **civil war** killed more than 50,000 people and created 500,000 mainly Hutu refugees. In 1994 President Cyprien Ntaryamira died in a rocket attack and the **genocide** continued. In 1996 the Tutsi army seized power. In 2002 Jean Minani, a Hutu, led a transitional assembly.

AREA: 27,830 sq km (10,745 sq mi)
POPULATION: 7,396,000
CAPITAL (POPULATION): Bujumbura (846,000)
GOVERNMENT: Transitional
ETHNIC GROUPS: Hutu 85%, Tutsi 14%, Twa (pygmy) 1%
LANGUAGES: French and Kirundi (both official)
RELIGIONS: Roman Catholic 61%, Protestant 7%, indigenous beliefs 13%, Muslim 10%
NATIONAL MOTTO: "*Unité, Travail, Progrès*" "Unity, Work, Progress"
NATIONAL ANTHEM (DATE): "*Uburundi Bwacu*" "Beloved Burundi" (1962)

On July 1, 1962, Burundi gained independence under King Mwambutsa IV.

44

FLAG RATIO: 2:3 **USE:** National/Civil **DATE ADOPTED:** 1948 **REINTRODUCED:** 1993

Cambodia adopted the present national flag in 1948. In 1970 the **Khmer Republic** introduced a new flag with three white stars. In 1993 the monarchy and the old flag were restored. The central emblem, a stylized representation of the 12th-century temple of **Angkor Wat** has been a symbol of the Khmer monarchy since the 19th century. **Red** is the traditional colour of Cambodia. The **blue** is said to represent the wealth of the land. The flag reflects the Khmer royal motto of "Nation, Religion, King".

HISTORY

The **Angkor period** (889–1434) was the 'golden age' of Khmer civilization. In 1434 the **Thai** captured Angkor and the capital moved to **Phnom Penh**. In 1887 Cambodia became part of the French Union of **Indochina**. Japan occupied it during World War II. In 1953 Cambodia gained **independence** from **France** and **Norodom Sihanouk** became King. The **Vietnam War** (1954–75) dominated Cambodian politics. In 1970 Lon Nol overthrew Norodom and US and South Vietnamese troops entered Cambodia to destroy North Vietnamese camps. Civil war ensued. In 1975 the **Khmer Rouge** (Cambodian communists) seized Phnom Penh and renamed the country **Kampuchea**. The Khmer Rouge, led by **Pol Pot**, killed between 1 and 4 million people in purges. In 1979 Vietnamese and Cambodian troops overthrew Pol Pot. Sihanouk returned as king in 1993.

AREA: 181,040sq km (69,900sq mi)
POPULATION: 11,437,656
CAPITAL (POPULATION): Phnom Penh (998,000)
GOVERNMENT: Constitutional monarchy
ETHNIC GROUPS: Khmer 92%, Chinese 3%, Cham 2%, Vietnamese, Thai, Lao, Kola
LANGUAGES: Khmer (official)
RELIGIONS: Theravada Buddhist 93%, Muslim (mainly Shafeite Sunni) 6%
MOTTO: "Nation, Religion, King"
NATIONAL ANTHEM (DATE): "*Nokoreach*" (1941, restored 1993)

Khmer dancers at the temple mountain of Bayon, built at Angkor by Jayavarman VII.

45

CAMEROON

FLAG RATIO: 2:3 USE: National/Civil DATE ADOPTED: 1975 LAST MODIFIED: 1975

Cameroon's tricolour flag uses the Pan-African colours of **red**, **green**, and **yellow**. They represent freedom from colonialism and a united Africa. The colours also represent the vegetation of the south (green) and the savannahs of the north (yellow). Red stands for union and freedom. In 1975 a **five-pointed yellow star** replaced the two stars that had been on the flag's green stripe since 1961. The star stands for national unity.

HISTORY

In 1472 **Portuguese** explorers reached the coast. Cameroon gets its name from the explorers, who fished for *camarões* (prawns). From the 17th century, southern Cameroon was a centre of the **slave trade**. In the early 19th century, Britain abolished slavery and established the **ivory** trade. After World War I, Cameroon divided into two zones, ruled by **Britain** and **France**. In 1960, following civil unrest, **French Cameroon** gained **independence**. In 1961 **northern British Cameroon** voted to join French Cameroon, forming the Federal Republic of Cameroon. **Ahmadou Ahidjo** served as president from 1960 to 1982. In 1966 Cameroon became a one-party state. In 1972 the federation became a unitary state. In 1984 **Paul Biya** made Cameroon a republic. In 1995 Cameroon joined the **Commonwealth of Nations**.

AREA: 475,440sq km (183,567sq mi)

POPULATION: 15,906,000

CAPITAL (POPULATION): Yaoundé (1,122,500)

GOVERNMENT: Multi-party republic

ETHNIC GROUPS: 200 tribes, including Fang 20%, Bamileke and Bamoun 19%, Douala, Luanda and Bass 15%, Kirdi 11%, Fulani 10%

LANGUAGES: French and English (both official)

RELIGIONS: Indigenous beliefs 40%, Roman Catholic 20%, Protestant 20%, Muslim 20%

NATIONAL MOTTO: "*Paix, Travail, Patrie*" "Peace, Work, Fatherland"

NATIONAL ANTHEM (DATE): "*Chant da Ralliement*" "Rallying Song" (1957)

Cacao, grown mainly in the south and centre, is Cameroon's major cash crop.

CANADA

FLAG RATIO: 1:2 **USE:** National/Civil **DATE ADOPTED:** 1965 **LAST MODIFIED:** 1965

In 1965 Canada raised its present **red** and **white** flag with a central, stylized **11-pointed red maple leaf** as the national flag. It replaced the Canadian Red Ensign, which featured the British Union Jack and Canada's coat of arms on a red field. The new flag sought to promote unity among Canadians. The maple leaf has been a national symbol since 1860. In 1921 King George VI proclaimed red and white as Canada's national colours and added the maple leaf to its coat of arms in recognition of Canadian sacrifice during World War I.

HISTORY

Ancestors of today's **Native Americans** arrived from Asia *c.*20,000 years ago. In the 10th century, the **Vikings** landed in Canada. In 1534 **Jacques Cartier** discovered the St Lawrence River and claimed Canada for **France**. The French established the first European settlement in 1605, and founded **Québec** in 1608. In 1759 Britain captured Québec, and it gained all of French Canada at the end of the **French and Indian War** (1754–63). Canada remained loyal to the British during the American Revolution (1775–83). The British North America Act (1867) established the Dominion of Canada. Canadians fought as part of Allied forces in both World Wars. Prime minister **W.L. Mackenzie King** did much to promote national unity. In 1982 **Pierre Trudeau** passed the Canada Act that made Canada a fully sovereign nation.

AREA: 9,976,140sq km (3,851,788sq mi)
POPULATION: 30,007,094
CAPITAL (POPULATION): Ottawa (774,072)
GOVERNMENT: Federal, multi-party constitutional monarchy
ETHNIC GROUPS: British 34%, French 26%, German 4%, Italian 3%, Ukrainian 2%, Native American 1.5%, Chinese, Dutch
LANGUAGES: English and French (both official)
RELIGIONS: Roman Catholic 47%, Protestant 36%, Eastern Orthodox 1%, Jewish 1%, Muslim 1%, Hindu, Buddhist
MOTTO: *"Mari usque ad mare"* "From Sea to Sea"
NATIONAL ANTHEM (DATE): "O Canada" (1980)

The Great Peace of Montréal *(1701) ended the Iroquois Wars with the French.*

47

CAPE VERDE

FLAG RATIO: Not fixed USE: National/Civil DATE ADOPTED: 1992 LAST MODIFIED: 1992

In 1992 Cape Verde, off the west coast of Africa, finally abandoned attempts to unite with Guinea-Bissau and adopted a new national flag. The **blue**, **white** and **red striped** flag replaced the design that had been in use since independence in 1975, and which was almost identical to the flag of Guinea-Bissau. Both were based on the flag of the *Partido Africano da Independência da Guiné e Cabo Verde* (PAIGC), which led the struggle for independence, and used the Pan-African colours. The blue symbolizes the sea and sky. The **ten, yellow five-pointed stars** represents each of Cape Verde's ten main islands. The **circle** stands for the unity of Cape Verde. White signifies peace, and red denotes national effort.

HISTORY

In 1462 **Portugal** began to settle the uninhabited islands of Cape Verde. The Portuguese imported **slaves** from west Africa to work on sugar plantations, and the islands prospered as a staging post in the Atlantic slave trade. In the 19th century, the abolition of slavery and persistent drought brought economic collapse and starvation. In 1956 the Cape Verdean **Amilcar Cabral** cofounded the PAIGC, which fought against Portuguese colonialism from mainland Portuguese Guinea (now **Guinea-Bissau**). In 1975 Cape Verde gained **independence**. A coup (1980) in Guinea-Bissau dented hopes of unification. **Aristides Pereira** served as President from 1975 to 1991.

AREA: 4033sq km (1557sq mi)
POPULATION: 449,100
CAPITAL (POPULATION): Praia (106,052)
GOVERNMENT: Multi-party republic
ETHNIC GROUPS: Creole (mulatto) 71%, African 28%, European 1%
LANGUAGES: Portuguese, Crioulo (a blend of Portuguese and West African)
RELIGIONS: Roman Catholic (infused with indigenous beliefs) 95%, Protestant (mostly Church of the Nazarene) 5%
NATIONAL ANTHEM (DATE): "*Cântico da Liberdade*" "Song of Liberty" (1975)

In 1898 Mindelo, on São Vicente island, was the world's fourth largest coaling station.

CENTRAL AFRICAN REPUBLIC

FLAG RATIO: 3:5 **USE:** National/Civil **DATE ADOPTED:** 1958 **LAST MODIFIED:** 1958

In 1958 the Central African Republic became a self-governing republic within the French Community and adopted its present flag. By combining the **yellow**, **green** and **red** colours of the **Pan-African** movement with the **blue** of the French flag, it acknowledges the history of the Central African Republic while looking forward to a united Africa. The **red** vertical stripe running through the centre of the flag symbolizes the common blood of humanity. The **yellow, five-pointed** star in the blue stripe stands for progress and unity.

HISTORY

Between the 16th and 19th centuries slavery greatly reduced the population of what is now the Central African Republic. In 1887 **France** occupied the area, and in 1894 established the colony of Ubangi-Shari at **Bangui**. In 1906 the colony united with Chad, and in 1910 it joined **French Equatorial Africa**. Post-1945, the colony received representation in the French parliament. In 1960 the **Central African Republic** declared **independence**. **David Dacko** was the first president. In 1966 **Jean-Bédel Bokassa** overthrew Dacko in a military coup. In 1976 Bokassa proclaimed himself Emperor. Dacko deposed Bokassa in a French-backed coup in 1979. **André-Dieudonné Kolingba** ruled from 1981 to 1993.

Subsistence agriculture dominates the economy of Central African Republic.

AREA: 622,980sq km (240,533sq mi)
POPULATION: 3,885,800
CAPITAL (POPULATION): Bangui (652,900)
GOVERNMENT: Multi-party republic
ETHNIC GROUPS: Baya 33%, Banda 27%, Mandje 13%, Sara 10%, Mboum 7%, Mbaka 4%, Takoma 4%
LANGUAGES: French (official), Sango (national)
RELIGIONS: Indigenous beliefs 35%, Roman Catholic 25%, Protestant 25%, Muslim 8%
NATIONAL MOTTO: "*Unité, Dignité, Travail*" "Unity, Dignity, Work"
NATIONAL ANTHEM (DATE): "*La Renaissance*" "The Revival" (1960)

CHAD

FLAG RATIO: 2:3 USE: National/Civil DATE ADOPTED: 1959 LAST MODIFIED: 1959

Chad's flag is identical to the flag of Andorra and Romania. It combines the **blue** of the French *tricolore* with the **yellow** and **red** of the **Pan-African** movement. The blue represents the sky and hope. Yellow symbolizes the Sahara Desert, and red stands for the blood shed for national liberation.

HISTORY

Chad straddles two, often conflicting worlds: the **Muslim** north and the sedentary **Christian** or animist south. In *c.*AD 700 North African nomads founded the **Kanem Empire**. In the 14th century, the kingdom of **Bornu** expanded to incorporate Kanem. In the late 19th century, the region fell to **Sudan**. In 1900 **France** defeated Sudan, and in 1908 Chad became the largest province of **French Equatorial Africa**. In 1920 it became a separate colony. In 1960 Chad gained **independence**. In 1965 northern Muslims, led by the Chad National Liberation Front (**Frolinat**) rebelled against the government of **François Tombalbaye**. By 1973 the government, helped by the French, quashed the revolt. In 1980 **Libya** occupied northern Chad. In 1982 **Hisséne Habre** and Goukouni Oueddi formed rival regimes. Libya's bombing of Chad in 1983 saw the deployment of French troops. In 1990 **Idriss Déby** overthrew Habre. Déby won elections in 1996 and 2001.

AREA: 1,284,000sq km (495,752sq mi)
POPULATION: 7,114,400
CAPITAL (POPULATION): Ndjamena (601,500)
GOVERNMENT: Transitional
ETHNIC GROUPS: Sara, Bagirmi and Kreish 33%, Sudanic Arab 26%, Teda 7%, Mbum 6%
LANGUAGES: French and Arabic (both official)
RELIGIONS: Muslim (mainly Tidjani Sufi) 50%, Christian (mainly Catholic) 25%, African traditional beliefs 18%
NATIONAL ANTHEM (DATE): "*La Tchadienne*" "The Song of Chad" (1960)

Armour, *clothes and weapon of a Moundang warrior from southern Chad.*

FLAG RATIO: 2:3 USE: National/Civil DATE ADOPTED: 1817 LAST MODIFIED: 1912

Chile's flag dates from 1817, during the war of independence against Spain. Adopted by the government of Bernardo O'Higgins, it was apparently designed by the Minister of War José Ignacio Zenteno. The **blue canton** represents the sky. The **white** symbolizes the snow-capped **Andes** Mountains, while the **red** stands for the blood shed by the nation's patriots. The **white five-pointed star** stands for unity, progress and honour.

HISTORY

In 1520 Portuguese navigator **Ferdinand Magellan** became the first European to sight Chile. In 1541 **Pedro de Valdivia** founded **Santiago**. Chile became a **Spanish colony**, ruled as part of the Viceroyalty of Peru. In 1817 an army, led by **José de San Martín**, surprised the Spanish by crossing the Andes. In 1818 **Bernardo O'Higgins** proclaimed Chilean **independence**. Chile gained mineral-rich land from Peru and Bolivia in the **War of the Pacific** (1879–84). In 1973 soaring inflation and public disturbances led to a military coup, with covert US support, against the government of **Salvador Allende**. The coup left more than 3000 people dead or missing, and **General Augusto Pinochet** assumed control. In 1977 Pinochet banned all political parties. His regime was characterized by repression and human rights' violations. In 2000 **Ricardo Lagos** became the first socialist president since Allende.

AREA: 756,950sq km (292,258sq mi)
POPULATION: 15,598,500
CAPITAL (POPULATION): Santiago (5,034,500)
GOVERNMENT: Multi-party republic
ETHNIC GROUPS: Mestizo 92%,
Native American 7%
LANGUAGES: Spanish (official)
RELIGIONS: Roman Catholic 81%,
Protestant 6%
NATIONAL MOTTO: "*Por la razon o la fuerza*"
"By reason or by force"
NATIONAL ANTHEM (DATE): "*Himno Nacional de Chile*" "National Song of Chile" (1941)

The Mapuche of central Chile are renowned for their textile handicraft.

51

CHINA

FLAG RATIO: 2:3 **USE:** National/Civil **DATE ADOPTED:** 1949 **LAST MODIFIED:** 1949

China adopted its present flag in 1949, when Mao Zedong founded a communist republic. **Red** is a traditional colour of China and communism. The **large gold star** represents the leading role of the **Communist Party of China**. The **four smaller gold stars** symbolize the main social classes: workers, peasants, bourgeoisie, and capitalists.

HISTORY

Qin Shihuangdi unified China. The **Qin** dynasty (221–206 BC) also built the majority of the **Great Wall**. The **Han** dynasty (202 BC–AD 220) developed the Empire, a bureaucracy based on **Confucianism**, and also introduced **Buddhism**. **Genghis Khan** conquered most of China in the 1210s, and established the **Mongol Empire**. **Kublai Khan** founded the **Yüan** dynasty (1271–1368), an era of dialogue with Europe. The **Ming** dynasty (1368–1644) reestablished Chinese rule. The Manchu **Qing** dynasty (1644–1912) initially expanded the empire. Britain occupied Hong Kong after the **Opium War** (1839–42). In 1912 **Sun Yat-sen** established a **republic**. In 1937 the warring nationalist Kuomintang and communists united to fight Japanese invasion. In 1966 Mao launched the **Cultural Revolution**. In 1976 **Deng Xiaoping** succeeded Mao. **Jiang Zemin** succeeded Deng in 1997.

AREA: 9,596,960 sq km (3,705,386 sq mi)
POPULATION: 1,295,330,000
CAPITAL (POPULATION): Beijing (7,129,500)
GOVERNMENT: Single-party communist republic
ETHNIC GROUPS: Han (Chinese) 92%, 55 minority groups
LANGUAGES: Mandarin Chinese (official)
RELIGIONS: The government encourages atheism. People practise Confucianism, Buddhism, Taoism, and Islam.
NATIONAL ANTHEM (DATE): "*Yiyongjjun Jinxingqu*" "March of the Volunteers" (1949)

Emperor Sima Yan unifies China at the end of the "Romance of the Three Kingdoms".

Colombia's **tricolour** flag has the same colours as their neighbours Ecuador and Venezuela. It differs from Ecuador's flag only in its **ratio** – 2:3 rather than 1:2. In 1806 Venezuelan revolutionary Francisco de Miranda raised the flag in revolt against Spanish rule. In 1819 Simón Bolívar defeated the Spanish at the Battle of Boyacá and the flag became the national symbol of Greater Colombia (including Ecuador and Venezuela). After several changes, the government reverted to the original design in 1861. A popular Colombian children's song says of the national colours, "**yellow** is our gold, **blue** is our vast oceans, and **red** is the blood that gave us our freedom".

HISTORY

The pre-Colombian **Chibcha** civilization lived undisturbed in the eastern cordillera for thousands of years. In 1525 the **Spanish** established the first European settlement at Santa Marta. By 1538 conquistador Gonzalo Jiménez de Quesada conquered the Chibcha and established Bogotá. Colombia became part of the **New Kingdom of Granada**. In 1830 Ecudaor and Venezuela gained independence from **Greater Colombia**. In 1885 the **Republic of Colombia** was formed. Nearly 100,000 people died in the first civil war (1899–1902). The second civil war, **La Violencia** (1949–57), was even more bloody. The **Revolutionary Armed Forces of Colombia (FARC)** have waged a guerrilla war since 1958.

AREA: 1,138,910sq km (439,733sq mi)
POPULATION: 43,492,500
CAPITAL (POPULATION): Bogotá (6,668,500)
GOVERNMENT: Multi-party republic
ETHNIC GROUPS: Mestizo 58%, White 20%, Mulatto 14%, Black 4%, mixed Black and Native American 3%, Native American 1%
LANGUAGES: Spanish (official)
RELIGIONS: Roman Catholic 93%, Protestant 4%
NATIONAL MOTTO: "Libertad y orden" "Liberty and Order"
NATIONAL ANTHEM (DATE): "Oh! Gloria inmarcesible" "Oh! Unfading Glory" (1920)

Porro *is a form of Colombian dance music similar to calypso or rumba.*

COMOROS

FLAG RATIO: 3:5 USE: National/Civil DATE ADOPTED: 2002 LAST MODIFIED: 2002

In 2002 Comoros adopted a new flag as the islands reunited as the Union of the Comoros. The flag consists of **four horizontal stripes** in **yellow**, **white**, **red** and **blue**. The **green triangle** with a **white crescent** and **four white stars** on the hoist recalls the islands' previous flag. The colour green and the crescent are traditionally associated with **Islam**, the main religion of the Comoros. The four stars represent the three islands of Comoros (**Grande Comore**, **Anjouan**, **Mohéli**) and the French-adminstered island of **Mayotte**, over which Comoros claims sovereignty.

AREA: 1862sq km (719sq mi)
POPULATION: 670,000
CAPITAL (POPULATION): Moroni (30,365)
GOVERNMENT: Transitional
ETHNIC GROUPS: Antalote, Cafre, Makoa, Oimatsaha, Sakalava
LANGUAGES: Arabic (official), French (official), Comoran (a blend of Swahili and Arabic)
RELIGIONS: Sunni Muslim 99%, Roman Catholic 1%
NATIONAL MOTTO: "*Unité, Justice, Progrès*"
"Unity, Justice, Progress"
NATIONAL ANTHEM (DATE): "*Udzima wa ya Masiwa*"
"The Union of the Great Islands" (1978)

HISTORY

Traders from Arabia, East Africa and **Madagascar** built settlements for the selling of slaves or food. In the late 18th century Comorians fortified the trading towns to protect them from Malagasy slave raids. In 1866 the islands became a French protectorate, and plantations were established. In 1912 Comoros became a French colony governed by Madagascar. In **1975** the Comoros declared **independence**, while Mayotte chose to remain with France. From independence to 2002 Comoros witnessed 20 **coups**, and French troops and French-backed mercenaries intervened on several occasions. In 1997 Anjouan and Mohéli declared independence. In 2001 a new constitution sought to reunify the Comoros but with greater autonomy for each island.

Comorian stamp displaying the old national flag and four islands in the group.

54

CONGO, DEMOCRATIC REPUBLIC OF

FLAG RATIO: 2:3 USE: National/Civil DATE ADOPTED: 1960 LAST MODIFIED: 1997

The present national flag of the Democratic Republic of Congo (DRC) is similar to the flag adopted after it gained independence from Belgium in 1960. The **blue** represents the United Nations' role in securing independence for the country. The **six small gold stars** stand for the original provinces of the independent state. The flag derives from the 1877 flag of the Congo Free State, a gold star on a blue background. The **large gold star** represents Congo as a guiding light for the continent of Africa.

HISTORY

Large **Bantu** kingdoms emerged in the 14th century. In 1482, a Portuguese navigator became the first European to reach the mouth of the River Congo. In the 19th century, traders in slaves and ivory formed powerful states. **Henry Morton Stanley**'s explorations (1874–77) established the route of the Congo. In 1885 King **Leopold II** of **Belgium** established the **Congo Free State**. In 1908 it became the colony of **Belgium Congo**. In 1960 the Republic of the Congo gained **independence** under **Patrice Lumumba**, but **Joseph Mobutu** seized power in a military coup. In 1971 he renamed the country **Zaïre**. In 1995 millions of Hutus fled into Zaïre from **Rwanda**. In 1996 **Laurent Kabila** overthrew Mobutu. Zaïre became the Democratic Republic of Congo. Between 1998 and 2001, a **civil war** killed 2.5 million people.

AREA: 2,344,885sq km (905,365 sq mi)
POPULATION: 54,995,500
CAPITAL (POPULATION): Kinshasa (6,301,100)
GOVERNMENT: Single-party republic
ETHNIC GROUPS: Luba 18%, Kongo 16%, Mongo 14%, Rwanda 10%, Azande 6%, Bandi and Ngale 6%, Rundi 4%
LANGUAGES: French (official)
RELIGIONS: Roman Catholic 48%, Protestant 29%, indigenous Christian churches 17%, traditional beliefs 3%, Muslim 1%
NATIONAL ANTHEM (DATE): "*Debout Congolais*" "Arise Congolese" (1991)

***Stamp** marking the 50th anniversary of the International Labour Organization (ILO).*

CONGO, REPUBLIC OF

FLAG RATIO: 2:3 **USE:** National/Civil **DATE ADOPTED:** 1958 **REINTRODUCED:** 1991

Congo-Brazzaville adopted its present tricolour of **diagonal stripes** in 1958, when it became an autonomous republic within the French Community. In 1969 a new constitution established the People's Republic of Congo and adopted a Soviet-inspired flag with communist symbols. In 1991 the Congo abandoned communism and reverted to its original flag. It uses the **Pan-African** colours of **green**, **yellow**, and **red**.

HISTORY

The **Loango** and **Bakongo** kingdoms dominated the Congo when the first European arrived in 1482. The Congolese coast became a centre for the slave trade. In 1880 **Pierre Savorgnan de Brazza** explored the area and it became a **French protectorate**. In 1910 **Brazzaville** became the capital of the federation of **French Equatorial Africa**. In **1960** the Republic of Congo gained **independence**. In 1964 Congo adopted **Marxism-Leninism** as the state ideology. The military, led by **Marien Ngouabi**, seized power in 1968. Ngouabi was assassinated in 1977. Colonel **Denis Sassou-Nguesso** ruled Congo from 1979 to 1992. **Pascal Lissouba** became president in 1992 multi-party elections. In 1997 Sassou-Nguesso overthrew Lissouba and the Congo plunged into **civil war**. In 2002 the Congo adopted a new constitution and Sassou-Nguesso was re-elected.

AREA: 342,000sq km (132,046sq mi)
POPULATION: 3,258,400
CAPITAL (POPULATION): Brazzaville (1,133,800)
GOVERNMENT: Multi-party republic
ETHNIC GROUPS: Kongo 52%, Teke 13%, Mboshi 12%, Mbete 5%
LANGUAGES: French (official)
RELIGIONS: Roman Catholic 45%, Protestant 5%, traditional beliefs 48%, Islam 2%
NATIONAL MOTTO: "*Unité, Travail, Progrès*" "Unity, Work, Progress
NATIONAL ANTHEM (DATE): "*La Congolaise*" "Song of Congo" (1962)

Traditional marriage ceremony in the Republic of Congo.

FLAG RATIO: 3:5 **USE:** National/Civil **DATE ADOPTED:** 1848 **LAST MODIFIED:** 1848

Costa Rica based its flag on the French *tricolore*. First Lady Pacífica Fernández Oreamuno designed the national flag in 1848. It consists of **five horizontal stripes** of blue, white and red. **Blue** represents the sky and opportunity. **White** stands for wisdom and peace. **Red** symbolizes the warmth of Costa Rica's people and the blood shed in the fight for freedom. In 1964 Costa Rica amended its **coat of arms**, which sometimes appears on unofficial civil flags. It shows two sailing ships on the Pacific Ocean and the Caribbean Sea, separated by three volcanos. Also included are the rising sun and seven stars, one for each of Costa Rica's provinces.

HISTORY

In 1502 **Christopher Columbus** sailed along the Caribbean shore and named the land Costa Rica, Spanish for 'rich coast'. The first **Spanish** colonizers arrived in 1561. Spain ruled the country until 1821, when Spain's Central American colonies broke away to join the **Mexican Empire**. In 1823 the Central American states split from Mexico to set up the **Central American Federation**. In 1838 Costa Rica achieved **independence**. It prospered on its **coffee** and **banana** exports. Costa Rica is perhaps the most stable and democratic nation in Central America. **José Figueres Ferrer** served as president from 1953 to 1958 and again from 1970 to 1974. His son, **José María Figueres**, Olsen, was also president (1994–98).

AREA: 51,100sq km (19,730sq mi)
POPULATION: 3,906,742
CAPITAL (POPULATION): San José (313,262)
GOVERNMENT: Multi-party republic
ETHNIC GROUPS: White 85%, Mestizo 8%, Black and Mulatto 3%, East Asian (mostly Chinese) 3%
LANGUAGES: Spanish (official)
RELIGIONS: Roman Catholic 90%
NATIONAL ANTHEM (DATE): "*Himno Nacional*" "National Hymn" (1853)

Stamp celebrating the International Year of the Older Persons in 1999.

CÔTE D'IVOIRE

FLAG RATIO: 2:3 **USE:** National/Civil **DATE ADOPTED:** 1959 **LAST MODIFIED:** 1959

Côte d'Ivoire modelled its flag on the *tricolore* of France, the former colonial power. It is a mirror image of Ireland's flag. **Orange** represents growth and the soil of the savanna on the northern and central plateaux. **White** stands for peace emerging from righteousness, as well as the rapids of the Sassandra, Bandama, and Komoé rivers. **Green** symbolizes hope for the future and the dense tropical forests in the west. Côte d'Ivoire once had the largest rainforests in West Africa, until logging and plantation farming reduced the coverage of forests.

AREA: 322,460sq km (124,502sq mi)

POPULATION: 17,676,000

CAPITAL (POPULATION): Yamoussoukro (195,500)

GOVERNMENT: Multi-party republic

ETHNIC GROUPS: Akan 41% (Baule 25%), Malinke 17%, Voltaic 16%, Krou 15%, Southern Mande 10%

LANGUAGES: French (official)

RELIGIONS: Muslim 38%, Christian 26%, African traditional beliefs 19%

NATIONAL MOTTO: *"Union, Discipline, Travail"* "Union, Discipline, Labour"

NATIONAL ANTHEM (DATE): *"L'Abidjanaise"* "Song of Abidjan" (1960)

HISTORY

The first Europeans reached Côte d'Ivoire (French, 'Ivory Coast') in the 15th century and began trading in **ivory** and **slaves**. Tribal kingdoms such as the **Kong** and the **Baule** flourished inland and restricted European activity to the coastal region. In the 19th century, the French established forts, trading posts, and **coffee plantations**. In 1893 Côte d'Ivoire became a **French colony**, and in 1904 it was subsumed into the Federation of French West Africa. **Felix Houphouët-Boigny** led the country to **independence** in 1960. The longest-serving head of state in Africa, Houphouët-Boigny served as President of Côte d'Ivoire until 1993.

***Côte d'Ivoire** celebrated 24 years of independence in 1984.*

FLAG RATIO: 1:2 **USE:** National/Civil **DATE ADOPTED:** 1990 **LAST MODIFIED:** 1990

Croatia adopted a Russian-based **red, white** and **blue** flag in 1848. As part of the Federation of Yugoslavia, Croatia's flag had a red star at its centre. In 1990 the present **coat of arms** replaced the red star. The coat of arms consists of a **chequered shield**, dating from the 15th century, and a **crown**. The crown incorporates **four regional symbols** (from Dubrovnik, Dalmatia, Istria, and Slavonia) and the oldest-known Croatian coat of arms.

HISTORY

Croatia was one of six republics that made up the former **Yugoslavia**. An 800-year union of the Hungarian and Croatian crowns began in 1102. In 1699 all of Croatia came under **Habsburg** rule. In 1867 the Habsburg Empire became the **Austro-Hungarian Empire**.

After World War 1, Croatia was incorporated into Yugoslavia (1929). Occupied by Germany in World War II, Croatia became a pro-Nazi state (*Ustashe*). In 1990 nationalist **Franjo Tudjman** became president. In 1991 Croatia voted for independence but Croatian Serbs took up arms in favour of staying part of Yugoslavia. War broke out between **Serbia** and Croatia, and by 1992 Croatia lost more than a third of its land. In 1993 Croatian Serbs in eastern Slavonia voted to establish the separate Republic of **Krajina**. In 1995 Croatia seized the Krajina and 150,000 Serbs fled. In 2000, after Tudjman's death, Stipe Mesic became president.

Andrija Maurović *who drew this* Black Rider *is the 'father of Croatian comics'.*

AREA: 56,538sq km (21,824sq mi)
POPULATION: 4,381,352
CAPITAL (POPULATION): Zagreb (682,598)
GOVERNMENT: Multi-party republic
ETHNIC GROUPS: Croat 78%, Serb 12%, Bosnian, Hungarian, Slovene
LANGUAGES: Serbo-Croatian
RELIGIONS: Roman Catholic 77%, Serbian Orthodox 11%, Muslim 1%
NATIONAL ANTHEM (DATE): "*Lijepa Naša Domovino*" "Our Beautiful Homeland" (1891)

CUBA

FLAG RATIO: 1:2 **USE:** National/Civil **DATE ADOPTED:** 1902 **LAST MODIFIED:** 1902

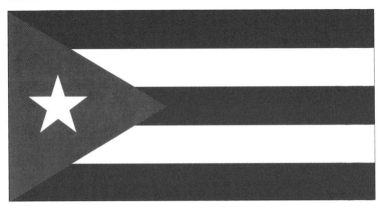

Cuba's flag was first used by Narciso Lopez, leader of a rebellion against Spanish rule in 1849. Cuba officially adopted the flag in 1902, when it gained independence from Spain. The **three blue horizontal stripes** represent the three original Cuban territories. The **red triangle** is of masonic origin and symbolizes liberty, equality, and fraternity. Red stands for the blood of the patriots. The **white star** signifies unity and the purity of revolutionary ideals. It has been suggested that the similarity between the Cuban flag and the 'Stars and Stripes' of the United States indicated Cuba's desire to join the union.

AREA: 110,860sq km (42,803sq mi)
POPULATION: 11,217,100
CAPITAL (POPULATION): Havana (2,328,000)
GOVERNMENT: Socialist republic
ETHNIC GROUPS: White 66%,
Mulatto 22%, Black 12%
LANGUAGES: Spanish (official)
RELIGIONS: Roman Catholic 40%,
Protestant 3%
NATIONAL MOTTO: *"Socialismo o muerte"*
"Socialism or death"
NATIONAL ANTHEM (DATE): *"La Bayamesa"*
"The Bayamo Song" (1902)

HISTORY

Christopher Columbus discovered Cuba in 1492, and Spanish settlers arrived in 1511. In 1895 **José Martí** led a war of independence. In 1898 the sinking of the US battleship *Maine* led to the **Spanish-American War**. Cuba was under **US occupation** (1898–1902) before becoming a republic. Cuba's economy flourished due to its **sugar plantations**. In 1933 **Fulgencio Batista** led a successful coup. **Fidel Castro** (supported by **Che Guevara**) launched a socialist revolution in 1956. In 1959 Castro became Premier. In 1961 the US government backed the disastrous **Bay of Pigs** invasion. Castro's attempt to export revolution to the rest of Latin America ended in diplomatic alienation. Between 1965 and 1973 more than 250,000 Cubans fled into exile.

The indigo hamlet *fish lives in the coral reefs around the island of Cuba.*

A dopted after gaining independence from Britain, the flag was designed to be a neutral symbol for the new Cyprus. The **white field** stands for peace between the fractious Turkish and Greek Cypriots. The **green olive branches** were also symbols of peace. At the centre of the flag is a **yellow silhouette** of the island of Cyprus. The colour yellow refers to the copper deposits for which the island was famous at the time. Although it is the official flag, use of the flag remains divided along lines of Greek and Turkish heritage.

HISTORY

From AD 330 Cyprus formed part of the **Byzantine Empire**. In the 1570s Cyprus became part of the **Ottoman Empire**. Turkish rule continued until 1878, when Turkey leased Cyprus to **Britain**. In 1925 it became a British colony. In the 1950s Greek Cypriots, who make up *c*.80% of the population, began a campaign for *enosis* (union) with Greece. In 1960 Cyprus gained **independence**. The new constitution provided for power-sharing between the Greek and Turkish Cypriots. The arrangement proved unworkable, and fighting broke out between the two communities. In 1983 **Turkish Cypriots** declared the northern part of the island the independent Turkish Republic of **Northern Cyprus**. Turkey is the only country to recognize it. Its **state flag** is a white field with a red crescent and star.

Village *of Agios Dimitrios (1400–1100 BC) near Kalavasos, southern Cyprus.*

AREA: 9250 sq km (3571 sq mi)
POPULATION: 762,000
CAPITAL (POPULATION): Nicosia (195,300)
GOVERNMENT: Multi-party republic
ETHNIC GROUPS: Greek Cypriot 81%, Turkish Cypriot 19%
LANGUAGES: Greek and Turkish (both official)
RELIGIONS: Greek Orthodox 78%, Sunni Muslim 18%
NATIONAL ANTHEM (DATE): "*Ymnos eis tin Eleftherian*" "Hymn to Freedom" (1960)

CZECH REPUBLIC

FLAG RATIO: 2:3 **USE:** National/Civil **DATE ADOPTED:** 1920 **LAST MODIFIED:** 1993

The original national flag was a red and white banner, but in 1920 Czechoslavakia adopted the **Pan-Slavic** colours of red, white and blue. The **white horizontal stripe** represents **Bohemia**, the **red horizontal stripe** represents **Moravia** and the blood shed for the freedom of the state, and the **blue triangle** on the hoist represents Slovakia. In 1993 Czechoslovakia split into two states. The Czech Republic kept the former flag. While the blue triangle no longer represents Slovakia, it does remain a symbol of impartiality and sovereignty.

HISTORY

In the 10th century Bohemia became part of the **Holy Roman Empire**. Emperor Charles IV (1316–78) made Prague his capital. In 1526 the Austrian **Habsburgs** assumed control. A Czech rebellion led to the **Thirty Years' War** (1618–48). **Tomáš Masaryk** was the first president (1918–35) of an independent Czechoslovakia. **Eduard Beneš** was the second president (1935–38). In 1939 Nazi Germany occupied the country. In 1948 the communists took control. In 1968 Soviet troops crushed the **Prague Spring** reforms of **Alexander Dubček**. The peaceful 'Velvet Revolution' saw the creation of a non-communist government in 1989, led by **Vaclav Havel**. In 1993 Czechoslovakia split into the Czech Republic and the **Slovak Republic**.

AREA: 78,864sq km (30,449sq mi)
POPULATION: 10,292,953
CAPITAL (POPULATION): Prague (1,178,576)
GOVERNMENT: Multi-party republic
ETHNIC GROUPS: Czech 90%, Moravian 4%, Slovak 2%, Romany, Polish, German, Silesian, Hungarian, Ukrainian
LANGUAGES: Czech (official)
RELIGIONS: Atheist 51%, Roman Catholic 39%, Protestant 4%, Eastern Orthodox 3%, Hussite 2%
NATIONAL ANTHEM (DATE): "*Kde Domou Múj?*" "Where is my Home?" (1920)

Czech woman in national costume holding painted Easter eggs.

The Danish flag is called the *Dannebrog* (Danish, 'flag of the Danes'). It is thought to be the oldest national flag in continuous use. In a Netherlandish book on heraldry (1370–86), a **white cross** on a **red field** appears on the coat of arms of King Valdemar IV Atterdag. According to legend, the flag fell from heaven during King Waldemar II's battle against the Estonians at Lyndanisse (June 15, 1219). It has long been associated with Christianity. The *Dannebrog* is the basis for the other Nordic flags bearing the 'Scandinavian cross'. A swallow-tailed version of the *Dannebrog* is the state flag and ensign.

ROSKILDE 1000 år

DANMARK 3.75

Viking *King Harald Bluetooth founded the town of Roskilde in 998.*

HISTORY

Between the 9th and 11th centuries, the **Vikings** conquered much of western Europe. From 1015 to 1034 King **Canute II** ruled over England. Queen **Margrethe I** unified Denmark, **Sweden** and Norway in 1397, but Sweden broke away in 1523. In 1536 Denmark adopted Lutheranism. **Christian IV** led Denmark into the costly **Thirty Years' War** with Sweden (1618–48). Denmark lost **Norway** to Sweden in 1814, and **Iceland** gained independence in 1918. In 1940 **Germany** occupied Denmark. In 1945 **Britain** liberated Denmark. Queen **Margrethe II** acceded to the throne in 1972. **Poul Rasmussen** has served as prime minister since 1993. In 2000 Danes voted against joining the **euro**. The **Faroe Islands** and **Greenland** are dependencies.

AREA: 43,070sq km (16,629sq mi)
POPULATION: 5,349,212
CAPITAL (POPULATION): Copenhagen (615,115)
GOVERNMENT: Parliamentary monarchy
ETHNIC GROUPS: Danish 97%
LANGUAGES: Danish (official)
RELIGIONS: Lutheran 91%, Roman Catholic 1%
NATIONAL ANTHEM (DATE): "*Der er et Yndigt Land*" "There is a Lovely Land" (1844)

63

DJIBOUTI

FLAG RATIO: 2:3 USE: National/Civil DATE ADOPTED: 1977 LAST MODIFIED: 1977

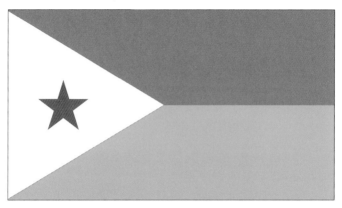

Djibouti's national flag is based on the banner of the African People's League for Independence, leaders in the struggle for liberation from France. The League adopted the flag in 1972. The **two horizontal stripes** represent the two main peoples of Djibouti. **Light blue** is the colour of the Issas people, and also represents the sky and the sea. **Green** is the colour of the Afars people and symbolizes the fertile earth. The **white triangle** represents peace and equality, while the **red**, **five-pointed star** symbolizes unity.

HISTORY

Islam arrived in the 9th century, and the conversion of the **Afars** led to conflict with Christian Ethiopians in the interior. By the 19th century, Somalian **Issas** moved into Djibouti and occupied much of the Afars' traditional grazing land. In 1888 France established the colony of **French Somaliland**. In 1917 the **railway** opened between Djibouti, the capital, and Addis Ababa, capital of Ethiopia. In a referendum in 1967, 60% of the electorate voted to retain links with France. The colony was renamed the **French Territory of the Afars and Issas**. In 1977 it gained **independence** as the Republic of Djibouti. **Hassan Gouled Aptidon** of the Popular Rally for Progress (RPP) was elected president. In 1981 Gouled declared a one-party state. By 1992 **Afar rebels** controlled more than two-thirds of Djibouti. Gouled was forced to adopt a multi-party constitution. In 1999 **Ismail Omar Guelleh** replaced Gouled as president.

AREA: 23,200sq km (8958sq mi)
POPULATION: 787,000
CAPITAL (POPULATION): Djibouti (524,700)
GOVERNMENT: Multi-party republic
ETHNIC GROUPS: Issa 47%, Afar 37%, Arab 6%
LANGUAGES: Arabic and French (both official)
RELIGIONS: Sunni Muslim 93%,
Roman Catholic 4%
MOTTO: "*Unité, Egalité, Paix*"
"Unity, Equality, Peace"
NATIONAL ANTHEM (DATE): Untitled (1977)

African nomads use headrests to prevent their hair becoming matted and dirty.

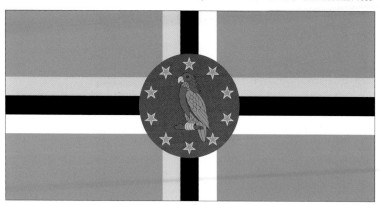

Chosen by national competition in 1978, the central emblem of the Dominican flag is the **sisserou parrot**, encircled by **ten stars** representing the ten parishes of Dominica. The sisserou parrot, an endangered species, is unique to Dominica and is the national bird. The **cross** is Christian, and the **yellow**, **black** and **white stripes** represent the Holy Trinity. The colours are also symbolic. **Yellow** represents the island's plentiful sunshine, its major agricultural crops (bananas and citrus), and the Carib people. **Black** represents the fertile soil and the African heritage of most Dominicans. **White** stands for the island's clear waters and the pure aspirations of its people. The **dark-green** field symbolizes the island's lush forests and vegetation.

HISTORY

Dominica is named after *dies dominica* (Latin 'the Lord's day'), the day **Christopher Columbus** sighted the island in 1493. Prior to Columbus' arrival, the **Arawak** people inhabited Dominica. The **Carib** displaced the **Arawak**. It was the last of the Caribbean islands colonised by Europeans, due mainly to the fierce resistance of the native **Caribs**. Dominica won **independence** from Britain in 1978. The republic's first prime minister was **Patrick R. John**. In 1980 **Mary Eugenia Charles** became the first woman prime minister in the Caribbean. She remained in power until 1995.

AREA: 750sq km (290sq mi)
POPULATION: 71,727
CAPITAL (POPULATION): Roseau (16,038)
GOVERNMENT: Multi-party republic
ETHNIC GROUPS: Black 90%, Mixed 7%, Native American 2%
LANGUAGES: English (official), French patois
RELIGIONS: Roman Catholic 70%, Seventh-Day Adventist 5%, Pentecostal 4%
NATIONAL MOTTO: "*Après Bondie, c'est la Ter*" "After God, the Earth"
NATIONAL ANTHEM (DATE): "Isle of Beauty, Isle of Splendor" (1967)

Dominican stamp marking the Year of the Elderly in 1999.

65

DOMINICAN REPUBLIC

FLAG RATIO: 2:3   **USE:** National   **DATE ADOPTED:** 1844   **LAST MODIFIED:** 1896

D ominican Republic adopted its flag upon gaining independence in 1844. The first flag took Haiti's flag of **blue** and **red**, and superimposed a **white** cross to signify the Christian faith of the Dominican people. The colours at the fly end of the flag were later reversed. Blue represents liberty. Red stands for the blood shed in the struggle for liberation, while the white cross is a symbol of sacrifice. On the **civil flag**, the national **coat of arms** appears at the centre of the white cross. The coat of arms includes a Bible open at the Gospel of Saint John, a symbol of the Trinitarian movement – the Christian secret society that led the movement for independence.

HISTORY

Christopher Columbus discovered the island of **Hispaniola** in 1492. **Santo Domingo**, capital of the Dominican Republic, was the first Spanish settlement in the New World. In 1697 Spain ceded the western third of the island (now **Haiti**) to France. In 1795 France gained control of the entire island. In 1821 the Dominican Republic declared **independence**, but it was soon occupied by Haiti. In 1844 it won independence. The dictatorship of **Rafael Trujillo** lasted from 1930 until 1961. President **Joaquín Balaguer** succeeded Trujillo, and mostly remained in power until 1978. Balaguer was also president from 1990 to 1996.

AREA: 48,734sq km (18,816sq mi)

POPULATION: 9,046,400

CAPITAL (POPULATION): Santo Domingo (2,061,200)

GOVERNMENT: Multi-party republic

ETHNIC GROUPS: Mixed 73%, White 16%, Black 11%

LANGUAGES: Spanish

RELIGIONS: Roman Catholic 95%

MOTTO: "*Dios, Patria, Libertad*" "God, Fatherland, Liberty"

NATIONAL ANTHEM (DATE): (1883)

Casandra Damiron *is known as the 'Queen of Song' in Dominican Republic.*

EAST TIMOR

FLAG RATIO: 1:2 **USE:** National/Civil **DATE ADOPTED:** 1975 **REINTRODUCED:** 2002

In 1975 Fretilin (*Frente Revolucionária do Timor-Leste Independente*) raised the present flag as the banner of the Democratic Republic of Timor. The republic proved short-lived as Indonesia invaded but the flag returned when independence was restored in 2002. **Yellow** represents the vestiges of East Timor's colonial past. **Black** stands for the darkness to be overcome, while **red** recalls the struggle for liberation. The **white, five-pointed star** is the guiding light of peace.

HISTORY

From *c.*1520, **Portuguese** spice traders began to settle on the island of Timor. In 1620 the **Dutch** landed and settled on the western side of Timor. **Japan** occupied Timor during World War II. In 1950 West Timor became part of **Indonesia**. In 1975 Portugal abandoned East Timor and the colony declared independence. Nine days later, Indonesia invaded. In 1976 Indonesia **annexed** East Timor as its 27th province. The **occupation** claimed the lives of *c.*200,000 Timorese people, most notably when Indonesia's army killed *c.*270 demonstrators in the capital, **Dili**. In 1999, after a vote in favour of independence, pro-Indonesian militias sought to destabilize East Timor. A United Nations' (UN) peacekeeping force restored order, and East Timor gained full independence on May 20, 2002. Former Fretilin leader **Xanana Gusmão**, jailed from 1992 to 1999, became the first President of East Timor.

According to legend, the island of Timor was formed out of a crocodile's back.

AREA: 14,874sq km (5743sq mi)
POPULATION: 891,000
CAPITAL (POPULATION): Dili (65,000)
GOVERNMENT: Multi-party republic
ETHNIC GROUPS: Malay and Papuan descent
LANGUAGES: Tetum, Portuguese (both official), Bahasa Indonesian, English
RELIGIONS: Roman Catholic 91%, Protestant 3%, Muslim 2%
NATIONAL ANTHEM (DATE): "*Pátria, Pátria*", "Motherland, Motherland" (2002)

ECUADOR

FLAG RATIO: 2:3 USE: National/Civil DATE ADOPTED: 1900 LAST MODIFIED: 1900

The revolutionary Francisco de Miranda created Ecuador's flag in 1806. The armies of Simon Bolívar, who liberated much of South America, fought under this flag. Colombia, Ecuador and Venezuela have **tricolours** of yellow, blue and red **horizontal stripes**, based on Miranda's design. The **yellow** stripe symbolizes the fertility of the land. The **blue** stripe represents the sea and the sky. The **red** stripe stands for the blood shed in the fight for liberation. At the centre of Ecuador's flag is the **coat of arms**, showing a **condor** soaring over Mount Chimborazo, Ecuador's highest peak at 6267m (20,561ft), and the Guayas River.

HISTORY

In 1532 **Spanish** forces, led by **Francisco Pizarro**, defeated the **Incas** at Cajamarca and established the Spanish Viceroyalty of Quito. A revolutionary war culminated in **Antonio José de Sucre**'s defeat of the Spanish at the Battle of Mount Pichincha (1822). **Simon Bolívar** negotiated the admittance of Quito to the **Federation of Gran Colombia** (Colombia, Ecuador, and Venezuela. In 1830 Ecuador seceded from the federation. In the **Treaty of Rio** (1942), Ecuador lost half its Amazonian territory to Peru. **José María Velasco Ibarro** served four terms as president (1944–47, 1952–56, 1960–61, 1968–72). In 1972 an army coup deposed Velasco. Ecuador returned to democracy in 1979. In 2000 **Gustavo Noboa** became president after an army coup and indigenous protests. Also in 2000, Ecuador adopted the **US dollar** as its national currency.

AREA: 283,560sq km (109,483sq mi)
POPULATION: 13,285,700
CAPITAL (POPULATION): Quito (1,648,100)
GOVERNMENT: Multi-party republic
ETHNIC GROUPS: Mestizo 40%, Amerindian 40%, White 15%, Black 5%
LANGUAGES: Spanish (official)
RELIGIONS: Roman Catholic 90%, Protestant 4%
NATIONAL ANTHEM (DATE): "Salve, O Patria!"
"We Salute You, Oh Fatherland!" (1948)

***The Andean condor**, the largest bird of prey, is Ecuador's national bird.*

EGYPT

FLAG RATIO: 2:3 **USE:** National/Civil **DATE ADOPTED:** 1984 **LAST AMENDED:** 1984

The **tricolour** of red, white and black horizontal stripes first appeared as Egypt's flag in 1958, when the country formed part of the short-lived **United Arab Republic**. In 1972 a hawk replaced the three stars on the central white band. In 1984 the **eagle of Saladin** replaced the hawk. **Red** symbolizes the struggle for liberation from Britain. **White** represents the bloodless overthrow of the monarchy in 1952. **Black** recalls the end of oppression from Britain and the monarchy.

HISTORY

The **Old Kingdom** saw the building of the Great **Pyramid** at Giza (*c.*2500 BC).

Queen Nefertari makes an offering to the goddess Hathor.

The **Middle Kingdom**'s capital at Luxor reveal Egypt's ancient power. In 322 BC, **Alexander the Great** conquered Egypt. **Rome** gained control after the fall of **Cleopatra**. The **Umayyad** dynasty conquered Egypt in 642, introducing Arabic and **Islam**. In 1517 the **Ottomans** came to power. In 1801 **Muhammad Ali** expelled the French and founded the modern state. The completion of the **Suez Canal** (1867) encouraged **Britain** to capture Cairo in 1882. In 1922 Egypt became a monarchy under **Fuad I**. In 1953 **Gamal Abdal Nasser** overthrew King **Farouk** and led (1954–70) the new republic. **Anwar Sadat** succeeded Nasser as President, but was assassinated in 1981. **Hosni Mubarak** replaced Sadat as President.

AREA: 1,001,450sq km (386,660 sq mi)
POPULATION: 67,786,300
CAPITAL (POPULATION): Cairo (7,764,700)
GOVERNMENT: Presidential republic
ETHNIC GROUPS: Egyptian 99%
LANGUAGES: Arabic (official), French, English
RELIGIONS: Sunni Muslim 94%,
Coptic Christian 6%
NATIONAL ANTHEM (DATE): "*Biladi, Biladi*"
"My Homeland, My Homeland" (1979)

69

EL SALVADOR

FLAG RATIO: 189:335 USE: National/State DATE ADOPTED: 1912 LAST MODIFIED: 1972

E¹ Salvador's tricolour flag of **blue-white-blue horizontal stripes** has its origins in the flag of the former Central American Federation (1823–39). Manuel José Arce chose the flag in 1822. The **coat of arms** consists of an equilateral triangle, symbolizing liberty, fraternity, and equality. Inside the triangle are five volcanoes, representing the five members of the federation, surrounded by the Atlantic and Pacific Oceans. Written in the sun's rays, above a Liberty cap on a pole, is "*15 De Septiembre De 1821*", the date of independence. Below the triangle is the national motto "*Dios, Union, Libertad*". Around the triangle appears "*República De El Salvador En La America Central*".

HISTORY

In 1524–26 **Spanish** explorer **Pedro de Alvarado** conquered Native American tribes and the region became part of the Spanish Viceroyalty of Guatemala. In 1821 El Salvador gained **independence**. In 1825 **Manuel José Arce** became the first President of the **Central American Federation**. In the late 19th century, El Salvador developed **coffee** plantations. **General Maximiliano Hernández Martínez** led a brutal dictatorship (1931–44). A 12-year long **civil war** (1979–92) between US-backed government forces and the **Farabundo Marti National Liberation Front (FMLN)** claimed 75,000 lives. In 2001 massive **earthquakes** killed *c.*1200 people.

AREA: 21,040sq km (8124sq mi)
POPULATION: 6,076,800
CAPITAL (POPULATION): San Salvador (496,000)
GOVERNMENT: Multi-party republic
ETHNIC GROUPS: Mestizo 89%, Native American 10%, White 1%
LANGUAGES: Spanish (official)
RELIGIONS: Roman Catholic 85%, Protestant 3%
NATIONAL MOTTO: "*Dios, Unión, Libertad*" "God, Union, Liberty"
NATIONAL ANTHEM (DATE): "*Saludemos la Patria orgilosos*" "Salute the Proud Motherland" (1953)

Stamp celebrating the Interamerican Day of Water in 1997.

EQUATORIAL GUINEA

FLAG RATIO: 2:3 USE: National/Civil DATE ADOPTED: 1968 REINTRODUCED: 1979

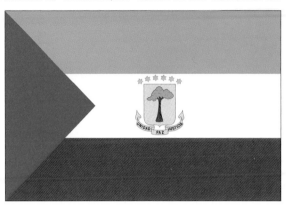

Equatorial Guinea's national flag consists of a **tricolour** of **horizontal stripes**, a **blue triangle** at the hoist, and the **coat of arms** at the centre. The **green stripe** represents agriculture, vitally important to the national economy. The **white stripe** symbolizes peace, while the **red stripe** stands for the blood shed in the struggle for independence. **Blue** represents the Pacific Ocean. The coat of arms features the **silk-cotton tree** on a **silver shield**. King Bonkoro of Bata signed the 1843 treaty with Spain under the tree. Above the shield are **six stars** representing the mainland and five islands of Equatorial Guinea. The national motto *"Unidad, Paz, Justicia"* appears below the shield. From 1972 to 1979, under the dictator **Macías Nguema**, Equatorial Guinea had a different coat of arms.

HISTORY

In 1471 Portuguese navigator **Fernando Póo** sighted the largest island of **Bioko**. In 1778 **Portugal** ceded the islands and mainland (**Mbini**) to Spain. From 1858 to 1959 it was known as **Spanish Guinea**. In 1959 it became an overseas province of Spain. Equatorial Guinea gained **independence** in 1968. **Francisco Macías Nguema**'s dictatorship killed more than 40,000 people. In 1979 **Colonel Teodoro Obiang Nguema Mbasogo** deposed Nguema in a military coup. Human-rights organizations accuse Obiang's regime of routine arrests and torture of opponents.

AREA: 28,050sq km (10,830 sq mi)
POPULATION: 465,800
CAPITAL (POPULATION): Malabo (112,800)
GOVERNMENT: Multi-party republic (transitional)
ETHNIC GROUPS: Fang 83%, Bubi 10%, Ndowe 4%
LANGUAGES: Spanish (official)
RELIGIONS: Roman Catholic 88%, African traditional beliefs 5%, Muslim 1%
MOTTO: "Unidad, Paz, Justicia" "Unity, Peace, Justice"
NATIONAL ANTHEM (DATE): "Himno Nacional" "National Hymn" (1968)

Cocoa, harvested mainly on Bioko, is a major cash crop of Equatorial Guinea.

71

ERITREA

FLAG RATIO: 1:2   USE: National/Civil   DATE ADOPTED: 1995   LAST MODIFIED: 1995

Eritrea's flag is based on the flag of the Eritrean People's Liberation Front (EPLF), leaders in the struggle for independence from Ethiopia. The **red triangle** symbolizes the blood shed in the fight for freedom. The **blue triangle** represents the resources of the Red Sea. The **green triangle** stands for agriculture. From 1952 to 1959 Eritrea flew a flag with a green wreath and olive branch in the centre of a field of United Nations' blue. On the new national flag, a **golden wreath** and **olive branch** replace the yellow star of the EPLF on the hoist side of the red triangle.

HISTORY

Eritrea was a dependency of **Ethiopia** until the 16th century, when it fell to the **Ottoman Empire**. In 1890 it became an **Italian** colony. From 1941 to 1952 it was under **British** military administration. In 1952 it federated with Ethiopia, and became a province in 1962. Eritrean separatists began a 30-year campaign of **guerrilla warfare**, and 700,000 **refugees** fled to Somalia. In 1991 the Eritrean People's Liberation Front (**EPLF**) helped topple **General Mengistu**'s Ethiopian government, and won a referendum on independence. Eritrea gained **independence** in 1993. The EPLF government, led by **Isaias Afwerki**, began reconstructing a country impoverished by war and famine. A **border war** with Ethiopia (1998–2000) claimed many lives: 40,000 in the Battle of **Badme** (1999) alone.

AREA: 117,599sq km (45,405sq mi)
POPULATION: 4,523,000
CAPITAL (POPULATION): Asmara (431,000)
GOVERNMENT: Transitional government
ETHNIC GROUPS: Tigrinya 48%, Tigre 35%, Afar 4%, Kunama 3%, Saho 3%
LANGUAGES: Afar, Amharic, Arabic, Tigre and Kunama, Tigrinya, other Kushitic languages
RELIGIONS: Sunni Muslim 50%, Eritrean Orthodox 40%, Roman Catholic 3%
NATIONAL ANTHEM (DATE): *"Ertra, Ertra, Ertra"* "Eritrea, Eritrea, Eritrea" (1993)

***Eritrean** stamp, issued in 1995, marking Independence Day (May 24, 1993).*

ESTONIA

FLAG RATIO: 7:11   USE: National/Civil   DATE ADOPTED: 1918   REINTRODUCED: 1990

Estonia's **tricolour** flag of blue-black-white **horizontal stripes** was originally the flag of the Estonian University Student Association (first flown in 1884). The flag and colours became unofficial national symbols. In 1918 the provisional government made it the national flag. The flag was banned under Soviet rule, but continued to be used as a nationalist symbol. It was readopted in 1990. **Blue** refers to the sky and fidelity of the nation. **Black** represents the peasantry and Estonia's historical suffering. **White** symbolizes the winter snow and freedom.

HISTORY

In 1217 the German **Order of the Brothers of the Sword** conquered southern Estonia (**Livonia**). By 1346 the **Teutonic Knights** controlled the country. In 1629 **Sweden** became the dominant power. **Russia** gained all of Estonia at the end of the **Great Northern War** (1700–21). In 1918 Estonia declared **independence**. In 1940 **Soviet** forces occupied Estonia. More than 60,000 Estonians were killed or deported in the first year of Soviet occupation. In 1941 **Germany** expelled the Soviets. Soviet troops returned in 1944. Between 1945 and 1953, the Soviets deported *c.*80,000 Estonians. Estonia became one of the 15 socialist republics of the Soviet Union. In 1990 Estonia declared **independence**, a status recognized by the Soviet Union in 1991. **Lennart Meri** became President in 1992.

AREA: 44,700sq km (17,300sq mi)
POPULATION: 1,439,197
CAPITAL (POPULATION): Tallinn (404,000)
GOVERNMENT: Multi-party republic
ETHNIC GROUPS: Estonian 62%, Russian 30%, Ukrainian 3%, Belorussian 2%, Finnish 1%
LANGUAGES: Estonian (official)
RELIGIONS: Evangelical Lutheran 80%, Apostolic Orthodox 8%, Baptist 2%
NATIONAL ANTHEM (DATE): *"Mu Isamaa, mu Õnn ja Rõõm"*
"My Native Land, My Joy, Delight" (1920)

Folk costumes from Muhu, Estonia's third largest island, north-east of Saaremaa.

73

ETHIOPIA

FLAG RATIO: 1:2 USE: National/Civil DATE ADOPTED: 1996 LAST MODIFIED: 1996

Emperor **Menelik II** adopted Ethiopia's **tricolour** flag of **horizontal stripes** in 1897 (in reverse order to today's flag). It changed to the present sequence in 1914. **Green** stands for the fertile land. **Yellow** represents religious freedom, while **red** symbolizes the blood shed in defending the country. The **Pan-African** movement used the colours of Ethiopia, Africa's oldest independent nation, to symbolize African unity. The central **golden pentangle** with **four radiant rays** was added in 1996. It represents equality for all Ethiopia's people. It is set against a **blue circle** to denote peace and democracy.

AREA: 1,128,000sq km (435,521sq mi)
POPULATION: 67,980,100
CAPITAL (POPULATION): Addis Ababa (2,674,200)
GOVERNMENT: Federal republic
ETHNIC GROUPS: Oromo (Galla) 40%, Semitic (Amhara and Tigre) 33%, Sidamo 9%, Shangalla 6%, Somali 5%, Afar 4%, Gurage 2%
LANGUAGES: Amharic (*de facto* official)
RELIGIONS: Sunni Muslim 45%, Coptic Christian 40%, African traditional beliefs 8%
NATIONAL ANTHEM (DATE): "*Whedefit Gesgeshi Woude Henate Ethiopia*" "March Forward, Dear Mother Ethiopia" (1992)

HISTORY

According to legend, **Menelik I**, son of King **Solomon** and the **Queen of Sheba**, founded Ethiopia in *c*.1000 BC. In AD 321, the Kingdom of **Axum** introduced **Coptic Christianity**. In 1930 **Ras Tafari Makonnen** was crowned Emperor **Haile Selassie**. In 1935 **Italy** conquered Ethiopia (Abysinnia), and it became part of **Italian East Africa**. In 1941 the Allies restored Haile Selassie. In 1962 Ethiopia annexed **Eritrea**. In 1974 Haile Selassie was killed in a coup. Major **Haile Mengistu**'s regime caused **civil war**. In 1984 **famine** led to the 'Live Aid' relief effort. In 1991 Mengistu fled into exile. **Menes Zenawi** became Prime Minister of the Federal Democratic Republic of Ethiopia in 1995. **War** with Eritrea (1998–2000) claimed many lives.

Ethiopians *were the first people to cultivate coffee for drinking.*

74

FIJI

FLAG RATIO: 1:2 USE: National/Civil DATE ADOPTED: 1970 LAST MODIFIED: 1970

The flag is a modified version of Fiji's colonial flag. It includes the flag of the **United Kingdom**, the former colonial power, and the **shield** from the coat of arms. The flag is **light blue** to represent the Pacific Ocean that surrounds Fiji. The **cross of Saint George** quarters the shield. Each quarter features products or symbols of Fiji: a **sugar-cane** plant, a **coconut palm**, a **bunch of bananas**, and a white **dove of peace**. A **lion** holding a **cocoa pod** crowns the shield.

HISTORY

Abel Tasman discovered the islands of Fiji in 1643. In 1874 Fiji became a **British colony**. The British brought in Indians to work on the **sugar plantations**, and by the 1950s **Indians** outnumbered the native Fijian population. In 1970 Fiji gained **independence**. The election of an Indian-majority government in 1987 prompted a military coup , led by Colonel **Sitiveni Rabuka**, and the proclamation of a republic. In 1992 Rabuka became prime minister. In 1997 Fiji adopted a **multi-racial** constitution. **Mahendra Chaudhry** defeated Rabuka in 1999 elections. In May 2000, **George Speight** led a coup, holding hostage the entire cabinet. The **Great Council of Chiefs** dismissed Chaudhry, and declared martial law. The **Commonwealth of Nations** suspended Fiji. In July 2000 Speight was arrested after freeing the hostages. Fiji was later readmitted to the Commonwealth.

AREA: 18,272sq km (7055sq mi)
POPULATION: 812,000
CAPITAL (POPULATION): Suva (77,366)
GOVERNMENT: Republic
ETHNIC GROUPS: Fijian 50% (predominantly Melanesian with a Polynesian admixture), Indian 45%, European, other Pacific Islanders, overseas Chinese, and other 5%
LANGUAGES: English (official), Fijian, Hindustani
RELIGIONS: Methodist 37%, Roman Catholic 9%, Hindu 38%, Sunni Muslim 8%, Sikh 1%
NATIONAL MOTTO: "*Rerevaka na Kalau ka Doka na Tui*" "Fear God and Honour the Queen"
NATIONAL ANTHEM (DATE): "*Meda Dau Doka*" "*God Bless Fiji*" (1970)

Fiji is famous for its decorated pottery, such as this Saqa drinking vessel.

75

FINLAND

FLAG RATIO: 11:18 **USE:** National/Civil **DATE ADOPTED:** 1918 **LAST MODIFIED:** 1918

Finland's flag developed from 1861, when Tsar Alexander II allowed the Nyland Yacht Club to fly a white flag with an upright blue cross to distinguish its vessels from Russian ships, which were subject to frequent attacks. In 1917 Finland provisionally adopted a lion flag, based on the coat of arms. In 1918, after the civil war, Finland acquired a flag with a **horizontal blue cross** against a **white field**. The blue represents Finland's more than 60,000 lakes. The white symbolizes the snow that blankets the land for five to seven months each year. Other Nordic countries use the 'Scandinavian cross', but Finland's flag colours are distinct. The **state flag** has Finland's coat of arms in the centre of the cross. The **coat of arms** consist of a **golden lion** holding a **sword** against a **red** background.

AREA: 338,130sq km (130,552sq mi)
POPULATION: 5,171,302
CAPITAL (POPULATION): Helsinki (551,123)
GOVERNMENT: Multi-party republic
ETHNIC GROUPS: Finnish 93%, Swedish 6%
LANGUAGES: Finnish, Swedish (both official)
RELIGIONS: Evangelical Lutheran 89%
NATIONAL ANTHEM (DATE): "Maamme"
"Our Land" (1848)

HISTORY

In the 8th century, Finnish-speaking settlers forced the Lapps into what is now **Lappland. Sweden** conquered Finland in the 13th century. **Lutheranism** took hold in the 16th century. **Russia** gained southeast Finland in the **Great Northern War** (1700–21). In 1809 Finland became a Grand Duchy of **Russia**. In 1917 Finland declared independence, and **Carl Mannerheim**'s forces won the resulting brutal **civil war** in 1918. More than 25,000 Finnish people died in the **Russo-Finnish War** (1939–40). In 1941 Finland allied with **Nazi Germany**. In 1944 Finland signed an armistice with the **Soviet Union**, and the country suffered greatly in the ensuing war with Germany. Finland remained **neutral** during the Cold War. **Urho Kaleva Kekkonen** led Finland from 1956 to 1981. Finland joined the **European Union** in 1995.

Finland's many lakes are a haven for birdlife. The willow ptarmigan is common.

The French *tricolore* first appeared during the French Revolution of 1789. French general Marquis de Lafayette is often credited with placing the **blue** and **red** colours of the arms of **Paris** with the **white** colours of the Bourbon royal family. The *tricolore* initially symbolized the reconciliation of the King with the city, but quickly became the symbol of the revolution. It was first used only as the jack and ensign of the French navy, with the colours in reverse order to the current flag – red at the hoist. On February 15, 1794, the National Convention adopted the present flag.

HISTORY

Hugh Capet, crowned in 987, is often regarded as the first King of France. **Joan of Arc** helped liberate France from English rule in the **Hundred Years' War** (1337–1453). In 1589 **Henry IV** became the first **Bourbon** king. **Louis XIV's** (1638–1715) court at **Versailles** was the richest in Europe. **Louis XVI** was executed in the **French Revolution** (1789–99), and France became a republic. Emperor **Napoleon I** conquered much of Europe before defeat in 1815. France was the battleground for much of **World War I** (1914–18), and Germany occupied it during **World War II** (1939–45). In 1958 **Charles de Gaulle** established the Fifth Republic. **François Mitterrand** served as president from 1981 to 1996.

Henri de Toulouse-Lautrec painted Yvette Gilbert singing "Linger, Longer, Loo" (1864).

AREA: 551,500sq km (212,934sq mi)
POPULATION: 58,145,400
CAPITAL (POPULATION): Paris (2,152,423)
GOVERNMENT: Multi-party republic
ETHNIC GROUPS: France 93%, Arab 3%, German 2%, Breton 1%, Catalan
LANGUAGES: French (official)
RELIGIONS: Roman Catholic 86%, Protestant 4%, Muslim 3%
MOTTO: "*Liberté, Egalité, Fraternité*" "Liberty, Equality, Fraternity"
NATIONAL ANTHEM (DATE): "*La Marseillaise*" (1795)

GABON

FLAG RATIO: 3:4 USE: National/Civil DATE ADOPTED: 1960 LAST MODIFIED: 1960

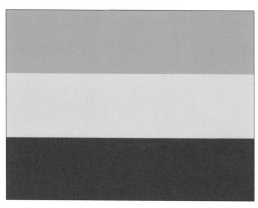

G abon's flag derives from the French *tricolore* and the colours of the Pan-African movement. It has **three horizontal stripes** of equal width. The **green** stripe represents the rainforests – the timber trade is very important to Gabon's economy. The **yellow** stripe stands for the sun and for the Equator which runs through Gabon. The **blue** stripe symbolizes the Atlantic Ocean. From 1958 to 1960 Gabon's flag had a French *tricolore* in the canton.

HISTORY

Portuguese explorers reached the Gabonese coast in the 1470s, and the area later became a source of **slaves**. In 1839 **France** established the first European settlement. In 1849 freed slaves founded **Libreville**. Gabon became a French colony in the 1880s, and part of **French Equatorial Africa** in 1910. It achieved **independence** in 1960. **Léon Mba** was Gabon's first president (1960–67). **Omar Bongo** became president on Mba's death in 1967. In 1968 he created a one-party state. Bongo won the first multi-party presidential elections in 1993, although accusations of fraud and corruption led to riots in Libreville. The international community condemned Bongo for his harsh suppression of popular demonstrations. He was re-elected in 1998.

AREA: 267,670sq km (103,347sq mi)
POPULATION: 1,308,500
CAPITAL (POPULATION): Libreville (541,000)
GOVERNMENT: Multi-party republic
ETHNIC GROUPS: Fang 36%, Mpongwe 15%, Mbete 14%, Punu 12%, Pygmy
LANGUAGES: French (official)
RELIGIONS: Roman Catholic 65%, Protestant 19%, African Christian 12%, African traditional beliefs 2%, Muslim 2%
NATIONAL MOTTO: "*Union, Travail, Justice*" "Union, Work, Justice"
NATIONAL ANTHEM (DATE): "*La Concorde*" "The Concord" (1960)

Gabon's rainforests support up to *62,000 elephants – Africa's largest population.*

78

Gambia adopted its present flag upon gaining independence in 1965. The colours of its **horizontal stripes** represent features of the Gambian landscape. **Green** symbolizes the land and agricultural produce. **Blue** stands for the River Gambia, a vital trade route. **Red** represents the hot African sun. The two **narrow white bands** that separate the other stripes stand for peace and unity.

HISTORY

Portuguese navigators landed on the coast of Gambia in 1455, when the area was part of the **Mali Empire**. In 1664 England established a settlement. In 1765 **Britain** founded the colony of **Senegambia**, which included parts of present-day Gambia and **Senegal**. The British purchased Banjul Island from a local king in 1816, and founded the town of Bathurst (now **Banjul**). In 1894 Gambia became a **British Protectorate**. It remained under British rule until it achieved **independence** in 1965. **Dawda Jawara** was Gambia's first prime minister. In 1970 Gambia became a **republic**. In July 1994 Jawara was overthrown in a military **coup** led by **Yahya Jammeh**. Jammeh became president in 1996 elections. In 2000 more than 12 people were shot dead during student demonstrations. In 2001 Jammeh was re-elected and lifted the ban on opposition parties.

AREA: 11,300sq km (4363sq mi)
POPULATION: 1,417,800
CAPITAL (POPULATION): Banjul (57,800)
GOVERNMENT: Military, transitional
ETHNIC GROUPS: Mandinka (Mandingo or Malinke) 40%, Fulani (Peul) 19%, Wolof 15%, Dyola 10%, Soninke 8%
LANGUAGES: English (official)
RELIGIONS: Sunni Muslim 90%, Christian 4%, African traditional beliefs 4%
NATIONAL MOTTO: "Progress, Peace, Prosperity"
NATIONAL ANTHEM (DATE): "For The Gambia, Our Homeland" (1965)

Gambia is a popular destination for bird-watchers. The village weaver is common.

79

GEORGIA

FLAG RATIO: 3:5 USE: National/Civil DATE ADOPTED: 1918 REINTRODUCED: 1991

G eorgia first adopted its present flag in 1918. In 1921 Georgia became part of the Soviet Union and the flag was abandoned. In 1991 Georgia regained independence and reverted to the 1918 flag. **Dark red/maroon** is Georgia's national colour. The **canton of black** and **white** juxtaposes Georgia's dark past with the hope for a peaceful future.

HISTORY

From the 6th century BC, the two Black Sea kingdoms of **Iberia** and **Colchis** developed in eastern and western Georgia respectively. In 66 BC, the **Roman Empire** conquered both kingdoms. From the 4th to the 7th century, Georgia was a battleground for the **Byzantine** and **Iranian** empires. The Byzantines held Colchis, while the **Sasanians** controlled Iberia. The reign (1184–1213) of **Queen Tamar** saw Georgia build a mighty empire. The **Ottoman Turks** and **Safavid Iranians** fought for control from the mid-16th century. In 1783 Georgia accepted Russian protection, and by 1878 it formed part of the **Russian Empire**. The Red Army ended a brief era of **independence** (1918–21), and Georgia joined with Armenia and Azerbaijan to form the Soviet Republic of **Transcaucasia**. In 1936 Georgia became a separate republic. In 1991 it declared independence. President **Zviad Gamsakhurdia**'s authoritarian regime brought civil war. **Eduard Shevardnadze** became president in 1992 elections. In 1995 **Abkhazia** gained autonomy.

AREA: 69,700sq km (26,910sq mi)
POPULATION: 5,402,800
CAPITAL (POPULATION): Tbilisi (1,382,900)
GOVERNMENT: Multi-party republic
ETHNIC GROUPS: Georgian 70%, Armenian 8%, Russian 6%, Azerbaijani 5%, Ossetian 3%, Greek 2%, Abkhazian 2%, others 3%
LANGUAGES: Georgian (official)
RELIGIONS: Georgian Orthodox 65%, Sunni Muslim 11%, Russian Orthodox 10%
NATIONAL ANTHEM (DATE): *"Dideba zetsit kurthelus"* "Praise Be to the Heavenly Bestower" (1991)

In 1992 Georgian soldiers fighting in Abkhazia received coupons with this stamp.

GERMANY

FLAG RATIO: 3:5 USE: National/Civil DATE ADOPTED: 1918 REINTRODUCED: 1949

After defeat in the Napoleonic Wars (1803–15), the **black-red-gold** tricolour became linked with the German Revival, perhaps because the colours recalled the Holy Roman Empire. After the **Revolutions of 1848**, the German League adopted the tricolour. In 1867 **Otto von Bismarck** created the North German Confederation, which used a black-white-red tricolour. In 1918 the **Weimar Republic** (1918–33) revived the 1848 flag. In 1935 **Adolf Hitler** adopted a black **swastika** on a white circle against a red field as the national flag. In 1949 the Federal Republic of (**West**) Germany returned to the 1848 flag. From 1959 to 1990 the (**East**) German Democratic Republic flag had a hammer and compass in a ring of rye on the tricolour.

HISTORY

In 962 **Otto I (the Great)** created the Holy Roman Empire, the first *Reich*. Rudolf I founded the **Habsburg** dynasty in 1273. Charles V's reign (1519–58) saw the **Reformation**. Catholics and Protestants fought the **Thirty Years' War** (1618–48). **Frederick the Great**'s reign (1740–86) saw the growth of **Prussia**. The **Franco-Prussian War** (1870–71) created a second *Reich*. Emperor **William II** led Germany into **World War I** (1914–18). In 1933 Hitler declared a **third *Reich***. Nazi aggression led to **World War II** (1940–45). Defeat saw the division of Germany. In 1990 East and West Germany **reunified**. **Helmut Kohl** was chancellor from 1982 to 1998.

German composer J.S. Bach (1685–1750) was a master of Baroque counterpoint.

AREA: 356,910sq km (137,803sq mi)
POPULATION: 82,163,500
CAPITAL (POPULATION): Berlin (3,392,900)
GOVERNMENT: Federal multi-party republic
ETHNIC GROUPS: German 93%, Turkish 2%, Yugoslav 1%, Italian 1%, Greek, Polish
LANGUAGES: German (official)
RELIGIONS: Protestant 38% (mostly Evangelical Lutheran), Roman Catholic 35%, Muslim 2%
NATIONAL ANTHEM (DATE): *"Lied der Deutschen"* "Song of the Germans" (1922)

81

GHANA

FLAG RATIO: 2:3 USE: National/Civil DATE ADOPTED: 1957 REINTRODUCED: 1966

Ghana was the first decolonized African nation to take the colours of **Ethiopia** and the **Pan-African movement**. It adopted the **tricolour of horizontal stripes** upon independence from Britain in 1957. From 1964 to 1966 the middle band was white. **Red** stands for the blood shed in the struggle for liberation. **Green** represents the landscape. Gold symbolizes Ghana's mineral wealth and recalls the country's former identity as the Gold Coast. The **black five-pointed star** at the centre of the flag is the guiding star of African freedom.

HISTORY

Various African kingdoms existed in the region before the arrival of **Portuguese** explorers in 1471, who named it the **Gold Coast** after its precious mineral resource. In 1642 the **Dutch** gained control, and the Gold Coast became a centre of the **slave trade**. In 1874 **Britain** colonized the region excluding **Ashanti**, which fell in 1901. Britain established **cacao plantations**. In 1957 Gold Coast became the first African colony to gain **independence**. **Kwame Nkrumah** was the first prime minister and the country was **renamed** Ghana after a powerful, medieval West African kingdom. In 1960 Ghana became a **republic** with Nkrumah as its president. In 1966 a military **coup** deposed Nkrumah. In 1979 **Jerry Rawlings** led a coup, executing Ghana's previous military rulers. Rawlings became president in 1992 elections. **John Kufuor** succeeded him in 2001.

AREA: 238,540sq km (92,100sq mi)
POPULATION: 18,845,265
CAPITAL (POPULATION): Accra (1,605,400)
GOVERNMENT: Multi-party republic
ETHNIC GROUPS: Akan 49%, Moshe-Dagoma 16%, Ewe 13%, Ga-Dangme 8%, Gurma 3%
LANGUAGES: English (official)
RELIGIONS: Protestant 25%, African traditional beliefs 21%, Roman Catholic 19%, Sunni Muslim 16%, African churches 14%, Pentecostal 8%
NATIONAL MOTTO: "Freedom and Justice"
NATIONAL ANTHEM (DATE): "God Bless Our Homeland Ghana" (1957)

The bushbuck is the smallest spiral-horned antelope. It lives in central Africa.

GREECE

FLAG RATIO: 2:3   USE: National/State   DATE ADOPTED: 1833   LAST MODIFIED: 1978

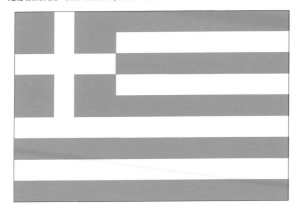

The blue and white flag of Greece has existed in various designs since the 19th century. The present flag consists of **nine horizontal stripes** in alternate lines of **blue and white**. There is a **white cross** on a **blue square** in the canton. The number of stripes apparently coincides with the syllables in the war cry of the War of Independence, "Freedom or Death". The blue and white colours symbolize Greece's crystal clear waters and the crests of the waves. The **Greek cross** represents the Greek Orthodox Church, the predominant faith in Greece.

HISTORY

Athens and **Sparta** led the city-states to victory in the **Persian Wars** (499–479 BC). **Corinth** and **Thebes** defeated Athens in the **Peloponnesian War** (431–404 BC). In 338 BC **Philip II of Macedon** became King of Greece. His son, **Alexander the**

Great, built a world empire. In 146 BC, Greece fell to the **Romans**. From AD 330 to 1453 it formed part of the **Byzantine Empire**. In 1456 the **Ottoman Turks** conquered Greece. Greece defeated the Ottomans in the **War of Independence** (1821–29). Greece remained neutral at the start of **World War II**, but **Germany** occupied it in 1941. **Konstantinos Karamanlis** became prime minister in 1955. In 1967 a **military junta** seized power. In 1973 **the Colonels** made Greece a **republic**. In 1974 civilian rule returned under Karamanlis. In 1981 Greece joined the **European Union** and **Andreas Papandreou** became the first socialist prime minister.

AREA: 131,990sq km (50,961sq mi)
POPULATION: 10,939,771
CAPITAL (POPULATION): Athens (757,400)
GOVERNMENT: Multi-party republic
ETHNIC GROUPS: Greek 96%, Macedonian 2%, Turkish 1%, Albanian, Slav
LANGUAGES: Greek (official)
RELIGIONS: Greek Orthodox 97%, Muslim 2%
NATIONAL MOTTO: "*Eleftheria i Thanatos*" "Freedom or Death"
NATIONAL ANTHEM (DATE): "*Ymnos eis tin Eleftherian*" "Hymn to Freedom" (1864)

The Greek Orthodox Church *stresses the divine nature of Christ the Saviour.*

83

GRENADA

FLAG RATIO: 1:2 USE: National/Civil DATE ADOPTED: 1974 LAST MODIFIED: 1974

Grenada's flag consists of a **rectangle of four triangles** in alternate **yellow** and **green** colours, framed by a **red border**. At the centre of the flag is a **yellow star** on a **red disc**, representing the borough of St. George's, Grenada's capital. On the red border are **six yellow stars**, denoting Grenada's six parishes. On the left-hand green triangle is a stylized **nutmeg**. Nutmeg is the largest export for the 'Spice Isle' of Grenada. The flag uses the **Pan-African colours**. Green represents the fertile land. Yellow stands for wisdom, sunshine, and the warmth of Grenadians. Red symbolizes the people's courage and vitality.

HISTORY

In 1498 **Christopher Columbus** sighted the islands. The **Carib** fiercely resisted colonization. In 1650 **France** founded St. George's. In 1783 **Britain** gained control. The British brought **slaves** from Africa to work on the sugar **plantations**. In 1795 **Julian Fedon** led a slave revolt. In 1877 Grenada became a **British colony**. In 1974 it gained **independence**. Eric M. Gairy was the first prime minister. In 1979 Gairy was overthrown in a **coup**. In 1983, after a second coup, **United States'** troops invaded and restored democratic government. **Keith Mitchell** served as prime minister from 1995 to date.

AREA: 344sq km (133sq mi)

POPULATION: 83,000

CAPITAL (POPULATION): St George's (4400)

GOVERNMENT: Constitutional monarchy

ETHNIC GROUPS: African 82% mixed race 13%, European and South Asian (East Indian) 15%, trace Arawak/Carib Amerindian

LANGUAGES: English (official), French *patois*

RELIGIONS: Roman Catholic 53%, Anglican 14%, other Protestant 33%

NATIONAL MOTTO: "Ever Conscious of God, We Aspire, Build and Advance as One People"

NATIONAL ANTHEM (DATE):
"Hail! Grenada" (1974)

***The Grenada dove** is an endangered species. It lives only in Grenada.*

GUATEMALA

FLAG RATIO: 5:8   USE: National/Civil   DATE ADOPTED: 1871   LAST AMENDED: 1997

Like many other nations in Central America, Guatemala has a **blue and white** flag. The flag of the **Central American Federation**, of which Guatemala was a member from 1823 to 1839, had blue and white horizontal stripes. The present flag of **three vertical stripes** (two blue, one white) dates from 1871. Blue stands for justice and loyalty, and recalls the blue of the sky. White symbolizes purity and integrity. The **shield of arms** at the flag's centre has two **laurel branches**, two **crossed swords**, two crossed **Remington rifles**, and a **quetzal bird** sitting atop a **scroll** inscribed with "*Libertad 15 de Septiembre de 1821*" (the date of independence).

HISTORY

Between AD 300 and 900 the Quiché **Mayas** ruled Guatemala. The ruins at **Tikal** are the tallest temple-pyramids in the Americas. In 1523–24 the **Spanish** *conquistador* **Pedro de Alvarado** defeated the native tribes. In 1821 Guatemala gained **independence**. **Rafael Carrera** dominated government until his death in 1865. The dictatorships of **Manuel Estrada Cabrera** and **Jorge Ubico** loomed over the early 20th century. From 1960 to 1996 a **civil war** claimed more than 200,000 lives. In 1976 an **earthquake** killed more than 22,000 people in the capital **Guatemala City**.

***Guatemala** is home to more than 600 species of orchids.*

AREA: 108,890sq km (42,042sq mi)
POPULATION: 13,385,334
CAPITAL (POPULATION): Guatemala City (823,301)
GOVERNMENT: Multi-party republic
ETHNIC GROUPS: Ladino (mixed Hispanic and Native American) 45%, Mayan 43%, White 5%, Black 2%, others (including Chinese) 3%
LANGUAGES: Spanish (official)
RELIGIONS: Roman Catholic 73%, Protestant 25%, indigenous beliefs 2%
NATIONAL MOTTO: "*Libertad!*" "Liberty!"
NATIONAL ANTHEM (DATE): "*Guatemala Feliz*" "Guatemala, Rejoice" (1896)

GUINEA

FLAG RATIO: 2:3 USE: National/Civil DATE ADOPTED: 1958 LAST MODIFIED: 1958

Like many former French colonies, Guinea based its flag on the French *tricolore*. Guinea's flag uses the colours of the **Pan-African** movement. It is the mirror image of Mali's flag. The colours are also symbolic of Guinea's national identity. **Red** symbolizes the blood shed in the struggle for independence and the desire for progress. **Yellow** represents the African sun, Guinean gold, and equality. **Green** stands for the lush vegetation and national prosperity. The colours also correspond to the national motto "*Travail, Justice, Solidarité*".

HISTORY

The Mali Empire dominated West Africa in the 12th century. The Songhai Empire supplanted it in the 15th century. **Portuguese** explorers arrived in the mid-15th century, and the **slave trade** began. In the 18th century, the **Fulani** embarked on a *jihad* (holy war). In 1849 France formed a protectorate on the Atlantic coast. It became the colony of **French Guinea**, and part of French West Africa in 1895. In 1958 Guinea declared independence. **Sékou Touré** was president from 1958 to 1984. In 1970 Portuguese Guinea (now **Guinea-Bissau**) launched an unsuccessful invasion of Guinea. In 1984 Colonel **Lansana Conté** became president. By 2000, Guinea was home to *c*.500,000 **refugees** from the wars in neighbouring Sierra Leone and Liberia.

AREA: 245,860sq km (94,927sq mi)
POPULATION: 7,830,000
CAPITAL (POPULATION): Conakry (1,508,000)
GOVERNMENT: Multi-party republic
ETHNIC GROUPS: Fulani (Peul) 40%, Malinke 26%, Susu 11%, Kissi 7%, Kpelle 5%
LANGUAGES: French (official)
RELIGIONS: Muslim (mainly Sunni) 80%, Christian 10%, African traditional beliefs 5%
NATIONAL MOTTO: "*Travail, Justice, Solidarité*" "Work, Justice, Solidarity"
NATIONAL ANTHEM (DATE): "*Liberté*" "Liberty" (1958)

***Demidoff's** dwarf galago or bushbaby is one of the smallest primates, 10 to 15 cm long.*

GUINEA-BISSAU

FLAG RATIO: 1:2 USE: National/Civil DATE ADOPTED: 1973 LAST MODIFIED: 1973

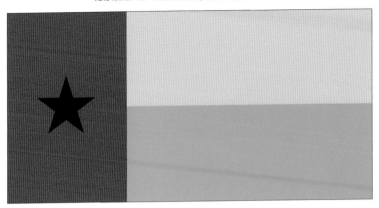

In 1973 Guinea-Bissau adopted a new flag to celebrate its independence from Portugal. Like many decolonized African nations, it took the colours of the **Pan-African** movement. The **red vertical band** symbolizes the blood shed in the liberation struggle. The **yellow horizontal stripe** stands for the hot African sun. The **green horizontal stripe** represents the fertile land and hope for the future. The **black star** on the red band represents the African continent and pays homage to the flag of **Ghana**, the first African colony to gain independence.

HISTORY

Portuguese navigators visited Guinea-Bissau in 1446. From the 17th to the early 19th century, Portugal used the coast as a **slave-trading** base. In 1836 Portugal joined Guinea-Bissau and **Cape Verde**.

Guinea-Bissau became the separate colony of **Portuguese Guinea** in 1879. In 1956 **Amilcar Cabral** founded the African Party for the Independence of Guinea and Cape Verde (PAIGC). In 1963 the PAIGC launched a guerrilla war. Within five years, it held more than two-thirds of Guinea-Bissau. In 1974 Guinea-Bissau gained **independence**. **Luís de Almeida Cabral**, Amilcar Cabral's brother, was the first president. In 1980 Major **João Veira** overthrew Cabral in a military coup. In 1999 a military coup toppled Veira. **Kumbala Yalá** became president at elections in 2000.

AREA: 36,120sq km (13,946sq mi)
POPULATION: 1,285,715
CAPITAL (POPULATION): Bissau (288,300)
GOVERNMENT: Multi-party republic
ETHNIC GROUPS: Balanta 32%, Fulani (Peul) 20%, Malinke (Mandingo or Mandinka) 13%, Mandyako 11%, Papel 10%
LANGUAGES: Portuguese (official), Crioulo
RELIGIONS: African traditional beliefs 45%, Sunni Muslim 38%, Roman Catholic 11%
NATIONAL MOTTO: *"Unidade, Luta, Progresso"* "Unity, Struggle, Progress"
NATIONAL ANTHEM (DATE): *"Esta é a Nossa Pátria Amada"* "This is our Beloved Country" (1975)

Guinea-Bissau has many villages in the mangrove swamps along the Atlantic coast.

87

GUYANA

FLAG RATIO: 3:5 USE: National/Civil DATE ADOPTED: 1966 LAST MODIFIED: 1966

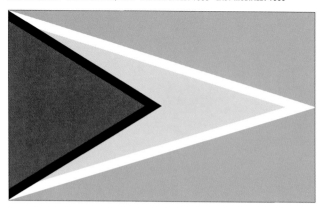

Guyana's flag is nicknamed 'the Golden Arrow'. It combines the colours of the **Pan-African** movement (red, yellow, green) and colours associated with **Marcus Garvey** (red, black, green). The **'golden arrow'** represents progress and Guyana's mineral wealth. The **red triangle** signifies the energy and potential of the Guyanese. The **green field** symbolizes the nation's forests and fertile land. The **white fimbriation** stands for its many rivers, and the **black fimbriation** denotes the endurance of the Guyanese.

HISTORY

In 1581 the **Dutch** built trading posts. They established **sugar plantations** in 1658, importing Africans as **slave labour**. In 1841 Britain captured the town of **Demerara**. The colony of **British Guiana** emerged in 1831. In 1834 Britain abolished slavery and began to use **indentured labour** from India and China. In 1953 **Cheddi Jagan** became prime minister. In 1961 British Guiana gained **self-rule** under Jagan. Guyana gained **independence** in 1966. **Forbes Burnham** led the country from 1964 to 1985. In 1970 Guyana became a **republic**. In 1978, 912 members of the **People's Temple cult**, led by Jim Jones, committed mass suicide. Cheddi Jagan became president in 1992 elections. His widow, **Janet Jagan**, was president from 1997 to 1999. **Ethnic tensions** snapped into **riots** in 1998. **Bharrat Jagdeo** became president in 1999.

AREA: 214,970sq km (83,000sq mi)
POPULATION: 861,200
CAPITAL (POPULATION): Georgetown (225,800)
GOVERNMENT: Multi-party republic
ETHNIC GROUPS: East Indian (South Asian) 49%, African 32%, Mixed 12%, Native American 6%
LANGUAGES: English (official)
RELIGIONS: Protestant 34%, Hindu 33%, Roman Catholic 16%, Sunni Muslim 9%
NATIONAL MOTTO: "One People, One Nation, One Destiny"
NATIONAL ANTHEM (DATE): "Dear Land of Guyana, of Rivers and Plains" (1966)

Caribbean manatees live in coastal waters and rivers. They grow to four metres long.

88

Haiti's **blue-and-red flag** originates from its war of independence against France. On May 18, 1803, Haitian rebel leader Jean-Jacques Dessalines tore up the French *tricolore*, discarding the white stripe. In 1807 General Alexandre Pétion changed the orientation of the stripes from vertical to **horizontal**. The **blue stripe** represents Haitians of African and French descent. The red stripe represents the blood shed in the struggle for liberation. At the centre of the flag is the **coat of arms** on a **white rectangle**. The coat of arms features a **Liberty cap** atop a **royal palm** tree and two cannons, flanked by flags. A **scroll** reads "*L'Union Fait la Force*" ("Strength in Unity"). At the 1936 Olympics, Liechtenstein noticed that it had the same flag as the civil flag (without arms) of Haiti and changed its flag.

HISTORY

Haiti and **Dominican Republic** share the island of Hispaniola. **Christopher Columbus** discovered Hispaniola in 1492. In 1697 Spain ceded Haiti to France. In 1790 **Toussaint L'Ouverture** led a slave revolt. Haiti gained **independence** in 1804. Dictator **'Papa Doc' Duvalier** came to power in 1957. In 1971 **'Baby Doc' Duvalier** succeeded his father. In 1986 'Baby Doc' fled into exile. In 1991 a military coup toppled President **Jean-Bertrand Aristide**, but he returned with US support in 1994.

AREA: 27,750sq km (10,714sq mi)
POPULATION: 8,003,000
CAPITAL (POPULATION): Port-au-Prince (1,082,800)
GOVERNMENT: Multi-party republic
ETHNIC GROUPS: African 95%, mixed race and white 5%
LANGUAGES: French (official)
RELIGIONS: Voodoo (non-exclusive) 90%, Roman Catholic 80%, Baptist 10%, Pentecostal 4%, Adventist 1%
NATIONAL MOTTO: "*Liberté, Egalité, Fraternité*" "Liberty, Equality, Fraternity"
NATIONAL ANTHEM (DATE): "*La Dessalinienne*" "The Song of Dessalines" (1904)

Haiti hosted the 25th General Assembly of the Organization of American States in 1995.

89

HONDURAS

FLAG RATIO: 1:2 USE: National/Civil DATE ADOPTED: 1866 LAST MODIFIED: 1866

L ike many other nations in Central America, Honduras has a **blue and white** flag in homage to the Argentine Generals Belgrano and San Martín. In 1823 Honduras, Costa Rica, El Salvador, Guatemala and Nicaragua united to form the Central American Federation, which adopted a flag with **three horizontal stripes** (**two turquoise**, **one white**). In 1839 the Federation dissolved, but Honduras retained the flag. In 1866 it added **five turquoise stars** in an X-pattern to the centre of its flag. The stars represent the five former members of the Federation. The turquoise bands stand for the Caribbean Sea and Pacific Ocean.

HISTORY

Christopher Columbus sighted the coast in 1502, and Pedro de Alvarado founded the first **Spanish** settlements in 1524. In 1576 the Spanish discovered the ruins of the **Maya** civilization at Copán, western Honduras, but they became covered in dense forest and were only rediscovered in 1839. In 1821 Honduras gained **independence**, forming part of the Mexican Empire. From 1823 to 1838 Honduras was a member of the Central American Federation. Britain controlled the **Mosquito Coast**. In the 1890s the United States developed **banana plantations**. From 1963 to 1982 the military ruled Honduras. In 1969 Honduras fought the 'Soccer War' against El Salvador. In 1998 **Hurricane Mitch** killed more than 5500 people.

AREA: 112,090sq km (43,278 sq mi)
POPULATION: 6,438,100
CAPITAL (POPULATION): Tegucigalpa (968,400)
GOVERNMENT: Multi-party republic
ETHNIC GROUPS: Mestizo 90%, Native American 7%, Garifunas (West Indian) 2%
LANGUAGES: Spanish (official)
RELIGIONS: Roman Catholic 95%, Protestant 5%
NATIONAL ANTHEM (DATE): *"Tu Bandera"* "Your Flag" (1915)

The scarlet macaw (Ara macao) *is the national bird of Honduras.*

Hungary's **tricolour** of **red, white** and **green** first appeared together on the cord of a seal in 1618, in the reign of Matthias II. The present tricolour of **horizontal stripes** was adopted during the Revolution of 1848. In 1849 Austria regained control and scrapped the flag. In 1867 Austria agreed to the joint Austro-Hungarian Empire and the tricolour returned with a royal coat of arms. In 1949 Hungary became a communist republic and the tricolour acquired a Soviet-style emblem. After the Hungarian Uprising in 1956, the plain tricolour was revived as the national flag. Red symbolizes strength. White stands for fidelity, while green represents hope.

HISTORY

In *c.*895 **Magyars**, led by **Árpád**, settled in Hungary. In 1699 Leopold I estab-

lished **Habsburg** rule. **Lajos Kossuth** declared Hungary's independence in 1848, but Emperor **Franz Joseph** regained control in 1849. Austrian defeat in the **Austro-Prussian War** (1866) led to the formation of the Austro-Hungarian Empire. In 1918 Hungary declared **independence**. In 1941 Hungary allied with **Nazi Germany**. Virulent **anti-Semitism** saw the murder of many Hungarian Jews. In 1948 **communists** overthrew the government of **Imre Nagy**. In 1956 a **revolt** led to the return of Nagy. The **Soviets** crushed the revolt and **János Kádár** came to power. In 1989 Kádár resigned and multi-party elections were held in 1990. In 1999 Hungary joined NATO.

Embroidery *from Kalocsa, southern Hungary, often has beautiful floral patterns.*

AREA: 93,030sq km (35,919sq mi)

POPULATION: 10,197,120

CAPITAL (POPULATION): Budapest (1,775,200)

GOVERNMENT: Multi-party republic

ETHNIC GROUPS: Magyar (Hungarian) 98%, Romany, German, Croat, Romanian, Slovak

LANGUAGES: Hungarian (official)

RELIGIONS: Roman Catholic 68%, Reformed Church 21%, Lutheran 4%, Jewish 1%

NATIONAL ANTHEM (DATE): *"Himnusz"* "National Anthem of Hungary" (1844)

ICELAND

FLAG RATIO: 18:25 USE: National/Civil DATE ADOPTED: 1915 CODIFIED: 1944

From 1380 to 1918 Iceland was under Danish rule and Denmark's flag was its national flag. In 1897 an unofficial flag appeared with a white cross on a blue field. In 1915 King Christian X of Denmark ruled that this flag was too similar to the flag of Greece, and instead approved a flag with a **red cross bordered in white** on a **blue field** for use on land and within Icelandic waters. In 1918 Iceland gained self-rule and adopted the 1915 flag. Iceland retained the flag upon becoming a republic in 1944. Blue stands for its mountains. White represents ice. Red symbolizes the fire from Iceland's volcanoes. The **Scandinavian cross** recalls Iceland's Nordic links.

HISTORY

In AD 874 Norwegian **Vikings** colonized Iceland, and in 930 the settlers founded the world's oldest parliament (***Althing***). In 1262 Iceland united with **Norway**. When Norway joined with **Denmark** in 1380, Iceland came under Danish rule. During the colonial period, Iceland lost much of its population due to migration, disease, and natural disaster. In 1918 it became a self-governing **kingdom**, united with Denmark. Iceland escaped Nazi German occupation during **World War II** (1940–45), largely due to the presence of United States' forces. In 1944, a referendum decisively voted to sever links with Denmark, and Iceland became an independent **republic**. In 1946 it joined NATO. The extension of Iceland's fishing limits in 1958 and 1977 led to the 'Cod War' with the United Kingdom. **Vigdis Finnbogadóttir** served as Iceland's first woman president from 1980 to 1996.

AREA: 103,000 sq km (39,768 sq mi)
POPULATION: 282,849
CAPITAL (POPULATION): Reykjavík (111,345)
GOVERNMENT: Multi-party republic
ETHNIC GROUPS: Icelandic 94%, Danish 1%
LANGUAGES: Icelandic (official)
RELIGIONS: Evangelical Lutheran 92%,
other Lutheran 3%, Roman Catholic 1%
NATIONAL ANTHEM (DATE): *"Lofsöngur"*
"Song of Praise" (1874)

Snaefell *volcano is the highest peak in Iceland outside of the glaciated regions.*

INDIA

FLAG RATIO: 2:3   USE: National/Civil   DATE ADOPTED: 1947   LAST MODIFIED: 1947

In 1931 the Indian National Congress, leaders of the struggle for independence from Britain, adopted a **horizontal tricolour** flag of **saffron, white** and **green**. Apparently designed by Congress leader 'Mahatma' Gandhi, the flag had a blue spinning wheel, a Gandhian symbol of self-sufficiency, on the white stripe. Saffron (orange) represented India's Hindu people, green stood for its Muslims, and white symbolized the peace between them. When India gained independence in 1947, the Assembly of India adopted the tricolour but replaced the spinning wheel with the *Dharma Chakra* ('Wheel of Law') on the 'lion capital' of King Ashoka at Sarnath, northern India.

HISTORY

In *c.*1500 BC **Aryans** conquered India and established **Hinduism**. King **Ashoka** unified India and established **Buddhism** in the 3rd century BC. In 1526 **Babur** founded the **Mogul Empire**. **Robert Clive** helped establish **British India** (1757–1947). Civil unrest culminated in the **Indian Mutiny** (1857–58). After World War I (1914–18), **'Mahatma' Gandhi** began his campaigns of passive resistance. In 1947, British India split into India and the Muslim state of **Pakistan**.

AREA: 3,287,590sq km (1,269,338sq mi)
POPULATION: 1,027,015,247
CAPITAL (POPULATION): New Delhi (294,783)
GOVERNMENT: Multi-party federal republic
ETHNIC GROUPS: Indo-Aryan 72%, Dravidian (Aboriginal) 25%, Other 3%
LANGUAGES: Hindi 30% and English (both official), Telugu 8%, Bengali 8%, Marati 8%, Urdu 5%, and many others
RELIGIONS: Hindu 83%, Sunni Muslim 11%, Christian 2%, Sikh 2%, Buddhist 1%
NATIONAL MOTTO: *"Satyam eva jayate"* "Truth alone triumphs"
NATIONAL ANTHEM (DATE): *"Jana-Gana-Mana"* "Thou Art The Ruler Of All Minds" (1950)

Chandragupta, grandfather of Ashoka, founded the Maurya Empire (321–185 BC).

93

INDONESIA

FLAG RATIO: 2:3 USE: National/Civil DATE ADOPTED: 1945 LAST MODIFIED: 1945

The Indonesian flag is known as the '*Sang Saka Merah Putih*' ('Grand bicolour of red and white'). The flag is based on the flag of the Javanese **Majapahit Empire**, which dominated Indonesia and Malaya from the 13th to the 16th century. **Red** and **white** are sacred colours, representing the physical and the spiritual worlds respectively. Red also symbolizes bravery and freedom. White also stands for purity and justice. From the 1920s, Indonesian nationalists adopted the colours to represent their struggle against Dutch rule. On August 17, 1945, Acmad Sukarno raised the flag to proclaim Indonesia's independence.

HISTORY

In the 7th century the Indian **Gupta dynasty** introduced **Buddhism** and built **Borobudur**. In 1511 the Portuguese seized **Malacca**. In 1799 Indonesia became a **Dutch** colony. **Krakatoa** erupted in 1883, killing *c*.50,000 people. In 1942 **Japan** occupied Indonesia. In 1945 Indonesia declared independence. In 1949 it became a republic. **Sukarno** was the first president. In 1965 General **Suharto** seized power. In 1975 Indonesia seized **East Timor**. **Megawati Sukarnoputri**, Sukarno's daughter, became president in 2001. In 2002 East Timor gained independence and a bomb in **Bali** killed nearly 200 people.

AREA: 1,904,570sq km (735,354sq mi)
POPULATION: 203,260,000
CAPITAL (POPULATION): Jakarta (8,385,000)
GOVERNMENT: Multi-party republic
ETHNIC GROUPS: Javanese 39%, Sundanese 16%, Indonesian (Malay) 12%, Madurese 4%
LANGUAGES: Bahasa Indonesian (official)
RELIGIONS: Muslim (mainly Sunni) 87%, Protestant 6%, Roman Catholic 3%, Hindu 3%, Buddhist 1%
NATIONAL MOTTO: "*Bhinneka Tunggal Ika*" "Unity in Diversity"
NATIONAL ANTHEM (DATE): "*Indonesia Raya*" "Great Indonesia" (1949)

Tari gamyong is a traditional dance in Central Java province (Jawa Tengah).

The colours represent the Islamic religion (**green**), peace (**white**), and courage (**red**). They first appeared in **tricolour** form on Iran's flag in 1907. After the abdication of the Shah in 1979, the symbol at the centre of the flag changed to **four crescents** and a **sword**. The five parts of the emblem symbolize the five precepts of Islam. The **inscription** "*Allah-u Akbar*" ("God is great") is written in ancient **Kufic script** along the horizontal borders of the white stripe. The inscription appears 22 times as a celebration of Iran's Islamic Revolution, which took place on the 22nd day of the 11th month of the Iranian calendar (February 11, 1979). The **hoist** of the flag should be to the viewer's right.

HISTORY

In 550 BC, **Cyrus the Great** conquered the **Median Empire**, and established the **Achaemenid** dynasty, rulers of Iran's first Empire. The Empire survived the **Persian Wars** (492–497 BC) against the Greek city-states, but fell to **Alexander the Great** in 331 BC. In AD 224, the **Sassanids** restored Iranian rule. **Arabs** conquered Iran in 641, introducing Islam. In the 1510s, Shah **Ismail** reunified Iran and founded a **Shi'a** theocracy. In 1921, **Reza Pahlavi** seized power. In 1941 British and Soviet forces occupied Iran, and **Muhammad Pahlavi** succeeded his father as Shah. In 1979 Pahlavi fled and **Ayatollah Khomeini** established an Islamic republic. **Muhammad Khatami** became president in 1997.

AREA: 1,648,000sq km (636,293sq mi)
POPULATION: 60,055,488
CAPITAL (POPULATION): Tehran (6,758,845)
GOVERNMENT: Islamic republic
ETHNIC GROUPS: Iranian 46%, Azerbaijani 17%, Kurdish 9%, Gilaki 5%, Arab 3%, Lur 2%
LANGUAGES: Iranian (or Farsi, official)
RELIGIONS: Shi'a Muslim 89%, Sunni Muslim 10%
NATIONAL ANTHEM (DATE): (1990)

The hawfinch (Coccothraustes coccothraustes) *is found throughout Iran.*

95

IRAQ

FLAG RATIO: 2:3 **USE:** National/Civil **DATE ADOPTED:** 1963 **LAST MODIFIED:** 1991

The **red**, **white** and **black** colours of the Iraqi flag are based on the **Pan-Arab** colours adopted by Hussein ibn Ali. The current design is similar to the design of the former United Arab Republic (UAR). The three **green stars** represent the members of the old UAR (Iraq, Egypt, Syria), and reflect Iraq's continuing desire for Arab union. The **green** *takbir* '*Allah-u Akbar*' ('God is Great'), written in Arabic script, was added during the Gulf War (1991). The **hoist** of the Iraqi flag should be to the viewer's right.

HISTORY

Ancient **Mesopotamia**, between the rivers Tigris and Euphrates, roughly equates to modern Iraq. **Hammurabi** founded the Empire of **Babylonia** in the 18th century BC. **Nebuchadnezzar** conquered Jerusalem in 597 BC, beginning the Babylonian Captivity of the Jews. In AD 637 Arab conquest introduced **Islam**. Baghdad served as capital of the **Abbasid** caliphate from 750 to 1258. Mesopotamia was part of the **Ottoman Empire** from 1534 to 1916. In 1921 Britain made **Faisal I** King of Iraq. In 1932 Iraq won **independence**. In 1958 Faisal was executed and a republic born. In 1963 the **Ba'ath Party** seized power. **Saddam Hussein** became president in 1979, purging the party and leading Iraq into the **Iran-Iraq War** (1980–88) and the **Gulf War** (1991). In 1991 Saddam crushed a Kurdish and Shi'a **rebellion**.

AREA: 438,320sq km (169,235sq mi)
POPULATION: 23,331,985
CAPITAL (POPULATION): Baghdad (4,832,477)
GOVERNMENT: Single-party republic
ETHNIC GROUPS: Arab 77%, Kurdish 19%, Turkmen, Iranian, Assyrian
LANGUAGES: Arabic (official), Kurdish
RELIGIONS: Shi'a Muslim 63%, Sunni Muslim 35%
NATIONAL ANTHEM (DATE): "*Ardulfurataini Watan*" "Land of Two Rivers" (1981)

***Ishtar Gate**, entrance to ancient Babylon, was built (600 BC) by King Nebuchadnezzar.*

IRELAND

The **tricolour** of **green**, **white** and **orange** was first flown as an emblem of the Young Ireland movement in 1848. It came into popular use after the Easter Rising of 1916. The colours represent aspects of Ireland's population. Green stands for the historic Gaelic and Anglo-Norman (Roman Catholic) section of society. Orange denotes the Protestant supporters of William of Orange. The white stripe symbolizes the hope for a lasting peace between the two traditions.

HISTORY

In *c*.432 **Saint Patrick** introduced **Christianity**. In 1014 **Brian Boru** defeated the Viking invaders. In 1171 **Henry II** of England conquered Ireland. In 1649 **Oliver Cromwell** brutally crushed an Irish rebellion. In the 1916 **Easter Rising**, Irish nationalists declared independence. The British Army's harsh breaking of the rebellion led to a landslide victory for Sinn Féin at elections in 1918. The Anglo-Irish Treaty (1921) saw the creation of the Irish Free State and the partition of Ireland. **Arthur Griffith** became the first *taoiseach* (prime minister). **Civil war** raged in 1922–23. In 1937 a new constitution declared the nation of Éire to be the whole island of Ireland. **Eamon de Valera** served as *taoiseach* (1932–48, 1951–54, 1957–59) and president (1959–73). Ireland remained neutral during **World War II**. In 1973 it joined the **European Union**.

Stamp *marking the 50th year of the organization to promote Irish traditional arts.*

AREA: 70,280sq km (27,135sq mi)
POPULATION: 3,626,087
CAPITAL (POPULATION): Dublin (953,000)
GOVERNMENT: Multi-party republic
ETHNIC GROUPS: Irish 94%
LANGUAGES: Irish and English (both official)
RELIGIONS: Roman Catholic 93%, Protestant 3%
NATIONAL MOTTO: "*Cead Mile Failte*" "One Hundred Thousand Welcomes"
NATIONAL ANTHEM (DATE): "*Amhrán Na bhFiann*" "The Soldier's Song" (1926)

97

ISRAEL

FLAG RATIO: 8:11   **USE:** National/Civil   **DATE ADOPTED:** 1948   **LAST MODIFIED:** 1948

According to legend, the six-pointed blue star made of two triangles at the centre of Israel's flag derives from the shield of **King David** (*c*.1000 BC). Often known as the 'Star of David', it also appeared on King Solomon's ring and is also called the 'Seal of Solomon'. In 1354 the Jewish community in Prague chose the Star of David as the symbol for their flag. In 1897 the World Zionist Organization adopted a flag with a **white field**, blue stripes and the Star of David. In 1948 Israel took the Zionist flag as its own. The **blue bands** come from the stripes of the *tallit* (Jewish prayer shawl). Blue and white are traditional Jewish colours symbolizing purity.

HISTORY

Israel forms most of the Biblical **Holy Lands**. In *c*.2000 BC Jews moved into **Palestine** from Egypt. In 63 BC the **Romans** conquered Palestine. In AD 640 it fell to Muslim Arabs. From 1516 to 1918 it was part of the **Ottoman Empire**. After World War I it came under **British** control. In 1947 the United Nations agreed to partition Palestine into an Arab and a Jewish state. On May 14, 1948, the State of **Israel** was proclaimed. **David Ben-Gurion** was the first prime minister. Hundreds of thousands of Palestinians fled. Israel successfully defended itself in the **Arab-Israeli Wars**. In 1967 it occupied Sinai, Golan Height, the West Bank, and Gaza Strip. In 1982 it returned Sinai to Egypt. In 1995 Prime Minister **Yitzhak Rabin** was assassinated.

AREA: 26,650sq km (10,290sq mi)
POPULATION: 5,899,940
CAPITAL (POPULATION): Jerusalem (622,091)
GOVERNMENT: Multi-party republic
ETHNIC GROUPS: Jewish 82%, Arab and others 18%
LANGUAGES: Hebrew and Arabic (both official)
RELIGIONS: Jewish 82%, Muslim 14%, Christian 2%, Druse and others 2%
NATIONAL ANTHEM (DATE): "*Hatikva*"
"The Hope" (1948)

Two dancers *on a stamp celebrating the festival of the Jewish Year 5762 (2001).*

Italy's flag was first established during the Napoleonic Wars and styled after the French *tricolore*. The colours apparently derived from the uniform of the Milan civic militia. In 1796 Emperor Napoleon ordered that the military flag of the Lombard Legion bear **vertical stripes** of **green**, **white**, and **red**. In 1797 the Cispadana Republic adopted a flag with red, white and green horizontal stripes. Later that year, the Cispadana and Transpadana Republics united to form the Cisalpine Republic, which adopted the present tricolour in 1798. In 1861 the Kingdom of Italy adopted the tricolour with the Savoy coat of arms at the centre. In 1946 the plain tricolour became the flag of the Republic of Italy.

the formation of the **Roman Empire** (27 BC) under Augustus. In 962 **Otto I** established the Holy Roman Empire. The 15th-century **Renaissance** profoundly affected western civilization. **Giuseppe Garibaldi** helped create the Kingdom of Italy under **Victor Emmanuel II** in 1861. The papacy refused to concede Rome, and **Vatican City** gained independence in 1929. Dictator **Benito Mussolini** came to power in 1922. Italy fought on the Axis side for much of World War II, but in 1943 Mussolini was dismissed and Italy surrendered. In 1948 Italy became a republic. **Alcide de Gasperi** was Prime Minister from 1945 to 1953. Media mogul **Silvio Berlusconi** became Prime Minister in 2001.

HISTORY

The assassination of **Julius Caesar** led to

Etruscan *tomb painting of a young girl from the 4th century BC.*

AREA: 301,270sq km (116,320sq mi)
POPULATION: 58,082,500
CAPITAL (POPULATION): Rome (2,649,500)
GOVERNMENT: Multi-party republic
ETHNIC GROUPS: Italian 94%, German, French, Greek, Albanian, Slovenian, Ladino
LANGUAGES: Italian 94% (official), Sardinian 3%
RELIGIONS: Roman Catholic 83%
NATIONAL ANTHEM (DATE): "*Inno di Mameli*" "Mameli's Hymn" (1946)

JAMAICA

FLAG RATIO: 1:2 USE: National/Civil DATE ADOPTED: 1962 LAST MODIFIED: 1962

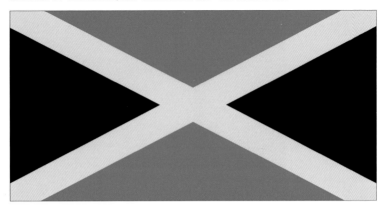

A committee of Jamaica's House of Representatatives designed the national flag. "The sun shineth, the land is green, and the people are strong and creative" sums up the flag's symbolism. It features a **gold saltire** (diagonal cross), representing Jamaica's sunshine and natural resources. The **green** triangles symbolize agriculture and the hope for the future. The **black** triangles on the hoist and flag stand for the hardships creatively faced and overcome and by its people.

HISTORY

Christopher Columbus made landfall on May 5, 1494. Spanish conquerors quickly eradicated the indigenous **Arawak** population. In 1509 the first

Spanish settlement appeared in the St Ann's Bay area. In 1655 **England** captured Jamaica, and the freed Spanish slaves (**Maroons**) took to the hills. **Port Royal** became a haven for buccaneers such as **Henry Morgan**. The English established **sugar plantations** using **slave labour** from Africa. The frequent slave rebellions precipitated the **abolition** of the slave trade in 1834. In 1865 Governor **Edward John Eyre** crushed the Morant Bay Rebellion. In 1872 **Kingston** became the island's capital. In 1962 Jamaica gained independence. **Sir Alexander Bustamante** was the nation's first prime minister. **Michael Manley** led Jamaica into the Caribbean Community and Common Market (CARICOM). Musician **Bob Marley** exported Jamaican **reggae** to Europe.

AREA: 10,962sq km (4232sq mi)
POPULATION: 2,735,000
CAPITAL (POPULATION): Kingston (538,900)
GOVERNMENT: Constitutional monarchy
ETHNIC GROUPS: Black 91%, Indian 1%
LANGUAGES: English, Patois
RELIGIONS: Church of God 21%, Seventh-Day Adventists 9%, Baptist 9%, Pentecostal 8%, Anglican 6%, Roman Catholic 4%
MOTTO: "Out of Many, One People"
NATIONAL ANTHEM (DATE): "Jamaica, Land We Love" (1962)

The bird of paradise or crane flower is native to South Africa.

JAPAN

FLAG RATIO: 2:3 USE: National/Civil DATE ADOPTED: 1870 CODIFIED: 1999

Japan's flag is called the *Hinomaru* ('Sun Circle'). The Japanese word for the country is *Nihon* or *Nippon* ('Land of the Rising Sun'). According to legend, the sun goddess founded the state and gave birth to the first Emperor, **Jimmu**, in the 7th century BC. The flag was officially adopted in 1870. In 1999, Japan's parliament set the proportions of the flag and the position of the **red sun** disc on the **white field**.

HISTORY

The **Yamato** clan established the Japanese state, with **Kyoto** as its capital, in the 5th century. From the 12th to the 19th century, **shoguns** (warrior-kings) ruled Japan. European contact dates from the arrival of Portuguese navigators in 1543. Under the **Tokugawa** shogunate (1603–1867), Japan isolated itself from the rest of the world. During Emperor **Meiji**'s reign (1868–1912), Japan modernized and industrialized. Japan gained Korea in the **Russo-Japanese War** (1904–05). In 1923, an **earthquake** in **Tokyo** claimed 123,000 lives. In 1937 Japan invaded China, starting the Second **Sino-Japanese War**. Japan allied itself with Germany and Italy during **World War II** (1939–45). In 1941 Japan attacked the US base at **Pearl Harbor**. In 1945, the US dropped **atomic bombs** on the cities of **Hiroshima** and **Nagasaki**. Emperor **Hirohito** surrendered and the US occupied Japan from 1945 to 1952. Today, Japan is the world's second largest economic power.

The **gujou odori** *dance festival takes place every year in the prefecture of Gifu.*

AREA: 377,800sq km (145,869sq mi)
POPULATION: 127,300,000
CAPITAL (POPULATION): Tokyo (8,130,408)
GOVERNMENT: Constitutional monarchy
ETHNIC GROUPS: Japanese 99%, Chinese, Korean, Ainu
LANGUAGES: Japanese (official)
RELIGIONS: Shintoist 50%, Buddhist 45%, Christian 1%
NATIONAL ANTHEM (DATE): "*Kimigayo*" "His Majesty's Reign" (2001)

JORDAN

FLAG RATIO: 1:2 USE: National/Civil DATE ADOPTED: 1921 LAST MODIFIED: 1946

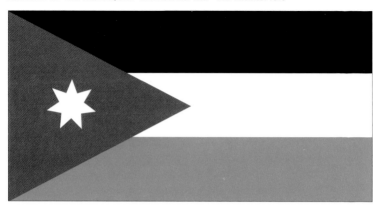

In 1916 Hussein ibn Ali raised the flag of the Great Arab Revolt against Ottoman rule in Arabia. The colours represented the **Pan-Arab** nature of the rebellion, which Lawrence of Arabia assisted. The colour of the **three stripes** stood for Arab dynasties of the Early Middle Ages: **black** for the Abbasid dynasty from Baghdad, **white** for the Umayyad dynasty from Damascus, and **green** for the Fatimid dynasty from Morocco. The **crimson triangle** joining the stripes is the colour of the Hashemite dynasty, rulers of Jordan. The revolt was successful but Arab unity rapidly disintegrated. In 1923 Hussein's son, Abdullah, became Emir of Transjordan. Abdullah added the **seven-pointed white star**, symbolizing both the unity of Jordan's people and the *Fatiha* – the first seven verses of the **Koran**.

HISTORY

In 1946 **Abdullah** became King of the **independent Hashemite Kingdom** of Jordan. In 1950, after the first of the **Arab-Israeli Wars**, Jordan annexed the **West Bank** and **East Jerusalem**. In 1951 Abdullah was assassinated. His son succeeded as **Hussein I** in 1953. The **Six-Day War** (1967) ended in the Israeli occupation of the West Bank and East Jerusalem. Jordan became home to more than one million **Palestinian** refugees. In 1970 Jordan fought a bloody **civil war** against the Palestinian Liberation Organization (PLO). In 1994 King Hussein signed a peace treaty with Israel. In 1999 Hussein died and was succeeded by his son as **Abdullah II**.

AREA: 89,210sq km (34,444sq mi)
POPULATION: 4,900,000
CAPITAL (POPULATION): Amman (1,864,450)
GOVERNMENT: Constitutional monarchy
ETHNIC GROUPS: Arab 99% (of which about 50% are Palestinian), Circassian
LANGUAGES: Arabic (official)
RELIGIONS: Sunni Muslim 95%, Christian 4%
NATIONAL ANTHEM (DATE): *"Asha al-Maleek"* "Long Live the King" (1946)

***Madaba Mosaic** is a 6th-century map of Palestine, discovered in Jerusalem in 1897.*

Kazakstan's flag has a **sky-blue** field, a traditional colour of Central Asian nomads. At the flag's centre is a **golden sun**, symbolizing Kazakstan's glorious future. The sun has **32 rays**. Underneath the sun and its rays is a soaring, golden **steppe eagle** (berkut), standing for the freedom of Kazak people. At the hoist is a band of gold 'national ornamentation'.

HISTORY

In 1218 **Genghis Khan** conquered the area. Upon his death in 1227, present-day Kazakstan was split between the khanate of his son **Jagatai** and the Empire of the **Golden Horde**. In the early 16th century, **Kazak nomads** united to create a mighty empire under **Kasim Khan**. The empire rapidly fragmented into three khanates. In 1742, devastated by attacks from the **Dzungars**, the Kazak khanates accepted Russian protection. By 1848 the **Russian Empire** had absorbed the three khanates. Mass emigration of Russians sped the process of Russification. In 1922 Kazakstan became an autonomous republic of the **Soviet Union**. More than 1.5 million Kazaks were murdered or died of starvation under the dictatorship of **Joseph Stalin**. In the 1950s, the 'Virgin Lands' project sought to turn vast areas of grassland into cultivated land to feed the Soviet Union. In December 1991, Kazakstan declared **independence** under President **Nursultan Nazarbayev**. In 1997 **Astana** replaced Almaty as capital. The first pipeline carrying **oil** direct from the **Caspian Sea** opened in 2001.

Bukhar Zhirau Kalkamanov is a famous 18th-century Kazak poet.

AREA: 2,717,300sq km (1,049,150sq mi)
POPULATION: 15,507,000
CAPITAL (POPULATION): Astana (280,500)
GOVERNMENT: Presidential republic
ETHNIC GROUPS: Kazak 53%, Russian 30%, Ukrainian 4%, Uzbek 3%, German 2%
LANGUAGES: Kazak (official), Russian
RELIGIONS: Sunni Muslim 47%, Russian Orthodox 44%, Protestant 2%
NATIONAL ANTHEM (DATE): "Mamlekettik Gemni" "National Anthem" (1944)

103

KENYA

FLAG RATIO: 2:3 USE: National/Civil DATE ADOPTED: 1963 LAST MODIFIED: 1963

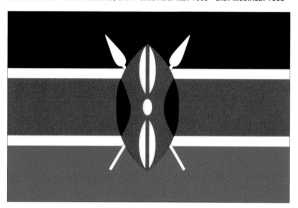

The flag of Kenya African National Union (KANU), the party that led the fight for independence, inspired the national flag. The **black** horizontal **stripe** stands for black majority rule, **red** symbolizes humanity and the struggle for liberation, and **green** represents the nation's fertile land. The thinner **white** dividing stripes, added on independence, signify peace. At the flag's centre is a traditional **Masai shield** and **two crossed spears**, symbolizing the defence of freedom.

HISTORY

From the 8th century, Arab traders began to settle on the coast of **East Africa**. By the 12th century, **Mombasa** had become an **Islamic** city-state. In 1498 **Vasco da Gama** explored the coast and **Portugal** soon dominated the trade routes. In 1698 **Oman** captured Mombasa. In the 18th century, the pastoralist Masai moved into central Kenya from the north. In the 19th century, the **Kikuyu** largely displaced them. In 1895 the **British** established the **East Africa Protectorate**. In 1903 the British completed a railway from Mombasa to **Lake Victoria**. In 1905 **Nairobi** became capital of the protectorate. After World War II (1939–45), some leaders of the Kikuyu formed a secret society, known as the **Mau Mau**, to fight for independence. In 1964 Kenya gained independence. **Jomo Kenyatta** was the first president. In 1978 **Daniel arap Moi** succeeded Kenyatta as president. A **bomb** attack (1998) on the US Embassy in Nairobi killed 230 people.

AREA: 580,370sq km (224,081sq mi)
POPULATION: 28,686,607
CAPITAL (POPULATION): Nairobi (2,143,254)
GOVERNMENT: Multi-party republic
ETHNIC GROUPS: Kikuyu 21%, Luhya 14%, Luo 13%, Kamba 11%, Kalenjin 11%
LANGUAGES: Swahili and English (both official)
RELIGIONS: Protestant 38%, Roman Catholic 28%, African traditional beliefs 19%, Sunni Muslim 10%
NATIONAL MOTTO: *"Harambee"* "Pull Together"
NATIONAL ANTHEM (DATE): *"Ee Mungu nguvu yetu"* "Oh God of All Creation" (1963)

Masai nomads wear distinctive red clothing and beaded necklaces.

FLAG RATIO: 1:2 **USE:** National/Civil **DATE ADOPTED:** 1979 **LAST MODIFIED:** 1979

Kiribati's flag was chosen by a national competition in 1979. Based on the colonial coat of arms, the College of Arms modified the design but the people of Kiribati successfully demanded a return to the original design. The **white** and **blue** wavy lines represent the Pacific Ocean. The **golden sun** rises from the waves into the **red sky**. A **frigate bird** flies over the sun, symbolizing control of the ocean.

HISTORY

Kiribati consists of 33 coral atolls divided among three island groups in the Pacific: the **Gilbert Islands** (including **Tarawa**, home to the capital Bairiki), the **Phoenix Islands**, and the **Line Islands**. Austronesian-speaking peoples settled Kiribati before the 1st century AD. In 1606 **Spanish** explorer Pedro Fernandez de Quiros sighted Butaritari, an atoll in what later became known as the Gilbert Islands. In 1788 British naval captains **Thomas Gilbert** and **John Marshall** discovered other islands. In the 19th century, missionaries spread **Christianity**. In 1892 the Gilbert Islands and the Ellice Islands became a **British protectorate**. In 1900 **phosphate** was found on **Banaba**. In 1942 Japan occupied the Gilbert Islands. United States' forces expelled the Japanese in 1943. In 1975, the mainly Polynesian Ellice Islands gained independence as **Tuvalu**. In 1979 the Gilbert Islands declared **independence** as Kiribati ('Gilberts' in the Kiribati language).

AREA: 717sq km (277sq mi)
POPULATION: 94,900
CAPITAL (POPULATION): Bairiki (2226)
GOVERNMENT: Multi-party republic
ETHNIC GROUPS: Micronesian 84%, Polynesian 14%
LANGUAGES: English (official), Kiribati
RELIGIONS: Roman Catholic 54%, Kiribati Protestant Church 38%
NATIONAL MOTTO: "*Te Mauri Te Raoi ao Te Tabomoa*" "Health, Peace and Prosperity"
NATIONAL ANTHEM (DATE): "*Teirake Kaini Kiribati*" "Stand, Kiribati" (1979)

The Moorish idol fish is native to the Pacific waters surrounding Kiribati.

KOREA, NORTH

FLAG RATIO: 1:2 **USE:** National/Civil **DATE ADOPTED:** 1948 **LAST MODIFIED:** 1948

The flag of the Democratic People's Republic of Korea consists of three **stripes** – blue, red, blue – separated by two narrow white lines. On the hoist of the red stripe is a **red five-pointed star** on a **white disc**. **Blue** symbolizes the desire for peace, **red** represents the blood of those who died in the socialist revolution, and **white** stands for the pure spirit of its people. The **red star** signifies the leading role of the 'Great Leader' Kim Il Sung in the transition to communism.

HISTORY

The name 'Korea' derives from the **Koryo dynasty**, which ruled from 918 to 1392. In 1910 **Japan** gained control. After Japan's defeat in World War II, Korea divided into two zones of occupation: Soviet forces north of the **38th** Parallel, and US troops south of this line. In 1948 North Korea established a communist government led by **Kim Il Sung**. In June 1950, North Korea invaded South Korea. The ensuing **Korean War** (1950–53) claimed c.4 million lives and ended in stalemate. After the Korean War (1950–53), several million Koreans fled Kim Il Sung's dictatorship, and North Korea became a secretive society. In the early 1990s, North Korea's **nuclear weapons**' programme gathered momentum. In 1994 Kim Il Sung died and his son, **Kim Jong Il**, succeeded as 'Dear Leader'. Aid agencies estimate that up to 2 million people died of **famine** in North Korea in the 1990s. In 2000 Kim Jong Il met South Korea's leader, Kim Dae Jong.

AREA: 120,540sq km (46,540sq mi)
POPULATION: 24,789,100
CAPITAL (POPULATION): Pyongyang (2,724,700)
GOVERNMENT: Single-party socialist republic
ETHNIC GROUPS: Korean 99%
LANGUAGES: Korean (official)
RELIGIONS: Government restricts religious freedom - no reliable figures available
NATIONAL ANTHEM (DATE): *"Aegukga"*
"Patriotic Song" (1947)

The Tale of Chun Hyang is a romantic masterpiece of Korean literature.

The Republic of Korea's flag is the *Taegeukgi*. The **blue lower-half** of the *taegeuk* **circle** at the flag's centre represents **yin** (negative cosmic forces), while the **red upper-half** stands for **yang** (positive cosmic forces). Yin and yang embody the concepts of continual movement, balance and harmony. **Four barred trigrams** (*kwae*) symbolize the elements. The *kwae* of unbroken bars on the top left represents *geon* (wind), the lower left *i* (fire), the top right *gam* (water) and the bottom right *gon* (earth).

HISTORY

The name 'Korea' derives from the **Koryo dynasty**, which ruled from 918 to 1392. The **Yi dynasty** succeeded the Koryo. In 1910 **Japan** gained control. After Japan's defeat in World War II, Korea divided into two zones of occupation: US forces south of the **38th Parallel**, and Soviet troops north of this line. In 1948 **Syngman Rhee** established a government in South Korea. In 1950 North Korea invaded South Korea. **The Korean War** (1950–53) claimed *c.*4 million lives and ended in stalemate. In 1961 **General Park** overthrew Rhee in a military coup. In 1979 Park was assassinated. In 1988 Seoul hosted the Olympic Games. In 1992 **Kim Young Sam** became South Korea's first civilian president. In 1998 **Kim Dae Jung** succeeded Kim Young Sam as President. In 2000 **Kim Dae Jung** received the Nobel Peace Prize for his efforts towards peace and reunification with North Korea, including a meeting with North Korea's President Kim Jong Il.

***The Courtesan's Sword Dance**, part of a series celebrating 5000 years of Korean art.*

AREA: 99,020sq km (38,2332sq mi)
POPULATION: 45,985,289
CAPITAL (POPULATION): Seoul (9,853,972)
GOVERNMENT: Multi-party republic
ETHNIC GROUPS: Korean 99%
LANGUAGES: Korean (official)
RELIGIONS: Buddhist 24%, Protestant 19%, Catholic 7%, Confucianist 1%
NATIONAL ANTHEM (DATE): "*Aegukga*" "Patriotic Song" (1948)

KUWAIT

FLAG RATIO: 1:2 USE: National/Civil DATE ADOPTED: 1961 LAST MODIFIED: 1961

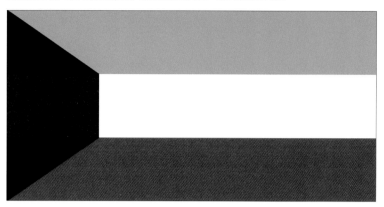

Kuwait's flag has **three horizontal stripes** and a **trapezoid** on the hoist side. Its colours are **Pan-Arab**. The colours derive from a poem by Safie Al-Deen Al-Hili. The top stripe is **green**, symbolizing Kuwaiti hospitality. The middle stripe is **white**, representing the commitment to peace. The bottom stripe is **red**, symbolizing Kuwait's determination to resist aggression. The trapezoid is **black**, signifying decisiveness.

HISTORY

The small Sheikhdom of Kuwait in the **north-east of Arabia** was founded in the early 18th century. In 1756 **Sabah al-Awal** established a Sheikhdom. During the 19th century, the **Ottoman** and **British Empires** fought for control of Kuwait. In 1899 it became a **British** protectorate. **Oil** was discovered in 1938, and Kuwait's huge oil reserves rapidly made it one of the richest countries in the world. In 1961 Kuwait gained **independence**. Kuwait supported **Saddam Hussein**'s Iraqi regime in the **Iran-Iraq War** (1980–88). In August 1990 **Iraq invaded** Kuwait, capturing the capital, Kuwait City, within a day. In the **Gulf War**, allied coalition troops, led by the United States, liberated Kuwait in February 1991. Iraqi troops set light to oil-wells as they retreated, causing widespread environmental damage. The cost of post-war reconstruction was *c*.US$100 billion. In 1992 Kuwait held its first parliamentary elections. The Amir, **Sheikh Jabir al-Sabah**, holds executive power.

AREA: 17,820sq km (6880sq mi)
POPULATION: 1,984,000
CAPITAL (POPULATION): Kuwait City (32,100)
GOVERNMENT: Constitutional monarchy
ETHNIC GROUPS: Kuwaiti Arab 45%, non-Kuwaiti Arab 36%, various Asian 18%
LANGUAGES: Arabic (official), English
RELIGIONS: Sunni Muslim 45%, Shi'a Muslim 40%
NATIONAL ANTHEM (DATE): (1978)

Kuwait stamp marking the sixth anniversary of Liberation Day (February 26, 1991).

At the centre of Kyrgyzstan's flag is a circular, stylized representation of the **roof of a yurt** (tent), the traditional home of Kyrgyz nomads. Surrounding the yurt is a **golden sun with 40 rays**, representing the 40 tribes united (according to an epic poem) by **Manas** to form Kyrgyzstan. The flag's **red field** recalls the banner of Manas.

HISTORY

The Kyrgyz, a forest-dwelling people who practiced shamanism, have inhabited the country since ancient times. In 1207 the Kyrgyz surrendered to Genghis Khan's son **Jöchi**. Under **Mongol** rule, the Kyrgyz preserved their **nomadic** and **shamanist** culture. In the 18th century, the **Qing** (Manchu) **dynasty** of China became nominal rulers of the region. In 1830 Muhammad Ali, Khan of **Kokand**, conquered the Kyrgyz and introduced Islam. In 1876 Kyrgystan became part of the **Russian Empire**. Russian emigration forced many Kyrgyz into the mountains of the **Tian Shan**. In 1916 Russia crushed a native rebellion and many Kyrgyz fled into China. In 1936 Kirgizia became a republic of the **Soviet Union**. The Soviets **forcibly resettled** most of the remaining Kyrgyz population onto collective farms. In August 1991, Kyrgyzstan declared **independence**. **Askar Akayev** was the new nation's first president. In 1993 Kyrgyzstan adopted its own national currency, the som.

Kyrgyz eaglers *(berkutchi)* *have been hunting with golden eagles for 6000 years.*

AREA: 198,500sq km (76,640sq mi)
POPULATION: 4,822,938
CAPITAL (POPULATION): Bishkek (762,308)
GOVERNMENT: Multi-party republic
ETHNIC GROUPS: Kyrgyz 57%, Russian 18%, Uzbek 14%, Ukrainian 3%, German 2%
LANGUAGES: Kyrgyz (official), Russian
RELIGIONS: Sunni Muslim 75%, Russian Orthodox 20%, Shi'a Muslim 5%
NATIONAL ANTHEM (DATE): *"Mamlekettik gimni"* "National Anthem" (1992)

LAOS

FLAG RATIO: 2:3 USE: National/Civil DATE ADOPTED: 1975 LAST MODIFIED: 1975

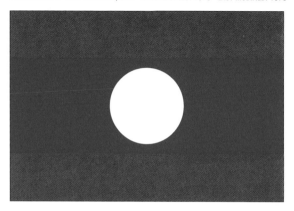

In 1975 the Republic of Laos adopted its present national flag. The flag was the banner of the Pathet Leo (Patriotic Front), the communist, republican movement that overthrew the royalist government. The large, horizontal central **blue stripe** represents the Mekong River that flows through Laos. It also symbolizes the nation's wealth. The **red stripes** stand for the two regions of Laos joined and separated by the river. It also denotes the blood shed in the struggle for independence. The **white disc** signifies the full moon over the Mekong River, the country's bright future, and the unity of its people.

HISTORY

In 1533 Prince **Fa Ngum** founded the Lao kingdom of Lan Xang ('**Land of a Million Elephants**'). **Burma** captured Lan Xang in 1571. Thailand gained control in 1778. In 1893 Laos became part of **French Indochina**. **Japan** occupied Laos during World War II. **France** regained control after the war. In **1953** Laos achieved independence but plunged into civil war between royalist forces, backed by the **United States**, and republican forces supported by the **Viet Cong**. During the **Vietnam War** (1954–75), the US bombed Laos in an effort to halt supplies to the Viet Cong. In 1975 Laos became a **republic**.

AREA: 236,800sq km (91,428sq mi)
POPULATION: 5,428,200
CAPITAL (POPULATION): Ventiane (189,600)
GOVERNMENT: Single-party republic
ETHNIC GROUPS: Lao 67%, Mon-Khmer 17%, Tai 8%, Hmong, Yao
LANGUAGES: Lao (official), French, English
RELIGIONS: Buddhist 58%, traditional beliefs 34%, Christian 2%, Muslim 1%
NATIONAL MOTTO: Peace, Independence, Democracy, Unity and Prosperity
NATIONAL ANTHEM (DATE): "Pheng Xat Lao" "Lao National Anthem" (1947)

Traditional wedding costumes of the Lao Theung (midland Lao), native people of Laos.

FLAG RATIO: 1:2   **USE:** National/Civil   **DATE ADOPTED:** 1918   **REINTRODUCED:** 1990

Latvia has one of the oldest national flags. In 1279 Latvian tribes carried a red banner with a white stripe into battle against the Estonians. The **white stripe** represents truth, trust, righteousness, and freedom. The **red field** stands for the blood shed for the nation's independence. Latvia adopted the current design after gaining independence in 1918, and it was declared the official flag in 1921. The flag was banned after the Soviet Union invaded Latvia in 1940. In 1990 Latvia declared independence and the Soviet flag was removed. In 1991 Latvia officially adopted the flag of 1918.

HISTORY

In the 13th century, the **Livonian Knights** conquered Latvia. Russian defeat in the **Livonian War** (1558–83) left Latvia partitioned between **Poland-Lithuania** and **Sweden**. Tsar **Peter the Great** gained parts of Latvia in the **Great Northern War** (1700–21) and all of Latvia fell under Russian rule after the **Partitions of Poland** (1772, 1793, 1795). In 1918 Latvia declared independence. Latvia was under Soviet and then German rule in World War II. Almost the entire Jewish population was exterminated in the Nazi Holocaust. In 1991 the Soviet Union recognized Latvia's **independence**. In 1993 **Guntis Ulmanlis** became Latvia's first directly elected president. In 1996 **Viara Vike-Freiberga** became the first woman head of state in post-communist Eastern Europe.

Latvian stamp of the traditional costume of peasants from Rietumvedzeme.

AREA: 24,938sq km (64,589sq mi)
POPULATION: 2,375,300
CAPITAL (POPULATION): Riga (764,328)
GOVERNMENT: Multi-party republic
ETHNIC GROUPS: Latvian 53%, Russian 34%, Belorussian 4%, Ukrainian 3%, Polish 2%
LANGUAGES: Latvian (official), Russian
RELIGIONS: Evangelical Lutheran 55%, Roman Catholic 30%, Russian Orthodox 10%
NATIONAL ANTHEM (DATE): *"Dies Sveti Latviju"* "God Bless Latvia" (1992)

LEBANON

FLAG RATIO: 2:3 USE: National/Civil DATE ADOPTED: 1943 LAST MODIFIED: 1943

The **green tree** at the centre of Lebanon's flag is the **cedar of Lebanon**. A symbol of Lebanon since Biblical times (Psalms 92:12), today precious few cedar trees survive in Lebanon. In 1918, after the collapse of Ottoman rule, Lebanon adopted a flag with a cedar tree on an entirely white field. In 1920 the flag changed to the French *tricolore* with a cedar tree in its central white band. Members of the Lebanese Parliament designed the present flag in 1943. The cedar tree is a symbol of immortality. The horizontal **red bands**, exactly half the width of the white band, represents the blood shed in the liberation struggle. The **white band** stands for peace and snow-capped Lebanese mountains.

HISTORY

Lebanon was the heart of ancient **Phoenicia**, which became part of the **Roman** province of Syria in 64 BC. Lebanon was a major battleground of the **Crusades** (1095–1291). In 1516 the **Ottoman** Turks conquered Lebanon, devolving power first to Druze dynasty of the **Maans** (1516–1697) and then to the **Shihab** dynasty (1697–1842), which converted to **Maronite** Christianity. In 1920 the League of Nations mandated Lebanon to **France**. In 1946 Lebanon gained **independence**. A **civil war** (1975–90) claimed *c.*130,000 lives. **Elias Hrawi**'s presidency (1989–98) saw the beginnings of reconstruction in Beirut. In 1982 **Israeli** troops invaded Lebanon. They withdrew in 2000.

AREA: 10,400sq km (4015sq mi)
POPULATION: 4,003,600
CAPITAL (POPULATION): Beirut (1,147,800)
GOVERNMENT: Multi-party republic
ETHNIC GROUPS: Lebanese 80%, Palestinian 12%, Armenian 5%, Syrian, Kurdish
LANGUAGES: Arabic (official), French
RELIGIONS: Muslim 70%, Christian 30%
NATIONAL ANTHEM (DATE): "An-Nashid Al-Watani Al-Lubnani"
"Lebanese National Anthem" (1927)

Stamp of 13th-century painting of The Lion and Jackal *folk tale, marking Childrens' Day.*

Lesotho adopted its present flag after a military coup in 1986. Its colours are based on the national motto: **white** for peace, **blue** for rain, and **green** for prosperity. White occupies the top **triangular** half of the flag. The **light-brown emblem** on the white field consists of a animal-skin **shield**, supported by an *assegai* (stabbing spear, left), a **plumed spine** (centre), and a **bludgeon** (right). These weapons signify the Lesotho nation's traditional safeguards of peace. The blue and green bands each occupy half the surface area of the lower half of the flag. They are not separated and appear to merge when viewed from a distance. The previous flag was based on the banner of the Basotho National Party (BNP), which led the nation to independence in 1966.

the Republic of **South Africa**. In 1824 **Moshoeshoe,** retreating from the terror unleashed by **Shaka**'s expansion of the **Zulu Empire**, formed a stronghold on the mountain of **Thaba Bosiu**. The settlement grew into the kingdom of Basotho. In 1871 Basutoland became part of **British Cape Colony**. In 1966 Lesotho gained **independence** under **Moshoeshoe II**. In 1970 Chief **Leabua Jonathan** seized control. In 1986 Moshoeshoe II returned to power in a coup. **Letsie III** succeeded Moshoeshoe in 1995. In 1998 South African troops restored order after an army mutiny. Many Sotho **migrate** to work in the **mines** of **South Africa**.

HISTORY

Lesotho is an **enclave kingdom** within

Nkho is a traditional water pot in Lesotho. It is dug into the ground to keep water cool.

AREA: 30,350sq km (11,718sq mi)

POPULATION: 2,456,500

CAPITAL (POPULATION): Maseru (169,200)

GOVERNMENT: Constitutional monarchy

ETHNIC GROUPS: Sotho 99%

LANGUAGES: Sesotho, English (both official)

RELIGIONS: Roman Catholic 63%, Protestant 27%

NATIONAL MOTTO: "*Khotso, Pula, Nala*" "Peace, Rain, Prosperity"

NATIONAL ANTHEM (DATE): "*Lesotho Fatse La Bontata Rona*" (1967)

LIBERIA

FLAG RATIO: 10:19 USE: National/Civil DATE ADOPTED: 1847 LAST MODIFIED: 1847

Liberia's flag is called 'Lone Star'. It is a replica of 'Old Glory', the flag of the United States. In 1822 the American Colonization Society founded Liberia as a colony for liberated slaves from the United States. Five years later, the colony adoped its own flag, similar to the present flag but with more stripes and bearing a cross, representing the Christian faith of the Society. In 1847 Liberia declared independence and adopted the current flag, designed by seven women. The 11 horizontal stripes, six red and five white, stand for the 11 signatories to Liberia's declaration of independence. In the canton, a white five-pointed star against a blue field symbolizes the shining example of Liberia as the first independent nation in Africa.

HISTORY

In 1822 Monrovia was built for freed slaves. In 1847 Joseph Roberts became the first president of independent Liberia. In 1926 the US Firestone Company opened a vast rubber plantation. William Tubman led Liberia from 1943 to 1971. In 1980 Samuel Doe came to power in a military coup. A civil war raged from 1989 to 1997, killing more than 150,000 people. Charles Taylor became president in 1997. Taylor's regime traded weapons for diamonds with rebels in Sierra Leone. In 2002 Taylor declared a state of emergency as fighting increased on the border with Guinea.

AREA: 111,370sq km (43,000sq mi)
POPULATION: 2,776,800
CAPITAL (POPULATION): Monrovia (543,000)
GOVERNMENT: Multi-party republic
ETHNIC GROUPS: Kpelle 19%, Bassa 14%, Grebo 9%, Gio 8%, Kru 7%, Mano 7%
LANGUAGES: English (official)
RELIGIONS: African traditional beliefs 34%, Protestant 20%, Muslim 20%
NATIONAL MOTTO: "The Love of Liberty Brought Us Here"
NATIONAL ANTHEM (DATE): "All Hail, Liberia Hail" (1847)

Liberia has one of the largest populations of the endangered western chimpanzee.

Libya has the simplest of national flags, consisting of a **single field of green**. Green is the national colour and the traditional colour of Islam. It also represents the hope for a 'green revolution' in agriculture. In 1969 Colonel Qaddafi overthrew King Idris and the new republic adopted a flag with the red, white and black colours of the Pan-Arab movement. In 1972 Libya joined the Federation of Arab Republics (FAR). It placed a golden eagle, the FAR's coat of arms, on the central white horizontal stripe of the Pan-Arab flag. The FAR proved still-born and Libya adopted its present flag in 1977.

HISTORY

The first inhabitants were the **Berbers**. In the 7th century BC, Greeks colonized **Cyrenaica**. **Carthage** gained Phoenician settlements in **Tripolitania** in the 6th century BC. Magnificent **ruins** survive from the **Roman** occupation. **Arabs** conquered Libya in 643, and Islam became the dominant religion. From 1551 Libya formed part of the **Ottoman Empire**. Power resided with local rulers known as **Janissaries**. During the 17th century, **Barbary** pirates attacked ships from bases on Libya's **Mediterranean** coast. In 1914 **Italy** conquered Libya. Libya was a battleground for many of the North Africa campaigns in World War II. In 1951 Libya became an **independent monarchy**, led by **King Idris**. In 1969 **Colonel Muammar al-Qaddafi** established a socialist Islamic state. In 1986, after evidence of Libya's involvement in international **terrorism**, the United States bombed **Tripoli**. In 1999 Libya sent for trial two Libyans suspected of the 1992 bombing of Pan-Am Flight 103 over **Lockerbie**, Scotland.

AREA: 1,759,540sq km (679,358sq mi)
POPULATION: 6,984,400
CAPITAL (POPULATION): Tripoli (1,223,300)
GOVERNMENT: Single-party socialist republic
ETHNIC GROUPS: Libyan Arab and Berber 89%
LANGUAGES: Arabic (official)
RELIGIONS: Sunni Muslim 97%
NATIONAL ANTHEM (DATE): "Allahu Akbar"
"God is Great" (1969)

Unity is strength stamp. Qaddafi long championed the cause of Arab unity.

115

LIECHTENSTEIN

FLAG RATIO: 3:5 **USE:** National/Civil **DATE ADOPTED:** 1937 **LAST MODIFIED:** 1957

L iechtenstein's flag consists of **two equal horizontal stripes** of **blue** (top) and **red** with a **gold crown** on the hoist side of the top stripe. The origin of the colours is unknown but probably derive from the livery colours of the ruling House of Liechtenstein. Blue is the colour of a radiant sky and red symbolizes the glow of the hearth at evening gatherings. At the 1936 Olympics it was noticed that Liechtenstein's flag was identical to the flag of Haiti, and a gold crown was added to the standard in 1937. In 1957 the design of the crown was modified. The crown represents the unity of the nation under the royal house.

HISTORY

In 1719 Emperor Charles VI merged the County of **Vaduz** and the Seigniory of **Schellenberg** to create the Principality of Liechtenstein in 1719. It remained part of the **Holy Roman Empire** until 1806, when it joined the Confederation of the Rhine. From 1815 to 1866 it formed part of the **German Confederation**. In 1866 Liechtenstein gained **independence**. In 1921 Liechtenstein entered into a currency **union** with **Switzerland** and in 1923, a customs union. Until 1990 Switzerland also handled its foreign policy. **Women** finally received the **vote** in 1984. In **1990** it joined the **United Nations**. Liechenstein has a constitutional and hereditary monarchy; the ruling family is the Austrian House of Liechenstein. Liechtenstein is the **fourth-smallest** country in the world, but is among the richest (GDP per capita, US$23,000).

AREA: 157sq km (61sq mi)
POPULATION: 28,000
CAPITAL (POPULATION): Vaduz (5200)
GOVERNMENT: Constitutional monarchy
ETHNIC GROUPS: Alemannic 88%
LANGUAGES: German (official), Alemmannic
RELIGIONS: Roman Catholic 80%,
Protestant 7%
NATIONAL ANTHEM (DATE): *"Oben am jungen Rhein"* "High Above the Young Rhine" (1963)

Liechtenstein is famous for its beautifully illustrated stamps.

Lithuania adopted its present flag in 1989, shortly before gaining independence from the Soviet Union. The design is the same as the flag adopted in 1918, but it has the ratio 1:2 rather than 2:3. It consists of **three horizontal bands**: yellow (top), green (middle) and red (bottom). The colours are common in Lithuanian folk art and costume. **Yellow** stands for grain and wealth, **green** for forests and hope, and **red** for the blood shed in the struggle for independence. In 1953, as a republic of the Soviet Union, it adopted a **tricolour** flag of red, white, and green with a hammer and sickle on the thicker red band.

HISTORY

In 1253 Pope Innocent IV crowned **Mindaugas** as Grand Duke of Lithuania. In 1386 Lithuania united with **Poland**, and the two countries **merged** in 1569. The Battle of **Tannenberg** (1410) marked the defeat of the Teutonic Knights. **Russia** gained most of Lithuania in the Second and Third Partitions of Poland (1793, 1795). In 1918 Lithuania declared **independence**. From 1926 to 1940 it was ruled by the dictator **Antonas Smetona**. In 1941 Germany occupied Lithuania. The Nazis murdered more than 165,000 Lithuanian Jews. In 1944 the **Soviet Union** occupied Lithuania. President **Vytautas Landbergis** declared independence in 1990. Soviet troops completed a withdrawal in 1993.

Aukstaiciai *(Uplanders) traditional costume. Aukstaiciai have their own dialect.*

AREA: 65,200sq km (25,200sq mi)
POPULATION: 3,490,800
CAPITAL (POPULATION): Vilnius (543,000)
GOVERNMENT: Multi-party republic
ETHNIC GROUPS: Lithuanian 80%, Russian 9%, Polish 7%, Belorussian 2%
LANGUAGES: Lithuanian (official)
RELIGIONS: Roman Catholic 80%, Russian Old Believers, Russian Orthodox
NATIONAL ANTHEM (DATE): "*Lietuva Teyvne Musu*" "Lithuania, Our Homeland" (1918)

117

LUXEMBOURG

FLAG RATIO: 3:5   USE: National   DATE ADOPTED: 1845   LAST MODIFIED: 1972

Luxembourg's tricolour flag derives from its coat of arms, which shows a **red** lion in front of **blue** and **white** horizontal **stripes**. The first recorded use of the coat of arms is on the banner of Earl Heinrich VI in 1228. Luxembourg's flag is identical to the tricolour of the **Netherlands**, except for the flag ratio and the lighter shade of its blue band.

HISTORY

The Grand Duchy of Luxembourg has the **highest GDP per capita** in the world (US$36,400). In the 11th century, the County of Luxembourg formed one of the largest fiefs of the **Holy Roman Empire**. In 1354 Luxembourg became a Duchy. In 1482 it passed to the **Habsburg** dynasty, and in the 16th century it became part of the **Spanish Netherlands**. In 1714 it passed to **Austria**. Occupied by **France** during the Napoleonic Wars, it became a Grand Duchy at the Congress of Vienna (1815). In 1839 **Belgium** acquired much of the Duchy. In 1867 Luxembourg gained **independence**. **Germany** occupied Luxembourg in both World Wars. In 1960 Belgium, the Netherlands and Luxembourg formed the economic union of **Benelux**. Luxembourg was a founder member of the **European Union (EU)**. In 1964, **Prince Jean** became Grand Duke. In 2000, he **abdicated** in favour of his son, **Henri**.

AREA: 2590sq km (1000sq mi)

POPULATION: 439,764

CAPITAL (POPULATION): Luxembourg City (76,687)

GOVERNMENT: Constitutional monarchy

ETHNIC GROUPS: Luxembourger 71%, Portuguese 10%, Italian 5%, Belgian 3%, German 2%

LANGUAGES: Letzeburgish (Luxembourgian, official), French, German

RELIGIONS: Catholic 95%, Protestant 1%

NATIONAL MOTTO: *"Mir wëlle bleiwe wat mir sin"* "We want to remain what we are"

NATIONAL ANTHEM (DATE): *"Ons Hémécht"* "Our Motherland" (1895)

Grand Duke Jean *was the fifth King of the Nassau-Weilbourg dynasty.*

The flag of the Former Yugoslav Republic of Macedonia is **red** with a stylized **golden-yellow sun**. The sun has **eight yellow rays** emerging from its disk. The rays thicken towards the edge of the flag. In 1992 Macedonia won independence and adopted a flag with the 'Sun of Vergina' on a red field. Vergina is the historic capital of ancient Macedonia. Greece objected to use of the symbol, which they argued was an emblem of Philip II of Macedon who united Greece in the 4th century BC. In 1995 Macedonia agreed to redesign its flag.

HISTORY

Philip II's son, **Alexander the Great**, built a mighty empire that broke up after his death (323 BC). The **Romans** defeated Macedon in the Macedonian Wars. In AD 395, Macedonia became part of the **Byzantine Empire**. It was under **Ottoman** rule from the 14th to the 19th century. The **Balkan Wars** (1912–13) saw Macedonia divided between Greece, Bulgaria, and Serbia. At the end of World War I, Serbian Macedonia joined what became known as **Yugoslavia**. Between 1941 and 1944, **Bulgaria** occupied all Macedonia. In 1946, Macedonia became a republic of **President Tito**'s federal Yugoslavia. In 1991 Macedonia declared **independence**. In 1999, war in the neighbouring Serbian province of **Kosovo** led to an influx of c.250,000 ethnic Albanian refugees. In 2001 fierce fighting between government forces and **Albanian rebels** displaced 100,000 people.

Embroidery from a Debar folk garment adorns this Macedonian stamp.

AREA: 24,900sq km (9600sq mi)
POPULATION: 2,095,800
CAPITAL (POPULATION): Skopje (288,217)
GOVERNMENT: Multi-party republic
ETHNIC GROUPS: Macedonian 65%, Albanian 21%, Turkish 5%, Romanian 3%, Serb 2%
LANGUAGES: Macedonian
RELIGIONS: Macedonian Orthodox 66%, Muslim 30%, Protestant 3%, Roman Catholic 1%
NATIONAL ANTHEM (DATE): (1992)

119

MADAGASCAR

FLAG RATIO: 2:3 USE: National/Civil DATE ADOPTED: 1958 LAST MODIFIED: 1958

Madagascar adopted its present flag in 1958, when it became a self-governing republic under French rule. The colours emphasize Madagascar's links with south-east Asia – many of Madagascar's population are ancestors of settlers from Malaysia and Indonesia *c*.2000 years ago. In the 19th century, the Merina kingdom used a flag of red and white. **Red** and **white** stand for sovereignty and purity respectively, while **green** represents the Betsimisaraka people of the coast and symbolizes hope.

HISTORY

Madagascar is the world's **fourth-largest island**. Africans and Indonesians arrived *c*.2000 years ago, and Muslims came in the 9th century. By the 1880s the **Merina** controlled nearly all the island. In 1896, the French defeated the Merina and **Malagasy** became a **French colony**. In 1946–48 France crushed a **rebellion**, killing *c*.80,000 islanders. Malagasy achieved full **independence** in 1960. In 1972 the military overthrew President **Philibert Tsiranana**'s autocratic regime. In 1975 Malagasy was **renamed** Madagascar, and **Didier Ratsiraka** became president. In 1993 Ratsiraka was defeated in Madagascar's first free elections for 17 years. He returned to power in 1997. In 2000 **floods** and **tropical storms** devastated Madagascar. Violence followed **Marc Ravalomanana**'s victory over Ratsiraka in presidential elections in 2001.

AREA: 587,040sq km (226,656sq mi)
POPULATION: 14,900,700
CAPITAL (POPULATION): Antananarivo (875,200)
GOVERNMENT: Multi-party republic
ETHNIC GROUPS: Merina 23%, Betsimisaraka 13%, Betsileo 10%, Tsimihety 7%, Sakalava 5%
LANGUAGES: Malagasy (official), French, English
RELIGIONS: Roman Catholic 28%, indigenous beliefs 24%, Church of Jesus Christ 22%, Lutheran 13%, Sunni Muslim 7%, Anglican 6%
NATIONAL MOTTO: "*Fahafahana, Tanindrazana, Fandrosoana*" "Liberty, Fatherland, Progress"
NATIONAL ANTHEM (DATE): "*Ry Tanindrazanay Malala O*" "O, Our Beloved Fatherland" (1958)

REPOBLIKA DEMOKRATIKA MALAGASY

PAOSITRA 1989

5
FMG
ARIARY

Heniochus acuminatus

The bannerfish *(Heniochus acuminatus) lives in the coral reefs of the Indian Ocean.*

FLAG RATIO: 2:3 **USE:** National/Civil **DATE ADOPTED:** 1964 **LAST MODIFIED:** 1964

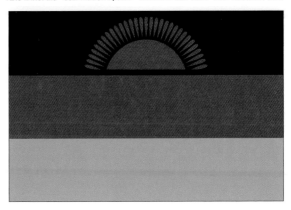

Malawi's flag derives from the old banner of the **Malawi Congress Party (MCP)**, which led the country to independence in 1964. It consists of **three horizontal bands** of black, red, and green. **Black** (top) represents Africa's people. **Red** (middle) symbolizes the blood spilled in the struggle to liberate Africa. **Green** stands for Malawi's forests and grassland. A **rising red sun** was added to the black band on the MCP banner. It symbolizes the *kwacha* or 'dawn' of a bright new era in Africa's history. Malawi gained its name, which means 'flaming waters', from the appearance of Lake Malawi at sunset.

HISTORY

The **Maravi** kingdom existed from the 15th to the 18th century. In the early 19th century, Malawi was a centre of the **slave trade**. In 1891, it became a **British Protectorate**. Britain abolished slavery and established **coffee plantations**. In 1907 it became known as **Nyasaland**. In 1953 Nyasaland became part of the **Federation of Rhodesia**. In 1964 Nyasaland achieved **independence** as Malawi. In 1966 Malawi became a republic. **Dr Hastings Banda**'s repressive rule in Malawi lasted from 1964 to 1994. **Bakili Muluzi** of the United Democratic Front defeated Banda and the MCP in 1994 elections. In 2002 Muluzi declared a state of national disaster with **famine** affecting 70% of the population.

AREA: 118,484sq km (45,745sq mi)
POPULATION: 9,933,868
CAPITAL (POPULATION): Lilongwe (440,471)
GOVERNMENT: Multi-party republic
ETHNIC GROUPS: Maravi (Chewa, Nyanja, Tonga, Tumbuka) 58%, Lomwe 18%, Yao 13%, Ngoni 7%
LANGUAGES: English (official), Chichewa
RELIGIONS: Protestant 34%, Roman Catholic 28%, Sunni Muslim 12%
NATIONAL MOTTO: "Unity and Freedom"
NATIONAL ANTHEM (DATE): "Oh! God, Bless Our Land of Malawi" (1964)

The bar tailed trogon lives in the grasslands of Malawi.

121

MALAYSIA

FLAG RATIO: 1:2 USE: National/Civil DATE ADOPTED: 1963 LAST MODIFIED: 1967

Malaysia's flag, the *Jalur Gemilang* ('Glorious Stripes'), resembles the flag of the United States. The **14 red and white horizontal stripes** represent the members of the federation. The **dark-blue canton** stands for Malaysia's unity and its place within the **Commonwealth**. The canton contains a **yellow crescent and star**, symbols of **Islam**. The star's 14 points symbolize the unity of the 13 states with the federal government. Yellow is the colour of the **Sultan** of Malaysia.

HISTORY

Britain conquered **Malacca** in 1795. In 1867 the Straits Settlement of **Penang**, Malacca and **Singapore** became a British colony. In 1888 **Sabah** and **Sarawak** became a British Protectorate. The states of **Perak**, **Selangor**, **Pahang**, and **Negeri Sembilan** federated in 1896. In 1909 **Johor**, **Kedah**, **Kelantan**, **Perlis**, and **Terengganu** formed the Unfederated Malay States. **Japan** occupied Malaysia during World War II. In 1948 Britain expanded the Federation of Malaya to include the Unfederated States and Malacca and Penang. Communists launched a guerrilla war, known as the **Malayan Emergency** (1948–60), and many **Chinese** were forcibly resettled. In 1957 Malaya gained **independence**. In 1963, Singapore, Sabah and Sarawak joined the Federation, which became known as Malaysia. In 1965 **Singapore seceded** from Malaysia. **Mahathir Muhammad** became President in 1981.

AREA: 329,750sq km (127,316sq mi)
POPULATION: 23,207,000
CAPITAL (POPULATION): Kuala Lumpar (1,297,526)
GOVERNMENT: Federal constitutional monarchy
ETHNIC GROUPS: Bumiptera 65%, Chinese 26%, Indian 8%
LANGUAGES: Malay (official)
RELIGIONS: Sunni Muslim 60%, Buddhist 19%, Christian 9%, Hindu 6%, Chinese 3%
NATIONAL MOTTO: "*Bersekutu bertambah mutu*" 'Unity is Strength"
NATIONAL ANTHEM (DATE): "*Negara ku*" "My Country" (1957)

The starfish (Oreaster occidentalis) is known as tapak sulaiman in Malaysia.

Like many other Islamic countries, the Maldives long used a plain red flag. By 1949, the Maldivian flag consisted of a green rectangle and white crescent on a red field with a band of black and white stripes on the hoist side. In 1965 the Maldives gained independence and the band of black and white stripes disappeared. The **green rectangle** represents the many palm trees, the life source of the islands. **Red** symbolises the blood sacrificed in the struggle for independence. The **white crescent**, in the centre of the green panel and pointing toward the fly, is a symbol of the **Islamic** faith of the Maldives.

HISTORY

The Sanskrit word 'Maladiv' means **'garland of islands'**, and the archipelago consists of 1196 islands in 26 atolls scattered across the Indian Ocean. In the 12th century, Arab traders introduced **Islam** to the Maldives. From the 14th century, the **ad-Din dynasty** ruled the Maldives. In 1518 the **Portuguese** claimed the islands. From 1665 to 1886 the Maldives were a dependency of **Ceylon** (now **Sri Lanka**). In 1887 they became a **British Protectorate**. In 1965, the Maldives gained **independence** under **Sultan Muhammad Farid Didi**. In 1968 the Sultan was deposed and the Maldives became a **republic**. **Maumoon Abdul Gayoom** became President in 1978. In 1982 Maldives joined the **Commonwealth of Nations**. In 1988 Indian troops helped suppress an attempted **coup** by Tamil mercenaries.

Yellowfin tuna is vitally important to the commercial fishing industry in the Maldives.

AREA: 298sq km (115sq mi)
POPULATION: 283,000
CAPITAL (POPULATION): Male (74,069)
GOVERNMENT: Presidential republic
ETHNIC GROUPS: Dravidian, Sinhalese, Arabs, Africans
LANGUAGES: Dhivehi (official, dialect of Sinhala, script derived from Arabic), English
RELIGIONS: Sunni Muslim
NATIONAL ANTHEM (DATE): (1972)

MALI

FLAG RATIO: 2:3 USE: National/Civil DATE ADOPTED: 1961 LAST MODIFIED: 1961

In 1959 French Sudan (now Mali) and Senegal formed the Federation of Mali. The Federation modelled its flag on the French *tricolore*. **Green**, **yellow** and **red** are the colours both of the African Democratic Rally, the party that led the fight for independence, and the colours of the **Pan-African** movement. Green stands for the vegetation, yellow for the mineral resources, and red for the blood shed in the liberation struggle. On the central band of the federation's flag was a stylized human figure in black, known as a *kanaga*. In 1960 Senegal seceded from the federation. In 1961 Mali adopted its present flag, removing the *kanaga* figure because of the **Islamic** stricture on the representation of nature. The new flag was identical to that of **Rwanda**, which promptly altered its flag.

HISTORY

The medieval **Empire of Mali** was one of the world's richest powers. The 14th-century reign of Emperor **Mansa Musa** saw the introduction of **Islam** and the development of **Timbuktu** as a great centre of learning and hub of the trans-Saharan trade. In 1893 it became the colony of **French Sudan**. In 1960 Mali became a one-party state under President **Modibo Keita**. In 1968 **Moussa Traoré** replaced Keita in a military coup. Mali returned to civilian rule under Alpha Konaré in 1992.

AREA: 1,240,190sq km (478,837sq mi)

POPULATION: 10,179,170

CAPITAL (POPULATION): Bamako (1,016,167)

GOVERNMENT: Multi-party republic

ETHNIC GROUPS: Bambara 32%, Fulani (Peul) 14%, Senufo 12%, Soninke 9%, Tuareg 7%, Songhai 7%, Malinke (Mandingo) 7%

LANGUAGES: French (official), Bambara

RELIGIONS: Sunni Muslim 90%, traditional African beliefs 5%, Christian 5%

NATIONAL MOTTO: "Un peuple, un but, une foi" "One People, One Goal, One Faith"

NATIONAL ANTHEM (DATE): "Hymne National Malien" "National Hymn of Mali" (1962)

The Tamasheq, a group of Tuareg nomads, produce fine metalwork such as this lock.

According to legend, the **white** and **red** colours of Malta's flag derive from the coat of arms of Roger I of Sicily, who conquered the islands in 1090. A red flag with a white cross was used by the **Knights of Malta** from the Middle Ages. In 1943 a **George Cross** on a blue canton was added to the flag after King George VI of Britain honoured the island for its brave defence against the Axis powers in World War II. In 1964 Malta gained independence from Britain, and a thin red edging replaced the blue canton around the George Cross.

HISTORY

Malta has three inhabited islands: **Malta**, **Gozo**, and **Comino**. The Phoenicians colonized Malta in *c*.850 BC. In AD 395

Malta became part of the Byzantine Empire. An Arab invasion brought Islam in 870, but **Roger I**, Norman King of Sicily, **restored Christian rule** in 1091. In 1530 the Holy Roman Emperor gave Malta to the **Knights Hospitallers**. In 1565 the Knights held Malta against a Turkish siege. In 1814 Malta became a **British colony** and a strategic military base. Italian and German aircraft bombed the islands in World War II. In 1942, in recognition of the heroism of the Maltese resistance, **George VI** awarded the George Cross to Malta. In 1964 Malta gained **independence**, and in 1974 it became a **republic**. The last British military base closed in 1979. **Tourism** dominates Malta's economy: the number of annual visitors is three times greater than its population.

Hoary rockrose *is endangered. It grows in the holm oak forest of Wied Hazrun.*

AREA: 316sq km (122sq mi)
POPULATION: 382,525
CAPITAL (POPULATION): Valletta (195,500)
GOVERNMENT: Multi-party republic
ETHNIC GROUPS: Maltese 96%, British 2%
LANGUAGES: Maltese, English (both official)
RELIGIONS: Roman Catholic 95%
NATIONAL ANTHEM (DATE): "*Innu Malti*"
"Hymn of Malta" (1945)

125

MARSHALL ISLANDS

FLAG RATIO: 1:2 **USE:** National/Civil **DATE ADOPTED:** 1979 **LAST MODIFIED:** 1979

The **deep-blue** background of the flag represents the Pacific Ocean. The **widening beams** symbolize the two chains of islands: **white** stands for Ratak (Sunrise) and **orange** for Ralik (Sunset). Orange represents bravery and white signifies peace. The **star** denotes the cross of Christianity, with each of its **24 points** representing a municipal district of the Marshall Islands. The **four longer points** of the star stand for the major towns of **Majuro**, **Ebeye**, **Jaluit**, and **Wotje**.

HISTORY

Inhabited by **Micronesians** for at least 2500 years, the Marshall Islands are named after British Naval **Captain William Marshall**, who sailed through the archipelago in 1788. In 1857 US explorer **Hiram Bingham, Junior**, founded a missionary post on Ebon. In 1885 **Germany** annexed the islands. In 1914 **Japan** captured the archipelago. After World War I, the League of Nations granted a mandate to Japan. In 1944 the **Allies occupied** the Marshall Islands. From 1946 to 1956 the **United States tested nuclear weapons** on the Marshall Islands, especially on **Bikini Atoll**. In 1947 the Marshall Islands became part of the US-administered **Trust Territory of the Pacific Islands**. In 1979 the Marshalls gained **self-government**. Trusteeship ended in 1990, and the **Compact of Free Association** with the United States expired in 2003.

AREA: 180sq km (70sq mi)
POPULATION: 68,126
CAPITAL (POPULATION): Majuro (19,664)
GOVERNMENT: Multi-party republic
ETHNIC GROUPS: Marshallese
LANGUAGES: Marshallese, English
RELIGIONS: United Church of Christ 55%, Assembly of God 26%, Roman Catholic 8%
NATIONAL MOTTO: *"Jepilpilin Ke Ejulaan"* "Accomplishment Through Joint Effort"
NATIONAL ANTHEM (DATE): *"Kej rammon Aelin Kein am"* "Forever Marshall Islands" (1991)

Marshallese *women make beautiful fans from sun-bleached coconut leaves.*

FLAG RATIO: 2:3 USE: National/Civil DATE ADOPTED: 1959 LAST MODIFIED: 1959

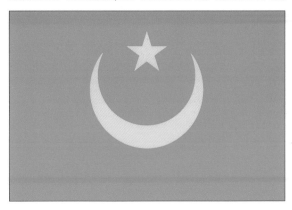

Mauritania's flag features a **crescent** and a **five-pointed star**, traditional symbols of **Islam**. **Green** and **yellow** are Islamic and **Pan-African** colours, reflecting Mauritania's position between the Arab countries of North Africa and the nations of sub-Saharan Africa.

HISTORY

Berbers migrated to the region in the first millennium AD. The **Hodh basin** lay at the heart of the ancient **Ghana Empire** (700–1200) and towns grew up along the **trans-Saharan** caravan routes. Mauritania was the cradle of the **Almoravid dynasty**, which spread Islam throughout north Africa. In the 14th and 15th century, it formed part of the ancient **Mali Empire**. In 1903

Mauritania became a **French protectorate**. In 1920 it became a colony of **French West Africa**. In 1960 Mauritania achieved full **independence**. President **Ould Daddah** established a one-party state. In 1973 Mauritania joined the **Arab League**. In 1976 Mauritania and Morocco occupied **Western Sahara**. In 1978 an army coup overthrew Ould Daddah. In 1979 Mauritania withdrew from Western Sahara. Recognition of Western Sahara's independence provoked civil unrest and **Ould Taya** came to power in 1984. Tension continues between the black African minority in southern Mauritania and Arabs and Berbers in the north.

Drought (secheresse *in French) devastated livestock farming in Mauritania.*

AREA: 1,025,520sq km (395,953sq mi)
POPULATION: 2,425,148
CAPITAL (POPULATION): Nouakchott (611,883)
GOVERNMENT: Multi-party Islamic republic
ETHNIC GROUPS: Moor (Arab-Berber) 70%, Wolof 7%, Tukulor 5%, Soninke 3%, Fulani 1%
LANGUAGES: Arabic (official)
RELIGIONS: Sunni Muslim 99%
NATIONAL MOTTO: "*Honneur, Fraternité, Justice*" "Honour, Fraternity, Justice"
NATIONAL ANTHEM (DATE): (1960)

MAURITIUS

FLAG RATIO: 1:2 USE: National DATE ADOPTED: 1968 LAST MODIFIED: 1968

The flag of Mauritius is unique in having **four equal horizontal bands**. Designed by the British College of Arms, the colours derive from Mauritius' coat of arms awarded by King Edward VII of Britain in 1906. **Red** represents the blood shed in the liberation struggle, **blue** for the Indian Ocean that surrounds the archipelago, **yellow** for the bright future afforded by independence, and **green** for the islands' lush vegetation. The **civil flag** has a blue field with the national flag on its canton and the **coat of arms** on the fly. The coat of arms includes the national motto and the **dodo**, a flightless bird hunted to extinction.

AREA: 2046sq km (790sq mi)

POPULATION: 1,201,000

CAPITAL (POPULATION): Port Louis (138,700)

GOVERNMENT: Multi-party republic

ETHNIC GROUPS: Indo-Mauritian 68%, Creole 27%, Sino-Mauritian 3%, Franco-Mauritian 2%

LANGUAGES: English (official), Creole, French, Hindi, Urdu, Hakka, Bojpoori

RELIGIONS: Hindu 50%, Roman Catholic 27%, Muslim (largely Sunni) 16%, Protestant 5%

NATIONAL MOTTO: "*Stella clavisque Maris Indici*" "The Star and Key of the Indian Sea"

NATIONAL ANTHEM (DATE): "Motherland" (1968)

HISTORY

The nation, *c.*800km (500mi) east of Madagascar, consists of the main island of **Mauritius**, 20 nearby islets, and the dependency islands of **Rodrigues**, **Agalega** and **Cargados Carajos**. The **Dutch** attempted to settle the islands from 1598, naming them after **Prince Maurice of Nassau**. In 1721 the **French East India Company** occupied Mauritius, which they renamed Île de France. The French established **sugarcane plantations** using **African slave labour**. In 1810 **Britain** seized Mauritius. It became a **British colony** in 1814. In 1833 slavery was abolished – **Indian indentured labour** took its place. In 1968 Mauritius achieved **independence**. Sir **Seewoosagur Ramgoolam** served as Prime Minister from 1968 to 1982. In 1992 Mauritius became a **republic**.

Shipwrights *(or* sarpantye pirog *in Creole) often work in the shade of a banyan tree.*

In 1823, the Constituent Congress of Mexico offically adopted the **tricolour** flag. The **green** band represents hope and victory, **white** stands for the purity of Mexico's ideals, and **red** symbolizes the blood shed in the struggle for independence. At the centre of the flag is the **state emblem**, which depicts an ancient Aztec legend about the founding of Mexico City. The god Huitzilopochtli guided the Aztecs to settle where an **eagle**, clutching a **snake**, landed on a **prickly-pear cactus**. In 1325 the Aztecs found the sign on an island in Lake Texcoco and named the site Tenochtitlán ('Place of the prickly-pear cactus'). On the emblem, the cactus has **red fruit**, an Aztec symbol for the heart. **Oak and laurel branches** are republican symbols.

HISTORY

The **Maya** flourished between AD 300 and 900. The **Toltecs** succeeded the Maya. In 1521 Spanish *conquistador* **Hernán Cortés** defeated **Aztec** Emperor **Montezuma**. In 1821 Mexico gained **independence** under Emperor **Augustín de Iturbide**. In 1823 it became a republic. The **Mexican War** (1846–48) saw Mexico lose half its territory to the United States. **Santa Anna** was president from 1832 to 1855, when civil war broke out. **Maximilian of Austria** was Emperor from 1864 to 1867. The dictator **Porfirio Díaz** ruled from 1876 to 1910. US troops helped defeat the peasant armies of **'Pancho' Villa** and **Emiliano Zapata** in the **Mexican Revolution** (1910–40). The Institutional Revolutionary Party (**PRI**) governed Mexico from 1929 to 2000.

AREA: 1,958,200sq km (756,061sq mi)
POPULATION: 97,361,711
CAPITAL (POPULATION): Mexico City (13,083,359)
GOVERNMENT: Federal multi-party republic
ETHNIC GROUPS: Mestizo 60%, Native American 30%, European 9%
LANGUAGES: Spanish (official)
RELIGIONS: Roman Catholic 90%, Protestant 5%
NATIONAL MOTTO: "*Arriba y adelante*" "Higher and Further"
NATIONAL ANTHEM (DATE): "*Mexicanos, al grito de guerra*" "Mexicans, to the War Cry" (1854)

In 1821 Mexico won independence. Its first flag had three diagonal stripes and stars.

129

MICRONESIA, FEDERATED STATES OF

FLAG RATIO: 1:2 **USE:** National/Civil **DATE ADOPTED:** 1962 **LAST MODIFIED:** 1979

The flag of the Federated States of Micronesia consists of **four white stars** on a **blue field**. The stars represent the four states of Micronesia (in order of population size): Chuuk, Pohnpei, Yap and Kusrae. From 1962 to 1977 Micronesia's flag had six stars, but the Marshall Islands and the Northern Mariana Islands left the federation and the present flag was adopted on November 30, 1979.

HISTORY

The 607 islands of the Federated States of Micronesia stretch across more than 2700 kilometres (1700 miles) of the **western Pacific Ocean**. **Spain** formally annexed the islands in 1874, and sold them to **Germany** in 1899. In 1914 **Japan** occupied Micronesia, and the League of Nations granted it a mandate to govern in 1920. In 1944 the **United States** occupied the islands. In 1947 the United Nations (UN) created the Trust Territory of the Pacific Islands, consisting of **Pohnpei** (including **Kusrae**), **Chuuk**, **Yap**, **Palau**, the **Marshall Islands**, and the **Northern Mariana Islands**. The United States acted as Trustee. In 1979 the Federated States of Micronesia was born. In 1986 Micronesia signed a **Compact of Free Association** with the United States. In 1991 Micronesia joined the United Nations (UN). The economy depends heavily on **aid** from the United States.

AREA: 705sq km (272sq mi)
POPULATION: 110,000
CAPITAL (POPULATION): Palikir (8600)
GOVERNMENT: Federal republic
ETHNIC GROUPS: Micronesian, Polynesian
LANGUAGES: English (official), Chuukese, Pohnpeian, Kosraean, Yapese
RELIGIONS: Protestant (largely United Church of Christ) 54%, Roman Catholic 45%
NATIONAL ANTHEM (DATE):
"Patriots of Micronesia" (1980)

The saddled butterflyfish lives in clear waters around Micronesia's coral reefs.

M oldova adopted its present flag upon proclaiming independence from the Soviet Union in 1990. The colours are the same as the **Romanian** flag, emphasising Moldova's close geographical, historical and cultural ties with Romania. On Romania's flag, the **blue** vertical **stripe** stands for the region of Transylvania, **yellow** for Wallachia, and **red** for Moldova. Moldova's flag incorporates its **coat of arms** on the central yellow band. An **eagle** holds an **Orthodox cross** in its beak and an **olive branch** and **sceptre** in its claws. The eagle was a symbol of the Byzantine Empire. On the shield are a **bison's head**, a **star**, a **rose** and a **crescent** – traditional symbols of the old medieval principality of Moldavia.

HISTORY

Moldavia formed part of the Roman province of **Dacia**. In the 14th century, it became an independent principality ruled by the **Vlachs**; its lands included **Bessarabia** and **Bukovina**. In 1504 the Turks conquered Moldavia, and it remained part of the **Ottoman Empire** until the 19th century. In 1859 Moldavia and **Wallachia** united to form Romania. In 1924 the Soviet republic of Moldavia formed. In 1991, after the collapse of the **Soviet Union**, Moldavia became the independent republic of Moldova. Many Moldovans wished to reunite with Romania, while Ukrainians and Russians east of the River **Dniester** declared independence as the **Transdniester Republic**.

Moldova produces fine Romanian folk art, especially ceramics and textiles.

AREA: 33,700sq km (13,010sq mi)
POPULATION: 4,247,200
CAPITAL (POPULATION): Chisinau (711,700)
GOVERNMENT: Multi-party republic
ETHNIC GROUPS: Moldovan 65%, Ukrainian 14%, Russian 13%, Gagauz 4%, Jewish 2%, Bulgarian
LANGUAGES: Moldovan (official)
RELIGIONS: Moldovan Orthodox/Bessarabian Orthodox 90%, Old Russian Orthodox 4%
NATIONAL ANTHEM (DATE): "*Limba Noastra*" "Our Tongue" (1912)

MONACO

FLAG RATIO: 4:5   USE: National/Civil   DATE ADOPTED: 1881   LAST MODIFIED: 1881

The colours of Monaco's flag derive from the coat of arms of the House of Grimaldi, rulers of the small principality since 1297. The Grimaldi family's use of **red** and **white** as heraldic colours dates back to 1339. Prince Karl III officially adopted it as the national flag in 1881. Except in its ratio, it is identical to the **bicolour** flag of **Indonesia**.

HISTORY

The Principality of Monaco, an **enclave** in **south-eastern France**, is the second smallest country in the world (after the Vatican). A battleground in the **Genoese** civil wars between the **Guelphs** and the **Ghibellines**, the Guelph **Rainier Grimaldi** captured Monaco from the Ghibellines in 1297. From 1525 to 1641 it was a **protectorate** of **Spain**. In 1641 it became a **protectorate** of **France**. In 1793 France overthrew the Grimaldis and annexed the principality. In 1815 Monaco became a protectorate of the **Kingdom of Sardinia**. In 1861 Monaco regained its independence under the guardianship of France. The principality flourished after the opening of the **Monte Carlo Casino** in 1863. In 1956 Prince **Rainier III** married the US film actress **Grace Kelly**. In 1993 Monaco joined the United Nations. The **absence of income tax** means that Monaco has become a haven for the super-rich.

AREA: 1sq km (0.4sq mi)

POPULATION: 30,000

CAPITAL (POPULATION): Monaco-Ville (1400)

GOVERNMENT: Constitutional monarchy

ETHNIC GROUPS: French 47%, Monégasque 16%, Italian 16%, other 21%

LANGUAGES: French (official), English, Italian, Monegasque

RELIGIONS: Roman Catholic 90%

NATIONAL MOTTO: "*Deo Juvante*" "With God's help"

NATIONAL ANTHEM (DATE): "*Le Marche de Monaco*" "The March of Monaco" (1867)

Monaco hosts the International Bouquet Competition (founded 1967) every April.

MONGOLIA

FLAG RATIO: 1:2 **USE:** National **DATE ADOPTED:** 1992 **LAST MODIFIED:** 1992

Mongolia's flag is red with a vertical blue stripe down the middle. **Red** is the colour of fire, symbolizing progress and prosperity. **Blue** represents the colour of the sky, and stands for peace and eternity. On the hoist band of the flag is a yellow *soyombo*, an ancient Mongolian ideogram. The three-tongued flame crowning the *soyombo* symbolizes the nation's past, present and future. The flame, together with the sun and the crescent, symbolizes the prosperity and progress of the Mongolian nation. The two downward-pointing triangles signify the defeat of the enemies of the Mongols. The horizontal rectangles symbolize honest and fair government. The yin and yang symbol signifies the unity of pairs of natural elements. The two vertical rectangles represent a fortress, indicating that the strength of the nation derives from the unity of its people.

HISTORY

Genghis Khan united Mongolia in the 13th century. His grandson, **Kublai Khan**, built up a mighty Mongol Empire. In 1650 the son of the Mongol Khan of Urga (now Ulan Bator) was named a **Living Buddha**. In the 17th century Mongolia came under **Chinese** control. In 1911 a Mongolian rising expelled China from **Outer Mongolia** and, with Soviet help, established the **independent** Mongolian People's Republic in 1924. **Inner Mongolia**, between the Gobi Desert and the Great Wall, remains part of communist China. **Yumzhagiyen Tsedenbal** led Mongolia from 1952 until 1984.

Living Buddhas *or* Khutuktu *governed Mongolia from 1696 to 1924.*

AREA: 1,566,500sq km (604,826sq mi)
POPULATION: 2,044,000
CAPITAL (POPULATION): Ulan Bator (691,000)
GOVERNMENT: Multi-party republic
ETHNIC GROUPS: Khalka Mongol 79%, Kazakh 6%
LANGUAGES: Khalka Mongolian (official)
RELIGIONS: Buddhist (mainly Tibetan) 93%, Sunni Muslim 4%
NATIONAL ANTHEM (DATE): *"Bügd Nairamdakh Mongol"* (1950)

MOROCCO

FLAG RATIO: 2:3 USE: National/Civil DATE ADOPTED: 1915 CODIFIED: 1956

The Alawite dynasty first adopted a red flag for Morocco in the 17th century. **Red** symbolizes the royal family's claim of descent from the prophet Muhammad. The **green pentagram** (five-pointed star), called the 'Seal of Solomon', first appeared in 1915. Morocco retained the design after gaining **independence** from France and Spain in 1956.

HISTORY

Berbers settled *c*.3000 years ago. In *c*.AD 685, **Arab** armies invaded Morocco, introducing Islam and Arabic. In 711 Moroccan Muslims invaded Spain. In 788 Berbers and Arabs united in an independent Moroccan state. In the mid-11th century, the **Almoravids** conquered Morocco. They built a Muslim empire.

The **Almohad** dynasty succeeded the Almoravids. The present ruling dynasty, the **Alawite**, came to power in 1660. In 1912 Morocco divided into **French Morocco** and the smaller protectorate of **Spanish Morocco**. **Abd al-Krim** led a revolt (1921–26) against European rule. In 1956 Morocco gained **independence**, although Spain retains the enclaves of Ceuta and Melilla. In 1957 Morocco became a constitutional monarchy. Sultan Sidi Muhammad changed his title to King **Muhammad V**. In 1961 Muhammad's son succeeded as King **Hassan II**. In 1979 Morocco assumed control of **Western Sahara**. In 1999 Hassan died, and his son became **Muhammad VI**.

AREA: 446,550sq km (172,413sq mi)
POPULATION: 28,238,000
CAPITAL (POPULATION): Rabat (652,000)
GOVERNMENT: Constitutional monarchy
ETHNIC GROUPS: Berber 59%, Arab 40%
LANGUAGES: Arabic (official), French
RELIGIONS: Sunni Muslim 99%, Christian 1%
NATIONAL MOTTO: "God, Country, King"
NATIONAL ANTHEM (DATE):
"*Hymne Cherifien*" (1956)

A copper water jug adorns this stamp celebrating the Red Crescent organization.

MOZAMBIQUE

FLAG RATIO: 2:3   USE: National/Civil   DATE ADOPTED: 1983   LAST MODIFIED: 1983

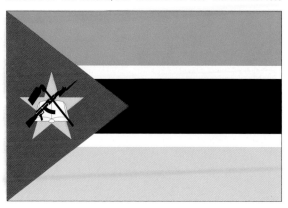

Mozambique's flag is based on the banner of the Front for the Liberation of Mozambique (Frelimo), the movement that led the struggle for self-determination. Frelimo's flag was in turn inspired by the banner of the African National Congress (ANC). The **green stripe** represents fertile land, the **white** for peace, the **black** for Africa, and the **yellow** for mineral wealth. The **red triangle** represents the blood shed in the fight for independence. Against the backdrop of a **yellow star** lie the national symbols: a **rifle**, a **hoe**, and a **book**.

HISTORY

Bantu speakers arrived in the first century AD. **Arab** traders settled from the 10th century. **Vasco da Gama** was the first European to discover Mozambique in 1498, and in 1505 **Portugal** established its first settlement. In the 16th century, the Portuguese built **plantations**. In the 18th and 19th centuries, Mozambique was a centre of the **slave trade**. In 1910 it became a Portuguese colony. In 1964 **Frelimo** launched a **guerrilla war** against Portuguese rule. In 1975 Mozambique gained **independence**, and **Samora Machel** became president. **Civil war** raged for 16 years, claiming tens of thousands of lives. In 1986 Samora Machel died and **Joachim Chissano** succeeded him. In 1995 Mozambique joined the **Commonwealth of Nations**. In 2000 the **River Limpopo** flooded leaving almost one million people homeless.

Estrelinhas *(Portuguese for 'little star') is the name for this haircut in Mozambique.*

AREA: 801,590sq km (309,494sq mi)
POPULATION: 19,371,007
CAPITAL (POPULATION): Maputo (2,000,000)
GOVERNMENT: Multi-party republic
ETHNIC GROUPS: Makua 47%, Tsonga 27%, Malawi 12%, Shona 11%, Yao 4%, Swahili 1%, Makonde 1%
LANGUAGES: Portuguese (official)
RELIGIONS: African traditional beliefs 50%, Roman Catholic 16%, Muslim 15%, Protestant 14%
NATIONAL ANTHEM (DATE): "*Patria Amada*" "Beloved Motherland" (2002)

135

NAMIBIA

FLAG RATIO: 2:3 USE: National/Civil DATE ADOPTED: 1990 LAST MODIFIED: 1990

A committee chose the flag design in 1990. The colours are those of the South West Africa People's Organisation (SWAPO), which led the struggle for independence, and of the Ovombo, the largest tribe in Namibia. The **red diagonal** band represents the heroism of Namibian people and their resolve for equal opportunity. The **white diagonals** stand for peace and unity. The **blue triangle** symbolizes the clear sky, the Atlantic Ocean, and Namibia's precious water resources. The **green triangle** signifies vegetation and agriculture. The **twelve-rayed golden sun** in the upper hoist represents life and energy.

HISTORY

The nomadic **San** were displaced by Bantu-speakers, such as the Ovambo, Kavango and Herero. In 1884 **Germany** claimed the region as a protectorate and subsumed it into the territory of **South-West Africa**. In 1908 the discovery of **diamonds** fuelled European settlement. Namibia was occupied by **South African** troops during World War I, and in 1920 South Africa gained a mandate. In 1966 SWAPO began a guerrilla war against South Africa. **Civil war** raged from 1977. SWAPO won multiparty elections in 1989, and Namibia gained **independence** in 1990. **Sam Nujoma** has served as president since independence.

AREA: 825,750sq km (318,694sq mi)
POPULATION: 1,791,900
CAPITAL (POPULATION): Windhoek (194,300)
GOVERNMENT: Multi-party republic
ETHNIC GROUPS: Ovambo 50%, Kavango 9%, Herero 7%, Damara 7%, White 6%, Nama 5%
LANGUAGES: English (official), Afrikaans, German, Oshivambo, Herero, Nama
RELIGIONS: Lutheran 51%, Roman Catholic 20%, African traditional beliefs 10%
NATIONAL MOTTO: "Unity, Liberty, Justice"
NATIONAL ANTHEM (DATE): "Namibia, Land of the Brave" (1991)

Issued for World Post Day, the stamp shows a San man carrying water and food.

FLAG RATIO: 1:2 USE: National/Civil DATE ADOPTED: 1968 LAST MODIFIED: 1968

Nauru's flag is a representation of the island's geographic position. The flag shows Nauru (the **white star**) just south of the line of the Equator (the **yellow stripe**), surrounded by the **blue** of the Pacific Ocean. The **12 points** of the star represent each of the original indigenous tribes of the island. Two of these tribes are now extinct.

HISTORY

Nauru is a **coral atoll** in the western Pacific Ocean, located halfway between Australia and Hawaii. It is the world's **smallest independent republic**. In 1798 British navigator **John Fearn** explored Nauru. In 1888 the atoll was annexed to **Germany**. It later formed part of the Protectorate of the **Marshall Islands**. Nauru has rich deposits of high-grade phosphate rock which began to be mined at the start of the 20th century by a joint British and German consortium. **Australian forces** occupied Nauru in World War I. The **Japanese** occupied Nauru from 1942 to 1945. After World War II, Australia resumed administration of the island. In 1968 the island became an **independent republic** within the **Commonwealth of Nations**. It joined the United Nations (UN) in 1999. **Hammer DeRoburt** was President from 1968 to 1976, and again from 1978 to 1989. Phosphate mining has left 80% of the island **uninhabitable**.

AREA: 21sq km (8sq mi)
POPULATION: 11,300
CAPITAL (POPULATION): No official capital, but government offices are in Yaren district
GOVERNMENT: Multi-party republic
ETHNIC GROUPS: Nauruan 58%, other Pacific Islander 26%, Chinese 8%, European 8%
LANGUAGES: Nauruan (official), English
RELIGIONS: Protestant 66%, Roman Catholic 33%
NATIONAL ANTHEM (DATE): "*Nauru Bwiema*" "Nauru, Our Homeland" (1968)

NAURU 30*C*

Common Eggfly (male) *Hypolimnas bolina*

The common eggfly butterfly lives throughout south-east Asia. The male is shown.

NEPAL

FLAG RATIO: 3:4 **USE:** National **DATE ADOPTED:** 1962 **LAST MODIFIED:** 1962

Nepal boasts the only non-rectangular flag in the world. Its unusual shape derives from two pennants representing political and royal authority. The **white crescent moon** with **eight rays** symbolizes the monarchy, while the **white, twelve-rayed sun** stands for the Rana family from which Prime Ministers were chosen from 1846 to 1951. The sun and moon symbolize the hope that Nepal's independence is as enduring as the heavenly bodies. **White** represents the pure, everlasting eyes of god. **Crimson** is the national colour and stands for energy. **Blue** denotes peace.

AREA: 140,800sq km (54,363sq mi)
POPULATION: 23,077,791
CAPITAL (POPULATION): Katmandu (696,852)
GOVERNMENT: Constitutional monarchy
ETHNIC GROUPS: Brahman, Chetri, Newar, Gurung, Sherpa, Tharu, and more than 60 others
LANGUAGES: Nepali (official, spoken by 90% of the population), 50 other languages
RELIGIONS: Hindu 86%, Buddhist 8%, Muslim 4%, Christian 2%
NATIONAL MOTTO: "The Motherland Is Worth More than the Kingdom of Heaven"
NATIONAL ANTHEM (DATE): "Ras Triya Gaan" "May Glory Crown Our Illustrious Sovereign" (1924)

HISTORY

In *c*.563 BC, **Buddha** was born in southwest Nepal. From the 10th to the 18th century, the **Malla dynasty** ruled Nepal. In AD 1769 Nepal united under **Gurkha** rule. **Britain** defeated the Gurkhas in a war (1814–16). In 1923 Britain recognized Nepal as a sovereign state. In 1951 the Rana government was overthrown and the monarchy re-established under **King Mahendra. Birendra** succeeded his father as King in 1972. In 2001 Birendra was shot and killed by his son, **Dipendra**, who then killed himself. **Gyanendra**, Birendra's brother, succeeded as King. Since the 1990s, a **Maoist revolt** has claimed more than 3500 lives.

Rana Tharu *are hunter-gatherer people of western Nepal. They are immune to malaria.*

The Dutch **tricolour** of **horizontal red, white, and blue stripes** derives from the orange, white and blue '*Prinsenvlag*' ('Prince's flag') of Prince William I of Orange, leader of the Revolt of the Netherlands (1567–79) against Spain. The orange stripe evolved into a deep red, perhaps because the orange was not bold enough for recognition at sea. Orange remains the national colour. The Dutch flag is almost identical to the flag of **Luxembourg**.

HISTORY

Philip II of Spain's attempt to impose Catholicism led to the **Revolt of the Netherlands**. The Union of Utrecht (1579) established the **United Provinces of the Netherlands**. The **Dutch East India Company** founded in 1602, and the **Dutch Empire** strengthened in two wars with Britain (1652–54, 1665–67).

In 1689 Prince William III became King **William III** of England. In 1815 the former United Provinces, Belgium, and Luxembourg united to form the **Kingdom of the Netherlands** under William I. Belgium left in 1830, and Luxembourg seceded in 1890. **Queen Wilhelmina** reigned from 1890 to 1948. The Netherlands was **neutral** in World War I. Most Dutch Jews were murdered under **Nazi occupation** during World War II. New Guinea and Surinam gained independence in 1962 and 1975. In 1980 **Queen Juliana** abdicated in favour of her daughter **Beatrix**. The Netherlands was a founder member of the European Union.

AREA: 41,526sq km (16,033sq mi)
POPULATION: 15,983,103
CAPITAL (POPULATION): Amsterdam (736,538)
GOVERNMENT: Constitutional monarchy
ETHNIC GROUPS: Netherlander 95%, Indonesian, Turkish, Moroccan, German
LANGUAGES: Dutch (official)
RELIGIONS: Roman Catholic 31%, Dutch Reformed Church 15%, Calvinist 6%, Muslim 4%
NATIONAL MOTTO: "*Je Maintiendrai*" "I Will Maintain"
NATIONAL ANTHEM (DATE): "*Wilhelmus van Nassouwe*" "William of Nassau" (1932)

Friesland, a province in northern Netherlands, unified in 1498.

139

NEW ZEALAND

FLAG RATIO: 1:2 USE: National/Civil DATE ADOPTED: 1902 LAST MODIFIED: 1902

New Zealand's **red, white** and **blue** flag recalls its historic links with Britain. Many former British colonies incoporate the **'Union Jack'** on the hoist of their flag. Like other countries in the southern hemisphere, New Zealand's flag features the stars of the **Southern Cross** constellation. The **blue field** represents the sky and the Pacific Ocean.

HISTORY

Maori settled in New Zealand more than 1000 years ago. The first European discovery was by the Dutch navigator **Abel Tasman** in 1642. British explorer **James Cook** landed in 1769. In 1840 the **British** built a settlement at **Wellington**. The Treaty of **Waitangi** (1840) promised to honour Maori land rights in return for recognition of British sovereignty. In 1841 New Zealand became a separate **colony**. Increasing colonization led to the first **Maori War** (1843–48). British seizure of land led to the protracted **Maori Wars** (1860–72). In 1893 New Zealand became the first country to give **women** the vote. In 1907 New Zealand became a **self-governing** Dominion. **William Massey** was Prime Minister from 1912 to 1925. More than 16,000 New Zealand soldiers died in **World War I**. Labour Party leaders **Michael Savage** and **Peter Fraser** guided government during World II. In 1951 New Zealand joined the **Anzus Pact**. It joined the South East Asia Treaty Organization (**SEATO**) in 1954. **Jenny Shipley** was New Zealand's first woman prime minister (1997–99).

AREA: 270,990sq km (104,629sq mi)
POPULATION: 3,737,277
CAPITAL (POPULATION): Wellington (163,824)
GOVERNMENT: Constitutional monarchy
ETHNIC GROUPS: New Zealand European 74%, New Zealand Maori 10%, Polynesian 4%
LANGUAGES: English and Maori (both official)
RELIGIONS: Anglican 21%, Presbyterian 16%, Roman Catholic 15%, Methodist 4%
NATIONAL ANTHEM (DATE): "God Defend New Zealand" (1940)

The kiwi, the national bird, is one of three flightless birds found only in New Zealand.

FLAG RATIO: 3:5   USE: National/Civil   DATE ADOPTED: 1908   LAST MODIFIED: 1971

Like many other nations in Central America, Nicaragua has a **blue and white** flag in homage to Argentina. In 1823 Nicaragua, Honduras, Costa Rica, El Salvador and Guatemala united to establish the **Central American Federation**, which adopted a flag with **three horizontal stripes**. In 1839 the Federation dissolved, but Nicaragua retained the flag. The arrangement of colours show Central America (**white stripe**) between the Atlantic and Pacific Oceans (**blue stripes**). The oceans also feature in the **triangular coat of arms**. Other symbols on the arms are **five volcanoes** (representing the members of the former federation), a **rainbow** (standing for hope), and a **red Liberty cap** (denoting freedom).

HISTORY

Christopher Columbus reached Nicaragua in 1502. **Spanish** colonization claimed the lives of *c*.100,000 **Native Americans**. In the 17th century, Britain secured control of the **Mosquito Coast**. In 1821 Nicaragua gained **independence**. In 1934 **US marines** helped **Anastasio Somoza García** to defeat **Augusto Sandino**. The Somoza family ruled Nicaragua until 1980, when the **Sandinistas** seized power from **Anastasio Somoza**. The United States aided the **Contra** rebels in a 10-year civil war against **Daniel Ortega**'s Sandinista socialist government. **Violeta Chamorro** defeated Ortega in 1990 elections. In 1998 **Hurricane Mitch** killed *c*.4000 people.

Footprints of Acahualinca *in Managua are more than 6000 years old.*

AREA: 130,000sq km (50,193sq mi)
POPULATION: 5,579,400
CAPITAL (POPULATION): Managua (1,106,600)
GOVERNMENT: Multi-party republic
ETHNIC GROUPS: Mestizo 77%, White 10%, Black 9%, Native American 4%
LANGUAGES: Spanish (official)
RELIGIONS: Roman Catholic 91%
NATIONAL ANTHEM (DATE): "*Salve a ti, Nicaragua*" "Hail to You, Nicaragua" (1939)

NIGER

FLAG RATIO: 2:3 USE: National/Civil DATE ADOPTED: 1959 LAST MODIFIED: 1959

Modelled on the French *tricolore,* the three horizontal stripes represent the three main geographic regions of Niger. Orange denotes the desert land in the north, white represents the central savannah, and green stands for the grassy plains in the south. The orange disc in the centre represents the hot sun shining over Niger. Niger's flag is very similar to the flag of Côte d'Ivoire, symbolic of the historical ties between the two nations.

HISTORY

The Hausa states ruled southern Niger from the 10th century to 1804, when Usman dan Fodio established the Fulani sultanate of Sokoto. In the 14th century, the Turaeg kingdom of Takedda developed west of the Aïr Mountains, flourishing on the trans-Saharan trade in copper. The Sultanate of Agadez succeeded Takedda. In the medieval period, the Kanem-Bornu Empire dominated eastern Niger, while the Songhai Empire commanded western Niger. Scottish explorer Mungo Park was probably the first European to reach Niger (1795). A French expedition arrived in 1891, but the Tuareg resisted French rule until 1922 – when Niger became a separate French colony. In 1960 Niger gained independence. Hamani Diori was Niger's first president. In 1975 Colonel Seyni Kountché overthrew Diori and founded a military dictatorship that lasted until his death in 1987. From 1990 to 1995 Tuaregs waged a civil war for a separate state in northern Niger.

AREA: 1,267,000sq km (489,189sq mi)
POPULATION: 11,825,400
CAPITAL (POPULATION): Niamey (723,200)
GOVERNMENT: Multi-party republic
ETHNIC GROUPS: Hausa 53%, Zerma-Songhai 21%, Tuareg 11%, Fulani (Peul) 10%
LANGUAGES: French (official), Hausa, Zarma, Fulfulde, Tamajaq
RELIGIONS: Sunni Muslim 82%, African traditional beliefs 8%, Christian 1%
NATIONAL ANTHEM (DATE): "*La Nigerienne*" "Song of Niger" (1961)

African ring-necked parakeet, a long-tailed parrot, lives in much of West Africa.

FLAG RATIO: 1:2 USE: National/Civil DATE ADOPTED: 1960 LAST MODIFIED: 1960

Nigeria's flag was the winning entry in a national competition held in 1959. The **green-white-green vertical stripes** are a stylized depiction of the River Niger (**white** stripe) flowing through the fertile fields of Nigeria (**two green stripes**). Green also symbolizes agriculture, the main source of income in Nigeria, and white stands for peace and unity. Nigeria adopted the flag upon independence from Britain in 1960.

HISTORY

The kingdom of **Kanem** arose in the 9th century, and in the 14th century merged into the kingdom of **Bornu**. In the 16th century, the Empire of Kanem-Bornu controlled the **Hausa states**. The **Yoruba** kingdom of **Ife** influenced the kingdoms of **Benin** and **Oyo**. The **Songhai Empire** dominated northern Nigeria in the early 16th century. In 1804 **Usman dan Fodio** created the **Fulani** sultanate of **Sokoto**. Nigeria was a centre of the **slave trade**. In 1861 **Britain** seized **Lagos**, ostensibly to stop the trade. By 1906 Britain conquered all of Nigeria. In 1960 Nigeria gained **independence** under **Sir Abubakar Tafawa Balewa**. In 1963 it became a republic, led by President **Tafawa Balewa**. In 1967 the **Ibo** declared the independence of **Biafra**. Civil war raged for three years before Biafra capitulated. Between 1960 and 1998 Nigeria enjoyed only nine years of civilian government. **Olusegun Obasanjo**, a former military ruler (1976–79), won elections in 1999.

Ibo from south-east Nigeria perform the acrobatic Nkpokiti dance.

AREA: 923,770sq km (356,668sq mi)
POPULATION: 105,000,000
CAPITAL (POPULATION): Abuja (350,000)
GOVERNMENT: Federal multi-party republic
ETHNIC GROUPS: Hausa 21%, Yoruba 21%, Ibo (Igbo) 19%, Fulani 11%, Ibibio 6%
LANGUAGES: English (official)
RELIGIONS: Muslim (mainly Sunni) 45%, Protestant 26%, Roman Catholic 12%
NATIONAL ANTHEM (DATE): "Arise, O Compatriots!" (1978)

NORWAY

FLAG RATIO: 8:11 USE: National/Civil DATE ADOPTED: 1821 CODIFIED: 1898

Frederik Meltzer, the member of Parliament from Bergen, designed Norway's flag in 1821. It was officially adopted as the national flag in 1898. The design combined the red-and-white *Dannebrog*, the flag of Denmark, with the blue of Sweden's flag. Its **red**, **white** and **blue** colours also recall the French *tricolore*, a symbol of liberty. The **Scandinavian cross** appears in blue.

HISTORY

From the 9th to the 11th century, **Vikings** raided western Europe. King **Olaf II**, patron saint of Norway, introduced **Christianity** in the early 11th century. **Lutheranism** became the state religion in the mid-16th century. In 1397 Norway, Sweden, and Denmark united in the **Kalmar Union**. Denmark ruled Norway from 1442 to 1814, when **Sweden** gained control. Norway declared independence, but Swedish troops forced Norway to accept union under the Swedish crown. In 1905 Norway became an **independent monarchy**. Norway remained neutral during World War I. In April 1940, **Germany** invaded. In 1942 the Nazis set up a puppet government under **Vidkun Quisling**. More than 50% of Norway's merchant fleet was destroyed during World War II. Liberation finally came in May 1945. Norway joined NATO in 1949, and was a co-founder (1960) of the European Free Trade Association (EFTA). It voted against joining the European Union (EU) in 1971 and 1994. In 1981 **Gro Harlem Brundtland** became Norway's first woman prime minister. In 1991 **King Olav V** was succeeded by his son as **Harald V**.

AREA: 323,900sq km (125,050sq mi)
POPULATION: 4,478,497
CAPITAL (POPULATION): Oslo (507,467)
GOVERNMENT: Constitutional monarchy
ETHNIC GROUPS: Norwegian 97%
LANGUAGES: Norwegian (official), Lappish, Finnish
RELIGIONS: Evangelical Lutheran 90%
NATIONAL ANTHEM (DATE): "*Ja, Vi Elsker Dette Landet*" "Yes, We Love This Land" (1864)

Bunad making is a Norwegian handicraft. Bunads are folk costumes.

FLAG RATIO: 1:2 **USE:** National/Civil **DATE ADOPTED:** 1970 **LAST MODIFIED:** 1995

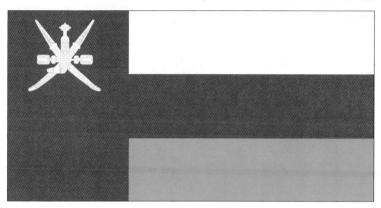

O man's flag was monochrome **red** until 1970, when **white** and **green** bands were added. White symbolizes peace. Green is a traditional **Islamic** colour, but also stands for the fertility of the land. Red represents the blood shed in the struggle for liberation. The Sultanate's **white coat of arms** on the upper hoist consists of two **crossed swords**, a *khnajar* (dagger), and **belt**. In 1995 the flag was altered by making the the white and green bands of equal width.

HISTORY

In ancient times, Oman was an important trading area on the main trading route between the Arabian (Persian) Gulf and the Indian Ocean. In 1507 the Portuguese captured several ports in Oman, including Muscat. **Portugal** controlled maritime trade until expelled by the **Ottomans** in 1659. The **al-Said** family have ruled Oman since taking power in 1741. During the 20th century, the Sultanate was often in conflict with religious leaders (*imams*) of the **Ibahdi** sect, who sought a more theocratic society. British colonial interference and economic inequality led to popular rebellions in the 1950s and 1960s. In 1970 Sultan **Sa'id bin Taimur** was deposed by his son, **Qaboos bin Sa'id**. In 1981 Oman was a founder member of the Gulf Cooperation Council (GCC).

AREA: 212,460sq km (82,278sq mi)
POPULATION: 2,176,000
CAPITAL (POPULATION): Muscat (350,000)
GOVERNMENT: Monarchy
ETHNIC GROUPS: Omani Arab 58%, expatriates (mainly South Asian) 27%, Baluchi 6%, Iranian 1%, Jibbali 1%
LANGUAGES: Arabic (official), English, Baluchi, Urdu, Indian dialects
RELIGIONS: Ibadhi Muslim 75%, other Muslim (Sunni and Shi'a) 20%, Hindu 3%, Roman Catholic 2%
NATIONAL ANTHEM (DATE): "*Nshid as-Salaam as-Sultani*" "The Sultan's Anthem" (1970)

Bahla, in northern Oman, is the centre for traditional Omani pottery.

PAKISTAN

FLAG RATIO: 2:3 USE: National DATE ADOPTED: 1947 LAST MODIFIED: 1947

The white and dark green flag of Pakistan represents the country's religious minorities (white) and Muslim majority (green). The **crescent moon** and **five-pointed star** are traditional motifs of **Islam**. The crescent also stands for progress. The star symbolizes light and knowledge.

HISTORY

In 712 **Arabs** conquered **Sind**, and introduced **Islam**. The **Delhi Sultanate** ruled from 1211 to 1526, when the **Mughal Empire** supplanted it. In the early 19th century, **Ranjit Singh** made **Punjab** the

centre of **Sikhism**. The **British** conquered Sind (1843), Punjab (1849), and much of **Baluchistan** in the 1850s. **British India** won independence in 1947, and split into India and Pakistan (Urdu, 'Land of the Pure'). **Muhammad Ali Jinnah** was Pakistan's first leader. In 1947 the long dispute with India over **Kashmir** began. **Muhammad Ayub Khan** was president from 1958 to 1969. In 1971 East Pakistan declared independence as **Bangladesh** and a bloody civil war ensued. **Zulfikar Ali Bhutto** was prime minister from 1973 to 1977. His daughter, **Benazir Bhutto**, was Pakistan's first woman prime minister (1988–90, 1993–96). In 1999 General **Pervez Musharraf** toppled **Nawaz Sharif** in a military coup.

AREA: 796,100sq km (307,374sq mi)
POPULATION: 130,578,000
CAPITAL (POPULATION): Islamabad (529,180)
GOVERNMENT: Federal multi-party republic
ETHNIC GROUPS: Punjabi 60%, Sindhi 12%, Pashtun (Pathan) 13%, Baluch 4%
LANGUAGES: Punjabi (official) 48%, Sindhi 12%, Saraiki (Punjabi variant) 10%, Pashto 9%, Urdu (official) 8%, Hindko 4%, Brahui 1%, English (official, lingua franca of political elite)
RELIGIONS: Sunni Muslim 77%, Shi'a Muslim 20%, Christian 2%, Hindu 1%
NATIONAL MOTTO: "Faith, Unity, Discipline"
NATIONAL ANTHEM (DATE): "*Qaumi Tarana*"
"National Anthem" (1954)

Terracotta jar (c.*2600 BC*) *from the Harappan site of Naushero, Baluchistan.*

PALAU

FLAG RATIO: 5:8 USE: National DATE ADOPTED: 1981 LAST MODIFIED: 1981

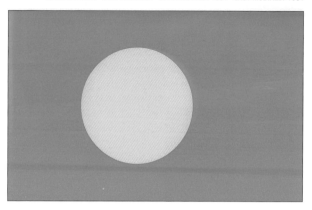

The flag was officially adopted in 1981 when the archipelago became self-governing. The **blue field** represents the geographic position of the islands in the northern Pacific Ocean. Blue also symbolizes independence. The **yellow disc** stands for the full moon and productivity – an ancient belief holds that the full moon is the best time for fishing and harvesting. Currently, eight of Palau's 16 states have their own **state flag**.

HISTORY

Ten of Palau's states and its capital, Korot, are on the largest island of **Babeldaob**. Settled by migrants from Southeast Asia *c*.3000 years ago, the **Spanish** arrived in 1710. In 1898 Spain sold the islands to **Germany**. In 1914 **Japan** occupied the archipelago. At the end of World War II, control passed to the **United States**, which administered Palau as part of the **US Trust Territory of the Pacific Islands**. In 1981 the islands gained self-government. In 1994 Palau became an **independent republic** in free association with the United States, which is responsible for its defence. **Migrant workers**, mainly from the **Philippines**, account for 30% of Palau's population.

The bai, *a meeting place for village chiefs, is a distinctive Microneisan architectural form.*

AREA: 460sq km (189sq mi)
POPULATION: 17,225
CAPITAL (POPULATION): Koror (9000)
GOVERNMENT: Federal multi-party republic
ETHNIC GROUPS: Palauan (Micronesian) 70%, Asian (mainly Filipinos) 28%, white 2%
LANGUAGES: English and Palauan (official) – except on Sonsoral (Sonsoralese, English), Tobi (Tobi, English), and Angaur (Angaur, Japanese, English)
RELIGIONS: Roman Catholic 40%, Modekngei 33% (indigenous), Evangelical Church 10%, Church of Jesus Christ of Latter-Day Saints 2%, Jehovah's Witness 2%, Baha'i 2%
NATIONAL ANTHEM (DATE): Untitled (1980)

147

PANAMA

FLAG RATIO: 2:3 USE: National/Civil DATE ADOPTED: 1903 RATIFIED: 1941

Panama's flag is a **rectangle** divided into **four quarters**. The lower-left quarter is **blue** and stands for the Conservative Party. The top-right quarter is **red** and represents the Liberal Party. Other quarters are **white**, symbolizing peace between the parties. The **blue star** in the top left quarter stands for purity and honesty. The **red star** in the bottom right quarter denotes government and law.

HISTORY

In 1502 **Christopher Columbus** landed in Panama. The indigenous population was soon wiped out and **Spain** asserted control. In 1821 Panama became a province of **Greater Colombia**. After a revolt in 1903, Panama declared **independence** from Colombia. The **Hay-Bunau-Varilla Treaty** (1903) gave the United States control of the proposed **Panama Canal**. The trans-isthmian canal opened in 1914. In 1977 a treaty confirmed Panama's sovereignty over the Canal, while providing for US bases in the Canal Zone. General **Manuel Noreiga** came to power in 1983. In 1989 Noreiga made himself president and declared war on the United States. The United States invaded and overthrew Noreiga, who received a 40-year prison sentence. **Pérez Balladares** became President in 1994 elections. In 1999 Panama gained control of the canal from the United States, and **Mireya Moscoso** became Panama's first woman President.

AREA: 77,080sq km (29,761sq mi)
POPULATION: 2,839,177
CAPITAL (POPULATION): Panama City (463,093)
GOVERNMENT: Multi-party republic
ETHNIC GROUPS: Mestizo 60%, Black and Mulatto 20%, White 10%, Native American 8%, Asian 2%
LANGUAGES: Spanish (official), English 14%
RELIGIONS: Roman Catholic 85%, Protestant 5%, Muslim 5%
NATIONAL MOTTO: "*Pro Mundi Beneficio*" "For the Benefit of the World"
NATIONAL ANTHEM (DATE): "*Himno Istmeño*" "Isthmus Hymn" (1925)

The full and flowing pollera dress is Panama's national costume for women.

PAPUA NEW GUINEA

FLAG RATIO: 3:4 USE: National/Civil DATE ADOPTED: 1971 LAST MODIFIED: 1971

Papua New Guinea's flag consists of two right-anged triangles. A yellow *kumul* bird of paradise is on the **upper red triangle**. It symbolizes Papua New Guinea's emergence as an independent nation. The plumes of the *kumul* are often used as ceremonial decoration in Papua New Guinea. The **white five-pointed stars** on the **lower black triangle** represent the constellation of the **Southern Cross**. The Southern Cross is a common motif of countries in the southern hemisphere. Black, red and yellow are the national colours of Papua New Guinea.

HISTORY

In 1526 the Portuguese became the first Europeans to sight New Guinea. In 1828 the **Dutch** took western New Guinea (now Irian Jaya province, **Indonesia**). In 1884 Germany captured north-east New Guinea, which became **German New Guinea**, while Britain created **British New Guinea** in south-east New Guinea. In 1906 British New Guinea passed to **Australia** as the **Territory of Papua**. In 1921 the League of Nations mandated German New Guinea to Australia as the **Territory of New Guinea**. In 1949 Papua and New Guinea combined to form the Territory of Papua and New Guinea. In 1973 the Territory achieved self-government as a prelude to full **independence** as Papua New Guinea in 1975. In the 1990s the government fought against separatists on the island of **Bougainville**. In 1998 a **tsunami** killed more than 1600 people.

AREA: 462,840sq km (178,073 sq mi)
POPULATION: 5,130,000
CAPITAL (POPULATION): Port Moresby (252,000)
GOVERNMENT: Constitutional monarchy
ETHNIC GROUPS: Papuan 84%, Melanesian 1%
LANGUAGES: English (official), more than 700 indigenous languages
RELIGIONS: Roman Catholic 22%, Evangelical Lutheran 23%, United Church 15%, Pentecostal 7%, Anglican 5%, Evangelical Alliance 4%, indigenous beliefs 34%
NATIONAL ANTHEM (DATE):
"O Arise, All You Sons" (1975)

Telefomin shield-carriers from West Sepik, Papua New Guinea, were unarmed.

PARAGUAY

FLAG RATIO: 3:5 **USE:** National/Civil **DATE ADOPTED:** 1842 **LAST MODIFIED:** 1988

In 1812 Paraguay adopted a **red, white and blue tricolour** as its national flag. It derived the design from the French *tricolore*, a popular symbol of liberty in the early 19th century. In 1842 it adopted the present flag with two different sides. The **obverse** of the flag displays the concentric circles of the **national shield**. At the centre of the shield is a **yellow** 'Star of May' on a **blue disc**, recalling the date of independence (May 14, 1811). **Laurel branches**, a traditional symbol of peace, surround the disc. The **reverse** of the flag shows the **seal** of the National Treasury, consisting of the national motto and a **lion** guarding a **red Liberty cap** on a pole.

AREA: 406,750sq km (157,046sq mi)
POPULATION: 5,496,560
CAPITAL (POPULATION): Asunción (546,800)
GOVERNMENT: Multi-party republic
ETHNIC GROUPS: Mestizo 90%,
Native American 3%
LANGUAGES: Spanish and Guaraní (both official)
RELIGIONS: Roman Catholic 90%,
Protestant 6%
NATIONAL MOTTO: *"Paz y Justice"*
"Peace and Justice"
NATIONAL ANTHEM (DATE): *"Himno Nacional"*
"National Anthem" (1846)

150

HISTORY

The earliest known inhabitants were the **Guaraní**. In 1537 the **Spanish** built a fort at Asunción, which became the capital of its South American colonies. In 1811 Paraguay won **independence**. **José Francia** was dictator from 1811 to 1840. Paraguay lost more than half of its population and much territory in the **War of the Triple Alliance** (1865–70) against Brazil, Argentina, and Uruguay. Paraguay regained some land in the **Chaco War** (1932–35) against Bolivia. General **Alfredo Stroessner**'s dictatorship lasted from 1954 to 1989. In 1993 elections **Juan Carlos Wasmosy** became the first civilian president for almost 40 years. The assassination of Vice President Luis María Argana led to **riots** in 1999.

The agouti paca, a tailless rodent, lives in the tropical forests of Paraguay.

FLAG RATIO: 2:3 USE: National/Civil DATE ADOPTED: 1825 LAST MODIFIED: 1825

In legend, Peru's **red and white striped** flag was inspired by a flock of flamingos that General José de San Martín spotted flying over his army when liberating Peru from Spain in 1820. Seeing this as a good omen, San Martín declared red and white to be the colours of liberty. Red also stands for the blood shed in the struggle for independence. White symbolizes peace. At the centre of the flag is the **coat of arms**. The tripartite shield, framed and topped by **green wreaths**, has a pile of **gold coins**, a **vicuña**, and a **keno tree**. Simon Bolívar defined the flag in 1825.

HISTORY

In 1500 the **Inca Empire** extended from Ecuador to Chile. Spanish conquistador **Francisco Pizarro** captured Inca King **Atahualpa** in 1532. By 1533 **Spain** ruled most of Peru. Spanish rule saw many native revolts, most notably that of **Tupac Amaru**. In 1821 Peru declared **independence**. Spain still held much of the interior, and **Simon Bolívar** completed Peru's liberation in 1826. Peru lost some of its land to Bolivia in the **War of the Pacific** (1879–84). **Civil war** between the government and rebels (such as **Shining Path** and Tupac Amaru) claimed more than 30,000 lives in the 1980s. In 1996 **guerrillas** held the Japanese Embassy in Lima for four months. In 2000, after a decade as president, **Alberto Fujimori** faced bribery charges and fled into exile.

***Cuzco**, southern Peru, hosts the annual* Inti Raymi *(June 24), Inca Festival of the Sun.*

AREA: 1,285,220sq km (496,223sq mi)
POPULATION: 26,657,300
CAPITAL (POPULATION): Lima (7,497,000)
GOVERNMENT: Multi-party republic
ETHNIC GROUPS: Quechua 47%, Mestizo 32%, White 12%, Aymara 5%
LANGUAGES: Spanish (official), Quechua (official), Aymara
RELIGIONS: Roman Catholic 93%, Protestant 6%
NATIONAL ANTHEM (DATE): "*Marcha Nacional*" "National March" (1822)

PHILIPPINES

FLAG RATIO: 1:2 **USE:** National/Civil **DATE ADOPTED:** 1898 **RATIFIED:** 1946

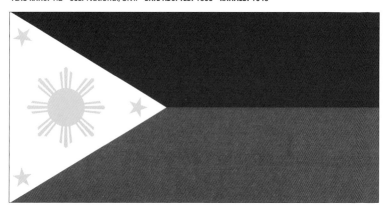

General Emilio Aguinaldo, leader of the revolt against Spain, designed Philippines' flag. The **equilateral triangle** at the hoist denotes equality. Its **white** colour symbolizes purity. The **yellow sun** stands for the giant steps made by Filipinos in building a nation. The sun's **eight rays** represent the first eight Filipino provinces to rebel against Spain. The **three yellow stars** represent the main geographical regions – Mindanao, Luzon, and Visayas. The **blue stripe** stands for the unity and noble aspirations of Filipinos. The **red stripe** symbolizes the blood shed in the fight for independence.

HISTORY

In 1565 **Spain** began its conquest of the islands, naming them *Filipinas* after King Philip II. In 1896 Filipinos revolted against Spanish rule. The **United States** gained the islands after victory in the Spanish-American War (1898). From 1899 to 1902, Filipinos vainly fought against US occupation. In 1935 **Manuel Luis Quezon** became the first president of the Commonwealth of the Philippines. **Japan** occupied the islands from 1941 to 1944. Philippines won **independence** in 1946. Dictator **Ferdinand Marcos** ruled from 1965 to 1986, when **Cory Aquino** came to power. Gloria Macaogal-Arroyo became president after a **rising** in 2001.

AREA: 300,000sq km (115,300sq mi)
POPULATION: 76,498,735
CAPITAL (POPULATION): Manila (1,581,082)
GOVERNMENT: Multi-party republic
ETHNIC GROUPS: Tagalog 30%, Cebuano 24%, Ilocano 10%, Hiligaynon-Ilongo 9%, Bicol 6%, Samar-Leyte 4%
LANGUAGES: Filipino (Tagalog) and English (both official)
RELIGIONS: Roman Catholic 84%, Philippine Independent Church (Aglipayan) 6%, Protestant 4%, Muslim 4%
NATIONAL MOTTO: "*Maka-diyos, maka-tao, makakalikasan at makabansa*"
"We are religious, we are friendly, we are rich, and we love our country"
NATIONAL ANTHEM (DATE): "*Lupang Hinirang*"
"Beloved Land" (1898)

Golden Tara *of Agusan (c.1400) is the earliest Indian artifact found in the Philippines.*

Poland's flag of **horizontal white and red stripes** dates back to the red banner with white eagle of Vladislav Jagiello at the Battle of Tannenberg (1410). Polish kings used various combinations of white and red in the 17th century. In 1831 the *Sejm* (Polish assembly) adopted white and red as national colours in the rising against Russian rule. In 1919 Poland adopted its present flag. The **state flag** has the coat of arms, a **white eagle** with a **golden crown** on a **red shield**, on the white band.

HISTORY

Mieszko I founded a Polish state in the 10th century. In 1386 Poland unified with **Lithuania**. In 1717 **Russia** conquered Poland. The **War of the Polish Succession** (1733–35) involved most of Europe. The **Partitions of Poland** (1772, 1793, 1795) erased Poland from the map. **Tadeusz Kosciuszko** led resistance. In 1918 Poland regained **independence** from Russia. In 1921 it became a republic. In 1939 **Germany** invaded Poland, prompting **World War II**. The **Nazis** established concentration camps in which more than 6 million Poles (mainly Jews) perished. Poland regained **independence** in 1945. In 1952 it adopted a Soviet-style constitution. **Vladislav Gomulka** led Poland from 1956 to 1970. In 1990 the trade union **Solidarity** toppled **General Jaruzelski**'s communist regime and **Lech Walesa** became president. In 1999 Poland joined NATO.

Krakowiak is a fast dance performed by several couples. Chopin wrote one in 1828.

AREA: 312,680sq km (120,726sq mi)
POPULATION: 40,366,000
CAPITAL (POPULATION): Warsaw (1,638,000)
GOVERNMENT: Multi-party republic
ETHNIC GROUPS: Polish 98%, German 1%, Ukrainian 1%
LANGUAGES: Polish (official)
RELIGIONS: Roman Catholic 95%
NATIONAL ANTHEM (DATE): "*Mazurek Dabrowskiego*" "Dabrowski's Mazurka" (1927)

153

PORTUGAL

FLAG RATIO: 2:3 **USE:** National/Civil **DATE ADOPTED:** 1911 **LAST MODIFIED:** 1911

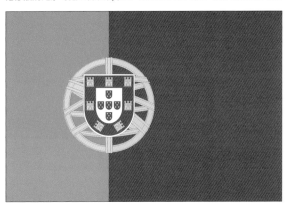

Portugal's national flag divides into two **vertical bands** of **green** and **red** representing hope and revolution respectively. The national **coat of arms** sits at the centre of an **armillary sphere** – an early navigational instrument and symbol of Portugal's leading role in early global exploration. The coat of arms includes important aspects of the nation's history and Christian beliefs. The **five blue shields** recall King Alfonso I victory over five Moorish princes in 1139. The five **white dots** on each shield are symbolic of the wounds of Christ at the crucifixion. The **seven gold castles** stand for the fortified cities conquered from the Moors.

HISTORY

In 711 **Moors** captured the entire country, except for the northern County of Portugal. **Alfonso I** drove out the Moors, and Spain recognized Portuguese **independence** in 1143. The reconquest ended with the Moors retreat from the **Algarve** in 1249. In 1385 **John I** founded the **Aviz dynasty**. The reign of **Manuel I** (1495–1521) was Portugal's 'golden age' when explorers such as **Vasco da Gama** built a vast **Portuguese Empire**. In 1500 **Pedro Cabral** conquered Brazil. The fall of the Aviz dynasty brought **Philip II** of Spain to the throne in 1580. For the next 60 years, **Spain** ruled Portugal. In 1640 **John IV** founded the **Braganza dynasty** which reigned until 1910. In 1910 Portugal became a **republic**. **António Salazar**'s dictatorship lasted from 1932 to 1968. In 1974 a military coup toppled **Marcelo Caetano**. In 1975 many Portuguese **colonies** won independence. In 1999 Portugal joined the **euro**.

AREA: 92,390sq km (35,670sq mi)
POPULATION: 10,230,603
CAPITAL (POPULATION): Lisbon (556,797)
GOVERNMENT: Multi-party republic
ETHNIC GROUPS: Portuguese 99%, Cape Verdean, Brazilian, Spanish, British
LANGUAGES: Portuguese (official)
RELIGIONS: Roman Catholic 95%
NATIONAL ANTHEM (DATE): "A Portugesa" "The Portuguese" (1910)

An amolador *(knife-grinder) was a familar figure in the streets of 19th-century Lisbon*

Qatar's national flag is very similar to the flag of **Bahrain**, a reflection of their close historical links. Until *c*.1860 the flag was monotone red. Qatar added a **vertical, serrated white stripe** at the request of the British, who sought to prevent piracy in the Arabian Gulf by including a white stripe for friendly Arab States. The **nine-point serrated** line indicates that Qatar is the ninth member of the 'reconciled Emirates' of the Arabian Gulf after the treaty with Britain in 1916. The **ratio** of the flag is different to that of Bahrain (11:28 rather than 3:5). In 1949 Qatar changed the colour of the right-hand band to **maroon** to differentiate it further from Bahrain. White also symbolizes peace, and maroon represents the blood shed in the 19th-century wars.

HISTORY

In the 1780s the **al-Khalifa** family gained control of Bahrain and Qatar. From 1872 to 1913 Qatar was part of the **Ottoman Empire**. In 1916 Qatar became a **British Protectorate**. Oil was first discovered in 1939. In 1971 Qatar gained **independence**. Sheikh **Khalifa bin Hamad Al-Thani** became Emir after a coup in 1972. Qatar was a founder member of the Gulf Cooperation Council (GCC) in 1981. Qatar allowed Allied coalition forces to use its territory to expel Iraqi forces from Kuwait in the **Gulf War** (1991). In 1995 Sheikh **Hamad bin Khalifa Al-Thani** overthrew his father and became Emir. A **coup** attempt failed in 1996.

Qatar is a liberal Islamic society where women can choose to cover their heads.

AREA: 11,437sq km (4415sq mi
POPULATION: 522,000
CAPITAL (POPULATION): Doha (264,000)
GOVERNMENT: Absolute monarchy
ETHNIC GROUPS: Arab 40%, Pakistani 18%, Indian 18%, Iranian 10%
LANGUAGES: Arabic (official), English (widely-spoken second language)
RELIGIONS: Muslim 95% (all native Qataris are Wahhabi Sunni)
NATIONAL ANTHEM (DATE): (1996)

155

ROMANIA

FLAG RATIO: 2:3 USE: National/Civil DATE ADOPTED: 1861 REINTRODUCED: 1989

In some accounts, Romania's **tricolour** of **blue**, **yellow** and **red vertical stripes** dates back to Michael the Brave, Prince of Wallachia (1593–1601). In 1834 Sultan Mahmud II allowed Wallachia to fly an ensign of red, blue and yellow horizontal stripes. After the Revolution of 1848, Wallachia adopted first a horizontal then a vertical tricolour of blue, yellow and red. In 1861 Wallachia and Moldavia united to form Romania. The new nation adopted Wallachia's flag. In 1948 Romania's communist government introduced a separate state flag with a coat of arms. In 1989 the communist regime collapsed and the flag was scrapped.

AREA: 237,500sq km (91,699sq mi)
POPULATION: 22,411,121
CAPITAL (POPULATION): Bucharest (2,016,131)
GOVERNMENT: Multi-party republic
ETHNIC GROUPS: Romanian 89%, Hungarian 7%, Romany (Gypsy) 2%
LANGUAGES: Romanian (official), Hungarian, German
RELIGIONS: Romanian Orthodox 70%, Roman Catholic 3%, Uniate Catholic 3%, Protestant 6%, Muslim 1%
NATIONAL ANTHEM (DATE): "Desteaptate, Romane" "Awake, Romanians" (1990)

HISTORY

Romania roughly corresponds to ancient **Dacia**, which the **Romans** conquered in AD 106. The principalities of **Wallachia** and **Moldavia** emerged in the 14th century. They formed part of the **Ottoman Empire** from the 15th to the 19th century. Russia gained control after the **Russo-Turkish War** (1828–29). In 1861 Wallachia and Moldavia merged to create Romania. In 1940 **Ion Antonescu** became dictator. Romania joined the German invasion of the Soviet Union in June 1941. More than 50% of Romanian Jews were killed during World War II. In 1944 **Soviet** troops occupied Romania. **Gheorghe Gheorghiu-Dej** replaced Antonescu. In 1965 the dictator **Nicolae Ceausescu** assumed power. In 1989 Ceausescu and his wife were executed. In 1990 **Ion Iliescu** became President.

Traditional Romanian *Easter eggs are hand painted in geometric designs.*

156

FLAG RATIO: 2:3 **USE:** National/Civil **DATE ADOPTED:** 1991 **LAST MODIFIED:** 1993

In 1991 Russia adopted a **tricolour** of **white**, **blue** and **red horizontal stripes**. In 1993 it changed the **ratio** from 1:2 to 2:3. White, blue and red are **Pan-Slavic** colours. A triband flag with these colours has been in use since the reign (1682–1721) of Tsar Peter the Great. In 1799 Tsar Alexander I adopted it as the civil ensign, and from 1883 it served as an alternative to the black-gold-white civil flag. In 1918 the Bolsheviks introduced a monochrome red flag with yellow Cyrillic letters. From 1954 the flag of the Soviet republic of Russia featured a red field with a blue stripe and a hammer and sickle on the hoist. According to tradition, white represents nobility, blue stands for honesty, and red represents courage.

HISTORY

The **Romanov** Tsarist dynasty ruled Russia from 1613 to 1917. **Peter the Great** founded **St Petersburg** in 1712. Tsarina **Catherine the Great** made Russia the greatest European power. In 1917, the **Bolsheviks,** led by **Lenin,** overthrew Tsar **Nicholas II** and Russia became part of the **Soviet Union**. In 1924 **Joseph Stalin** succeeded Lenin. In 1941 **Germany** invaded Russia. About 25 million Soviet people died in **World War II**. In 1991 **Boris Yeltsin** became President of Russia. In December 1991, the Soviet Union collapsed. In 1999 Yeltsin resigned in favour of **Vladimir Putin,** who relaunched the war in **Chechenia**.

In 1997 Vologda, north-west Russia, marked its 850th anniversary.

AREA: 17,075,000sq km (6,592,800sq mi)
POPULATION: 145,934,900
CAPITAL (POPULATION): Moscow (8,389,200)
GOVERNMENT: Federal multi-party republic
ETHNIC GROUPS: Russian 82%, Tatar 4%, Ukrainian 3%, Chuvash 1%
LANGUAGES: Russian (official)
RELIGIONS: Russian Orthodox 55%, Muslim 5%, Jewish 1%
NATIONAL ANTHEM (DATE): *"Gimn Rossiyskaya Federatsiya"* "Hymn of the Russian Federation" (2001)

RWANDA

FLAG RATIO: 2:3 USE: National DATE ADOPTED: 2002 LAST MODIFIED: 2002

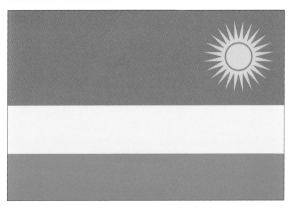

In 2002 Rwanda adopted a **tricolour** flag of **blue, yellow and green horizontal stripes**. The flag was part of an effort to forge a new national identity after the genocide of the 1990s. The previous flag, adopted in 1962, used the Pan-African colours of red, yellow and green with an 'R' on the central vertical stripe. The new flag recalls Rwanda's landscape of lush forests and desert under the African sun. Green symbolizes hope for prosperity. Yellow represents work, and blue stands for peace and happiness. The **sun** denotes unity and the fight against ignorance.

HISTORY

In the 15th century, **Tutsi** cattle herders moved into the area and soon dominated the **Hutus**. By the late 18th century, Rwanda and Burundi formed a single state, ruled by a Tutsi king (*mwami*). In 1890 it became part of **German East Africa**. In 1919 **Belgium** gained control. In 1959 the *mwami* died and a civil war claimed more than 150,000 lives. Hutu victory led to a mass exodus of Tutsis. In 1962 Rwanda won **independence**. In 1973 Juvénal **Habyarimana** ousted President **Grégoire Kayibanda**. In 1994 Habyarimana and President Ntaryamira of Burundi died in a rocket attack. The Hutu army began a war of **genocide** against the Tutsi minority, killing more than 800,000 people. The Tutsis toppled the regime, creating 2 million Hutu refugees.

AREA: 26,340sq km (10,170sq mi)
POPULATION: 8,170,100
CAPITAL (POPULATION): Kigali (290,600)
GOVERNMENT: Multi-party republic
ETHNIC GROUPS: Hutu 90%, Tutsi 9%, Twa 1%
LANGUAGES: Kinyarwanda, French, English (all official), Swahili
RELIGIONS: Roman Catholic 53%, Protestant 24%, Adventist 10%, African traditional beliefs 6%
NATIONAL ANTHEM (DATE): "Rwanda nziza" "Beautiful Rwanda" (2001)

Rwanda has many traditional instruments. The lulunga is an eight-stringed harp.

SAINT KITTS AND NEVIS

FLAG RATIO: 2:3 USE: National/Civil DATE ADOPTED: 1983 LAST MODIFIED: 1983

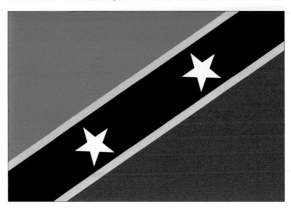

Saint Kitts and Nevis' flag has **green** and **red right-angled triangles**, separated by **three diagonal stripes** (two **yellow** and one **black**). The black stripe has **two white stars**. Yellow represents the nation's abundant sunshine. Green stands for its fertile lands. Red represents the islands' struggle for freedom from colonialism and slavery. Black symbolizes its African heritage, and the two white stars denote the freedom of the two islands.

HISTORY

Saint Kitts is a shortened form of its official name, Saint Christopher, given to it by **Christopher Columbus** when he discovered the island in 1493. In 1623 Saint Kitts became the first **English** colony in the West Indies. The French arrived in 1624. Europeans massacred the indigenous **Caribs**. In 1698 colonists settled on the neighbouring island of **Nevis** (Spanish, 'snow'). The Treaty of Paris (1783) confirmed British possession of the islands, which prospered through imported African **slave labour** on **sugar plantations**. Nevis became known as the 'Queen of the Caribees' because of its productive sugar industry. In 1918 Britain joined Saint Kitts and Nevis with Anguilla and the Virgin Islands. The islands gained self-government in 1967, and full **independence** in 1983. In 1998 Nevis held a referendum on independence, but failed to gain the two-thirds majority in favour of separation.

Pirates *plundered many pieces-of-eight from Spanish ships around Saint Kitts-Nevis.*

AREA: 311sq km (120sq mi)
POPULATION: 44,000
CAPITAL (POPULATION): Basseterre (11,600)
GOVERNMENT: Constitutional monarchy
ETHNIC GROUPS: Black African 96%
LANGUAGES: English (official)
RELIGIONS: Anglican 50%, Methodist 25%, Roman Catholic 10%, Jehovah's Witness 1%
NATIONAL MOTTO: "Country Above Self"
NATIONAL ANTHEM (DATE):
"Oh Land of Beauty" (1983)

SAINT LUCIA

FLAG RATIO: 1:2 **USE:** National/Civil **DATE ADOPTED:** 1967 **LAST MODIFIED:** 1979

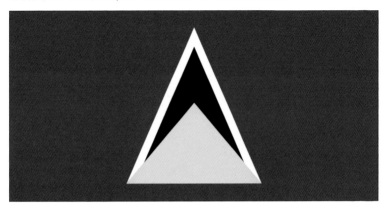

Dunstan St Omer, a local artist, designed Saint Lucia's flag in 1967. At the centre of a **blue field** are **three triangles** (**gold**, **black**, and **white**) superimposed on each other. Blue represents fidelity, the tropical sky, and the surrounding waters of the Caribbean Sea and Atlantic Ocean. Gold stands for the sunshine and prosperity. Black and white symbolize Saint Lucia's two cultures working together in unity. The superimposition of the triangles reflects the dominance of Saint Lucia's black African culture. The triangles also recall Saint Lucia's famous twin volcanic peaks of the Pitons.

AREA: 616sq km (238sq mi)
POPULATION: 155,996
CAPITAL (POPULATION): Castries (62,967)
GOVERNMENT: Constitutional monarchy
ETHNIC GROUPS: Black African 90%, mixed race 6%, European and East Indian 4%
LANGUAGES: English (official), French patois
RELIGIONS: Roman Catholic 80%, Seventh-Day Adventist 7%, Anglican 3%, Hindu 1%
NATIONAL MOTTO: "The Land, the People, the Light"
NATIONAL ANTHEM (DATE): "Sons and Daughters of Saint Lucia" (1967)

HISTORY

Euopeans discovered the island around 1500. In 1605 and 1638 the **Caribs** successfully resisted English attempts at colonization. In 1660 **France** signed a treaty with the Carib. The French built the first town, **Soufriere**, in 1746. The **British** attempted to capture the island at the **Battle of Cul de Sac** (1778). The British and French established **sugar plantations** using **slave labour** from Africa. After a series of conflicts, Britain gained Saint Lucia by the Treaty of Paris (1814). Saint Lucia achieved **self-government** in 1967, and full **independence** in 1979. **John Compton** was Prime Minister from 1964 to 1979 and from 1982 to 1996.

The banded butterflyfish lives on the coral reefs surrounding Saint Lucia.

SAINT VINCENT AND THE GRENADINES

FLAG RATIO: 2:3 **USE:** National/Civil **DATE ADOPTED:** 1985 **LAST MODIFIED:** 1985

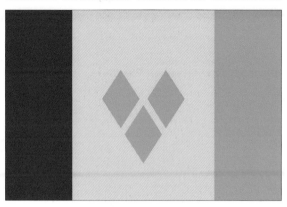

Saint Vincent and the Grenadines has a **tricolour** of **vertical stripes** of blue, yellow, and green. At the centre of the flag are **three green diamonds** in the shape of a letter 'V' for Vincent. The diamonds define the islands as "the gems of the Antilles". Blue represents the tropical sky and crystal clear waters around the nation. Yellow stands for the golden sands of the Grenadines, and green recalls the islands' lush vegetation. From 1979 to 1985 the flag had the coat of arms on a breadfruit leaf in the centre.

HISTORY

The nation consists of the volcanic island of **Saint Vincent** and the five islands of the **Grenadine** group, the best known of which is **Mustique**. Saint Vincent was probably visited and named by **Christopher Columbus** in 1498. The native **Carib** fiercely resisted settlement until the **British** established a colony in 1762. After a revolt in 1795, the British deported most of the Carib and imported **slave labour** from Africa. Saint Vincent and the Grenadines formed part of the British colony of the **Windward Islands** from 1833 to 1958 and of the **West Indies Federation** from 1958 to 1962. It gained self-government in 1969, and **independence** in 1979. **James Fitz-Allen Mitchell** was Prime Minister from 1972 to 1974 and 1984 to 2000.

AREA: 388sq km (150sq mi)
POPULATION: 128,000
CAPITAL (POPULATION): Kingstown (17,400)
GOVERNMENT: Constitutional monarchy
ETHNIC GROUPS: Black African 66%,
mixed race 19%, East Indian 6%, Carib 2%
LANGUAGES: English, French patois
RELIGIONS: Methodist 20%, Roman Catholic
10%, Seventh-Day Adventist 7%
NATIONAL MOTTO: *"Pax et Justitia"*
"Peace and Justice"
NATIONAL ANTHEM (DATE): "St Vincent! Land
so Beautiful" (1969)

Forestry logo of Saint Vincent and the Grenadines. Forest covers 30% of St Vincent.

SAMOA

FLAG RATIO: 1:2   USE: National/Civil   DATE ADOPTED: 1948   LAST MODIFIED: 1949

Samoa's national flag has a **red field** and a **blue canton** with **five white stars**. It adopted the national flag in 1948, but with four stars instead of five. A fifth was added in 1949 as a representation of the **Southern Cross**. It is common for countries in the southern hemisphere to use the constellation as a motif. The three colours stand for courage (red), purity (white), and freedom (blue).

HISTORY

First settled in *c.*1000, the islands are the cradle of **Polynesian** culture. Dutch navigator **Jacob Roggeveen** sighted the island in 1722, and **Louis Antoine de Bougainville** claimed them for France in 1768. European colonialism brought conflict and disease. British missionaries arrived in the 1830s, and soon converted the native population to **Christianity**. In 1899 **Western Samoa** became a **German Protectorate**, and the **United States** annexed Eastern Samoa (now **American Samoa**). In 1914 **New Zealand** seized Western Samoa, and the League of Nations mandated it to New Zealand in 1920. In 1929 New Zealand troops killed 11 members of the **Mau**, a passive resistance movement. In 1946 Western Samoa became a trust territory of New Zealand. In 1962 Western Samoa became the first Polynesian nation to gain **independence**. In 1997 it changed its name to **Samoa**.

AREA: 2840sq km (1097sq mi)

POPULATION: 171,000

CAPITAL (POPULATION): Apia (36,000)

GOVERNMENT: Constitutional monarchy under native chief

ETHNIC GROUPS: Samoan 93%, Euronesians (mixed European and Polynesian) 7%

LANGUAGES: Samoan (Polynesian), English

RELIGIONS: Congregational 43%, Roman Catholic 21%, Methodist 17%, Latter-Day Saints 10%, Seventh-Day Adventist 3%

NATIONAL ANTHEM (DATE): "The Banner of Freedom" (1962)

The many-coloured fruit dove *is a rare bird, found only in Polynesia.*

San Marino officially adopted its bicolour flag of **blue** and **white** **horizontal stripes** in 1862. It was first mentioned in 1797, after Napoleon's invasion of Italy. The colours originate from earlier versions of the state's coat of arms, which lies at the centre of the flag. The **coat of arms** features the **three peaks** and castle towers of Monte Titano, San Marino's highest mountain. An **ostrich feather** tops each tower. The upper white stripe symbolizes the snow covered peaks of Titano. The blue stripe represents the sky. San Marino also flies a **civil flag** without the coat of arms.

HISTORY

San Marino is the world's second smallest republic (after Nauru). According to legend, it was founded in the early 4th century AD, when a Christian stonemason named **Marinus the Dalmatian** fled there to escape the Roman Emperor Diocletian. Saint Marinus established a small Christian community on **Monte Titano**. The area became an independent commune in the 13th century. Until the 15th century, San Marino consisted solely of Mount Titano when **Pope Pius II** gave San Marino the towns of Fiorentino, Montegiardino, Serravalle, and Faetano. While San Marino has its own currency and stamps, Italian and Vatican equivalents are widely used. It possesses its own legislative assembly, the Great and General Council, which elects Captains Regent as heads of state.

The towers of the three fortresses on Monte Titano are the symbol of San Marino.

AREA: 61sq km (24sq mi)
POPULATION: 27,100
CAPITAL (POPULATION): San Marino (4400)
GOVERNMENT: Multi-party republic
ETHNIC GROUPS: Sammarinese, Italian
LANGUAGES: Italian
RELIGIONS: Roman Catholic 95%
NATIONAL MOTTO: "*Libertas*" "Liberty"
NATIONAL ANTHEM (DATE): "*Inno Nazionale*" "National Anthem" (1894)

SÃO TOMÉ AND PRÍNCIPE

FLAG RATIO: 1:2 **USE:** National/Civil **DATE ADOPTED:** 1975 **LAST MODIFIED:** 1975

São Tomé and Príncipe's national flag derives from the banner of the *Movimento de Liberacion de São Tomé and Príncipe* (MLSP), which led the struggle for liberation. The flag uses the **Pan-African** colours of **green**, **red**, and **yellow**. The **two five-pointed black stars** represent the islands of São Tome and Príncipe.

HISTORY

In *c*.1470 **Portugal** discovered the small (uninhabited) islands, and they built a settlement on **São Tomé** (Portuguese, 'Saint Thomas') in 1485. In 1522 the islands became a Portuguese colony. The **Dutch** controlled the islands from 1641 to 1740, but Portugal regained control and brought **slaves** from the African mainland to work on the **sugar plantations**. After the collapse of the sugar market, **Príncipe** (Portuguese, 'Prince') served as Portugal's staging post in the **slave trade** to Brazil. In 1822 Portugal introduced **cacao**, and São Tome soon became a leading world producer. In 1975 a military coup forced Portugal to grant **independence** to the islands. President **Manuel Pinto da Costa**, who ruled from 1975 to 1991, pursued a broadly communist agenda. In 1991 **Miguel Trovada** won the nation's first democratic elections. In 1995 Príncipe received **autonomy**. **Fradique de Menezes**, a wealthy cocoa exporter, became president in 2001 elections.

AREA: 1001sq km (387sq mi)
POPULATION: 151,000
CAPITAL (POPULATION): São Tomé (52,300)
GOVERNMENT: Multi-party republic
ETHNIC GROUPS: *Mestico, Angolares* (both Angolan slave descendants), *Forros* (freed slave descendants), *Servicais* (contract labourers), *Tongas* (*Servicais* descendants)
LANGUAGES: Portuguese (official)
RELIGIONS: Roman Catholic 83%, Protestant 15%, traditional African beliefs 1%
NATIONAL MOTTO: "*Unidade, Disciplina, Trabalho*" "Unity, Discipline, Work"
NATIONAL ANTHEM (DATE): "*Independência Total*" "Total Independence" (1975)

In 2000 São Tome celebrated the third anniversary of cooperation with China.

164

Saudi Arabia's flag consists of a **green field** with **Arabic script** and a **sword** pointing towards the hoist. The Arabic writing is the *shahada*, the profession of Muslim faith: "There is no God but Allah, and Muhammad is his Prophet". **Green** is a traditional colour of **Islam** and the Wahhabi sect. The *shahada* on a green field derives from the late 18th-century flag of the Wahhabi movement. In 1902 Ibn Saud became King of the Nejd, and added a sword to the flag. In 1973 the Saudi constitution defined the flag.

HISTORY

In 570 Prophet **Muhammad** was born in **Mecca**, western Saudi Arabia. In the 18th century, the **Wahhabi** (a strict Islamic sect) won the support of the **Saud** family, who formed a state in **Nejd**. In 1810 **Turkey** conquered the region. In 1902 **Ibn Saud** captured **Riyadh**, and by 1906 he ruled the entire Nejd. In 1913 **Al Hasa** province fell. In 1920 Ibn Saud seized the **Asir**, and by 1925 he gained the whole of the **Hejaz**. In 1932 Ibn Saud formed the **Kingdom of Saudi Arabia**, ruling in line with the *sharia* of Wahhabi Islam. In 1953 Ibn Saud died. His son succeeded as King **Saud**. In 1964 Prince **Faisal** overthrew Saud. He was assassinated in 1975, and **Khalid** became King. Saudi Arabia supported Iraq in the **Iran-Iraq War** (1980–88), but backed the Allied coalition against Iraq in the **Gulf War** (1991). In 1982 Prince **Fahd** succeeded Khalid.

Stamp *marking the Muslim victory at the Battle of Badr (624), near Medina.*

AREA: 2,149,690sq km (829,995sq mi)
POPULATION: 22,147,500
CAPITAL (POPULATION): Riyadh (3,627,700)
GOVERNMENT: Absolute monarchy
ETHNIC GROUPS: Saudi 82%, Yemeni 10%, other Arab 3%
LANGUAGES: Arabic (official)
RELIGIONS: Wahhabi (Sunni) Muslim 95%, Shi'a Muslim 5%
NATIONAL ANTHEM (DATE): "*Aash Al Maleek*" "Long Live our Beloved King" (1950)

SENEGAL

FLAG RATIO: 2:3 USE: National/Civil DATE ADOPTED: 1960 LAST MODIFIED: 1960

Based on the French *tricolore*, the Senegalese flag consists of **three equal, horizontal stripes**. At the centre of the flag is a **green star**. It uses the **Pan-African** tricolour of **green, gold,** and **red**. Green is a traditional colour of **Islam**, but also stands for fertility and hope. Gold represents prosperity and the hard work of the Senegalese people. Red symbolizes the blood shed in the struggle for independence. The **five-pointed** star represents Senegal's place among the nations of the five continents.

AREA: 196,720sq km (75,954sq mi)

POPULATION: 8,762,000

CAPITAL (POPULATION): Dakar (1,968,300)

GOVERNMENT: Multi-party republic

ETHNIC GROUPS: Wolof 35%, Fulani (Peul) 18%, Serer 17%, Diola 9%, Tukulor 9%, Mandinka 3%, Soninke 1%

LANGUAGES: French (official), Wolof, Pulaar, Serer, Diola, Mandinka, Soninke

RELIGIONS: Sunni Muslim 93%, Roman Catholic 4%, African traditional beliefs 1%

NATIONAL MOTTO: "*Un Peuple, Un But, Une Foi*" "One People, One Target, One Faith"

NATIONAL ANTHEM (DATE): "*Pincez Tous vos Koras, Frappez les Balafons*" "Pluck Your Koras, Strike the Balafons" (1960)

HISTORY

From the 6th to 10th century, Senegal formed part of the **Empire of Ghana**. The **Tukulor** state of **Tekrur** dominated the Senegal valley from the 11th to the 14th century. The **Almoravid** dynasty of Berbers introduced **Islam**. In 1444 **Portuguese** sailors reached Cape Verde. In 1658 **France** built the port of **St Louis**. In 1765 Senegal became part of the **British** colony of **Senegambia**. France regained control in 1783, and Senegal joined **French West Africa** in 1895. In 1959 Senegal united with French Sudan (now **Mali**) to form the Federation of Mali. In 1960 Senegal withdrew from the union and became an **independent** republic. **Léopold Senghor** was president from 1960 to 1980. In 2000 elections, **Abdoulaye Wade** defeated **Abdou Diouf**, ending 40 years of socialist rule.

Senegalese *women often wear beautiful cotton dresses and elegant headscarves.*

166

The Seychelles' flag consists of **five oblique bands** of **blue, yellow, red, white**, and **green**. Blue represents the sea and sky around and above the Seychelles. Yellow stands for the islands' abundant sunshine. Red denotes the Seychellois and their united determination for future prosperity. White symbolizes justice and harmony. Green represents the land. From 1976 to 1977 the Seychelles' flag had a white saltire dividing triangles of blue (top and bottom) and red (hoist and fly). From 1997 to 1996 the flag had red, green and white horizontal wavy bands.

HISTORY

In 1502 **Vasco da Gama** explored the islands and named them the "Seven Sisters". **France** colonized the islands in 1756, establishing **spice plantations** worked by slaves from Mauritius. The **British** captured the archipelago (1794) during the Napoleonic Wars and, in 1814, it became a dependency of **Mauritius**. In 1903 the Seychelles became a separate Crown Colony. In 1976 the islands gained **independence**. In 1977 a coup established **Albert René** as President. In 1981 South African mercenaries attempted to overthrow the government. Continued civil unrest and another failed coup (1987) led to the first **multi-party elections** in 1991. In 1998 René secured a fifth consecutive term as President.

The male Seychelles sunbird has a curved beak, blue throat, and yellow pectoral tufts.

AREA: 453sq km (175sq mi)
POPULATION: 75,000
CAPITAL (POPULATION): Victoria (22,800)
GOVERNMENT: Multi-party republic
ETHNIC GROUPS: Seychellois Creole (European, Asian, and African) 96%
LANGUAGES: English (official), French (official), Creole (official)
RELIGIONS: Roman Catholic 90%, Anglican 8%, Hindu 1%
NATIONAL ANTHEM (DATE): *"Koste Seselwa"* "Come Together All Seychellois" (1996)

SIERRA LEONE

FLAG RATIO: 2:3 USE: National/Civil DATE ADOPTED: 1961 LAST MODIFIED: 1961

Sierra Leone has a **tricolour** flag of **green**, **white** and **blue horizontal stripes**. Green represents the nation's agriculture and its lush mountain slopes. Blue stands for the waters of the Adriatic that lap Sierra Leone's coast. White symbolizes the desire for peace, justice and unity.

HISTORY

In 1460 **Portuguese** sailors reached the coast. In the 16th century Sierra Leone was a source for **slaves**. In 1787 the British Anti-Slavery Society founded **Freetown** as a settlement for freed slaves. In 1808 the settlement became a **British Crown Colony**. Britain made the interior a **Protectorate** in 1896. In 1951 the Protectorate and Colony united. In 1961 Sierra Leone gained **independence**. Sir **Milton Margai** was the nation's first prime minister. In 1971 Sierra Leone became a **republic**. From 1992 to 1999 **civil war** between the government and the Revolutionary United Front (RUF) claimed *c*.10,000 lives. Ahmed Kabbah became President in 1996 elections, but was deposed in a coup in 1997. He returned to power in 1999. In 2000 rebels, led by **Foday Sankoh** and backed by Liberia, abducted UN troops and renewed the war of terror. British soldiers captured Sankoh and disarmed the rebels in 2002.

AREA: 71,740sq km (27,699sq mi)
POPULATION: 4,768,900
CAPITAL (POPULATION): Freetown (1,032,100)
GOVERNMENT: Multi-party republic
ETHNIC GROUPS: Temne 30%, Mende 30%, Krio (Creole) 10%
LANGUAGES: English, Krio, Temne, Mende, and 15 other indigenous languages
RELIGIONS: African traditional beliefs 47%, Sunni Muslim 43%, Roman Catholic 3%
NATIONAL MOTTO: "Unity, Freedom, Justice"
NATIONAL ANTHEM (DATE): "High We Exalt Thee, Realm of the Free" (1961)

Jentink's duiker is an endangered small antelope found in Sierra Leone.

S ingapore first hoisted its **bicolour** flag in 1959, and retained it when breaking away from the Federation of Malaysia in 1963. It consists of a **red horizontal stripe**, symbolizing brotherhood and equality, and a **white horizontal stripe**, representing purity and virtue. The **crescent moon** denotes the emergence of the new nation, while the **five stars** stand for the five ideals of democracy, peace, justice, progress, and equality.

HISTORY

According to legend, Singapore was founded in 1299. It was first called Temasak (Sea Town), but was renamed **Singapura** (City of the Lion). In 1819 Sir **Thomas Stamford Raffles** of the **British East India Company** leased the island from **Johor**, and the Company founded the city of Singapore. In 1826 Singapore, Pinang, and Malacca formed the **Straits Settlement**. **Japan** seized the island in 1942, but British rule returned in 1945. In 1946 the Straits Settlement dissolved and Singapore became a separate colony. In 1959 Singapore won **self-government**. In 1963 it became part of the **Federation of Malaysia**, but separated to become an **independent republic** in 1965. **The People's Action Party (PAP)** has ruled Singapore since 1959. **Lee Kuan Yew** was Prime Minister from 1959 to 1990. **Goh Chok Tong** succeeded him.

AREA: 618sq km (239 sq mi)

POPULATION: 4,017,733

CAPITAL (POPULATION): Singapore City (2,812,000)

GOVERNMENT: Multi-party republic

ETHNIC GROUPS: Chinese 77%, Malay 14%, Indian 8%

LANGUAGES: English, Mandarin and other Chinese dialects, Malay, Tamil

RELIGIONS: Buddhist 41%, Christian 18%, Muslim 17%, Taoist 13%, Hindu 5%,

NATIONAL MOTTO: "*Majulah Singapura*" "May Singapore Prosper"

NATIONAL ANTHEM (DATE): "*Majulah Singapura*" "May Singapore Prosper" (1959)

The trishaw is a traditional form of transportation in Singapore.

169

SLOVAK REPUBLIC

FLAG RATIO: 2:3 **USE:** National/Civil **DATE ADOPTED:** 1992 **LAST MODIFIED:** 1992

Slovakia has a **tricolour** flag of **white, blue**, and **red horizontal stripes**. It first adopted a white, blue and red flag in 1848, and the present order of colours first appeared in 1868. As part of Czechoslovakia from 1919 to 1991, Slovakia used the flag currently flown by the **Czech Republic**. In 1992, after the break-up of Czechoslavakia, the present flag was officially adopted. The **coat of arms**, set slightly toward the hoist, was added to distinguish the flag from that of Russia. The coat of arms is taken from part of the Hungarian arms, and shows a **double cross** set on **three hills** to commemorate the arrival of Christianity to the Carpathian region in the 9th century. Red, white and blue are **Pan-Slavic** colours.

HISTORY

Slavic peoples settled in the region in the 5th and 6th centuries AD. Conquered by the **Magyars** in the 10th century, **Hungary** dominated the region for about 900 years. The **Austro-Hungarian Empire** emerged in 1867. After the defeat of Austria-Hungary in World War I, Slovakia became an autonomous region of **Czechoslovakia**. The Czechs dominated the union, and many Slovaks became dissatisfied. In 1939 Slovakia gained nominal independence as a Protectorate of **Nazi Germany**. In 1945 it returned to Czechoslovakia. In 1993 the federation dissolved, and Slovakia gained **independence**. Vladimír Mečiar was the first Prime Minister.

AREA: 49,035sq km (18,932sq mi)
POPULATION: 5,379,455
CAPITAL (POPULATION): Bratislava (428,672)
GOVERNMENT: Multi-party republic
ETHNIC GROUPS: Slovaks 86%, Hungarians 10%, Roma 2%, Czechs 1%
LANGUAGES: Slovak (official), Hungarian
RELIGIONS: Roman Catholic 69%, Evangelical Lutheran 6%, Greek Orthodox 4%
NATIONAL ANTHEM (DATE): "*Nad Tatrou sa Blyská*" "Storm above the Tatras" (1993)

Folk clothing from Detva, *central Slovakia, includes wide linen trousers and a fur cloak.*

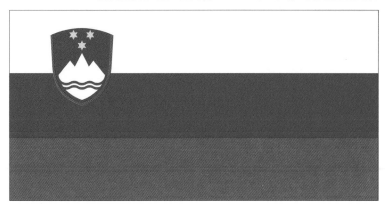

Slovenia's **tricolour** flag derives from the historical flag of the Duchy of Carniola (1848–1918). Blue, white and red are **Pan-Slavic** colours. On the upper hoist of the flag is the **coat of arms,** designed in 1991. The arms is a **shield** featuring a stylized depiction of the **three peaks** of Mount Triglav in **white** on a **blue background**. The **two wavy blue lines** below Triglav symbolize the **Adriatic Sea**. Above Triglav are **three six-pointed gold stars** in the pattern of a triangle. The stars derive from the coat of arms of the County of Celje, which united much of Slovenia in the Middle Ages.

HISTORY

The Slovenes, the western branch of the **South Slavs**, established a kingdom in the 7th century. From the 10th century they were enserfed by German lords. From the 13th century until 1918, the **Austrian Habsburgs** ruled Slovenia. In 1918 Slovenia became part of the **Kingdom of the Serbs, Croats, and Slovenes**, renamed **Yugoslavia** in 1929. During World War II, Slovenia was invaded and partitioned between Italy, Germany, and Hungary. After the war, Slovenia returned to Yugoslavia. In 1990 **Milan Kucan** led a non-communist government. In 1991 Slovenia declared **independence**, which led to brief fighting between the Slovenes and the Federal Yugoslav Army. In 1996 Slovenia applied to join the European Union (EU).

AREA: 20,251sq km (7817sq mi)

POPULATION: 1,990,094

CAPITAL (POPULATION): Ljubljana (270,500)

GOVERNMENT: Multi-party republic

ETHNIC GROUPS: Slovenes 88%, Croats 3%, Serbs 2%, Bosnians 2%

LANGUAGES: Slovene (official). Hungarian, Italian, Italian

RELIGIONS: Roman Catholic 71% (including Uniate 2%), Lutheran 1%, Muslim 1%

NATIONAL ANTHEM (DATE): *"Zdravljica"* "A Toast" (1990)

Decorated honey-cake ('loški' *or* 'mali kruhek') *is a traditional gift for Epiphany.*

SOLOMON ISLANDS

FLAG RATIO: 1:2 **USE:** National/Civil **DATE ADOPTED:** 1977 **LAST MODIFIED:** 1977

Solomon Islands' flag consists of a **blue right-angled triangle** and a **green right-angled triangle**, separated by a **yellow diagonal stripe**. On the hoist are **five white five-pointed stars**. Blue represents the Pacific Ocean around the islands. Green stands for the islands' lush vegetation. Yellow denotes the abundant sunshine of Melanesia. The five stars represent the five districts of the Solomon Islands at the time of the flag's adoption.

HISTORY

The Solomon Islands are spread across more than 1400 kilometres (900 miles) of the **Pacific Ocean**. **Spain** discovered the islands in 1568. The indigenous **Melanesians** resisted colonization until the late 19th century. In 1893 the southern islands became a **British Protectorate**. **Germany** controlled the northern islands from 1895. In 1900 Germany ceded its territory to Britain. During World War I, **Australian** troops occupied Bougainville and Buka (now part of **Papua New Guinea**), and the League of Nations mandated them to Australia in 1920. In 1942 the **Japanese** occupied the southern islands. In 1944, after heavy fighting, particularly on **Guadalcanal**, United States' troops liberated the islands. In 1976 the Solomon Islands achieved **self-government**, as a prelude to full **independence** in 1978. The Solomon Islands belong to the **Commonwealth of Nations**.

AREA: 27,900sq km (10,800sq mi)
POPULATION: 429,000
CAPITAL (POPULATION): Houiara (52,900)
GOVERNMENT: Constitutional monarchy
ETHNIC GROUPS: Melanesian 93%, Polynesian 4%, Micronesian 2%, European 1%
LANGUAGES: English (official), 90 vernaculars (including Solomon Islands pidgin)
RELIGIONS: Anglican 35%, Roman Catholic 19%, South Sea Evangelical 17%, United Church (Methodist) 11%, Seventh-Day Adventist 10%
NATIONAL MOTTO: "To Lead is to Serve"
NATIONAL ANTHEM (DATE): "God Save Our Solomon Islands" (1978)

Solomon Islanders use kastom *or custom dances to tell stories about the past.*

FLAG RATIO: 2:3 USE: National/Civil DATE ADOPTED: 1954 LAST MODIFIED: 1954

In 1954 Italian Somaliland adopted the current flag. The **blue** derived from the colour of the United Nations' (UN) flag – Italian Somaliland was a UN Trust Territory from 1950 to 1960. The **white five-pointed star** represents the five regions inhabited by Somali people (north and south Somalia, Djibouti, southern Ethiopia, and northern Kenya). White symbolizes peace and prosperity.

HISTORY

In the 7th century, Arab traders established coastal settlements and introduced **Islam**. The interest of European imperial powers increased after the opening of the **Suez Canal** in 1869. In 1887 **Britain** established a **Protectorate** in northern Somalia. By 1905, **Italy** controlled central and southern Somalia. In 1936 Italian Somaliland united with the Somali regions of **Ethiopia** to form **Italian East Africa**. In 1950 Italian Somaliland became a United Nations' (UN) Trust Territory, administered by Italy. In 1960 it united with British Somaliland to form an **independent** Somalia. In 1969 **Siad Barre** led a military coup, and Somalia became an Islamic republic. In 1991 Barre was overthrown, former **British Somaliland** declared independence, and Somalia disintegrated into civil war between rival clans. UN forces failed to restore peace but provided **famine** relief. In 1998 Puntland became self-governing. A **transitional** national government, the first for nine years, took office in 2000.

Somalia's coat of arms, shown on this stamp, is two leopards holding a shield.

AREA: 637,660sq km (246,201sq mi)
POPULATION: 11,101,800
CAPITAL (POPULATION): Mogadishu (1,183,100)
GOVERNMENT: Transitional
ETHNIC GROUPS: Somali 85%, non-Somali (Bantu and Arabs) 15%
LANGUAGES: Somali and Arabic (both official), English, Italian
RELIGIONS: Sunni Muslim 99%
NATIONAL ANTHEM (DATE): (2000)

SOUTH AFRICA

FLAG RATIO: 2:3 **USE:** National/Civil **DATE ADOPTED:** 1994 **LAST MODIFIED:** 1994

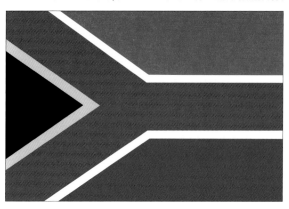

South Africa adopted a new flag after the **African National Congress** (ANC) won the country's first multi-racial elections in 1994. The flag combines the **black**, **green**, and **yellow** colours of the ANC with the **red**, **white**, and **blue** of the former colonial powers, **Britain** and the **Netherlands**. The Y-shape on the flag symbolises convergence and a united future.

HISTORY

The indigenous people are the **San**. In 1652 the **Dutch East India Company** founded a colony at Table Bay. Dutch **Afrikaners** (or **Boers**) established farms, employing slaves. In the early 19th century, **Britain** gained control of the Cape region. In 1833 the Boers embarked on the **Great Trek**. Britain defeated the **Zulu** in the **Zulu War** (1879) and the Boers in the **South African Wars** (1880–81, 1899–1902). In 1910 the **Union of South Africa** was formed, and won **independence** in 1931. In 1948 the Nationalist government adopted its racist policy of **apartheid**. The **ANC** resisted and its leader, **Nelson Mandela**, was jailed from 1964 to 1990. In 1994 he became president of the multiracial democracy. **Thabo Mbeki** succeeded him in 1999.

AREA: 1,219,916sq km (470,566sq mi)
POPULATION: 45,129,400
CAPITAL (POPULATION): Pretoria (executive, 1,228,200), Cape Town (legislative, 2,686,000), Bloemfontein (judicial, 371,200)
GOVERNMENT: Multi-party republic
ETHNIC GROUPS: Black 75%, White 14%, Coloured 9%, Asian 2%
LANGUAGES: Afrikaans, English, Ndebele, Sotho, Pedi, Swazi, Tsonga, Tswana, Venda, Xhosa, Zulu (all official)
RELIGIONS: Dutch Reformed 13%, traditional African beliefs 13%, Zion Christian 4%, Anglican 3%, Roman Catholic 3%, Methodist 3%, Lutheran 3%, Muslim 2%, Hindu 1%
NATIONAL ANTHEM (DATE): "The National Anthem of South Africa" (1995)

Thabo Mbeki *replaced Nelson Mandela as President of South Africa in 1999.*

174

Spain has a **bicolour** flag of **horizontal stripes** (two red, one yellow). The colours probably derive from its historic kingdoms. In 1785 King Charles III adopted the bicolour flag as the war ensign. In 1843 it became the state flag. From 1931 to 1939, Spain had a tricolour of red, yellow and purple. The **coat of arms** at the centre of the flag last changed in 1981. The **shield**, topped by a crown and flanked by **pillars**, features the **arms** of the regions of **Castile, León, Navarre,** and **Granada.** Wrapped around the pillars is a banner with the national motto.

HISTORY

Iberians and **Basques** were Spain's early inhabitants. In 1483 **Ferdinand V** and **Isabella I** launched the **Inquisition.** In 1492 the **reconquest** of Granada ended **Moorish** rule in Spain. **Christopher Columbus'** discovery of America (1492) helped Spain become the leading imperial power. In 1519 Charles I became Holy Roman Emperor **Charles V.** The accession of **Bourbon** King **Philip V** provoked the War of the **Spanish Succession** (1700–14). In 1923 **Primo de Rivera** formed a dictatorship. **General Franco's** victory in the **Spanish Civil War** (1936–39) crushed the **second republic.** Franco's dictatorship lasted until his death in 1975, when a constitutional monarchy emerged under **Juan Carlos.** In 1977 the Basque Country *(Pais Vasco)*, Catalonia and Galicia gained limited autonomy.

***Paper maché giants** parade at the September festival of La Mercé, Barcelona.*

AREA: 504,780sq km (194,896sq mi)
POPULATION: 40,974,359
CAPITAL (POPULATION): Madrid (2,957,058)
GOVERNMENT: Constitutional monarchy
ETHNIC GROUPS: Castilian Spanish 72%, Catalan 16%, Galician 8%, Basque 2%
LANGUAGES: Castilian Spanish (official), Catalan, Galician, Basque
RELIGIONS: Roman Catholic 97%
NATIONAL MOTTO: "*Plus Ultra*" "More Beyond"
NATIONAL ANTHEM (DATE): "*Marcha Real*" "Royal March" (1942)

SRI LANKA

FLAG RATIO: 1:2 USE: National/Civil DATE ADOPTED: 1951 LAST MODIFIED: 1978

In legend, Sri Lanka's 'Lion Flag' dates back to around 486 BC, when Prince Vijaya arrived on the shores of Sri Lanka. The last king to use the flag was Sri Vikrama Rajasinghe, whose reign ended in 1815. The **yellow border** represents the *Maha Singha*, chief advisers to the king. The **yellow lion holding a sword** in its right paw denotes justice and righteousness. The **crimson field** symbolizes immortality. The **four bo leaves** represent the four **Brahma *Viharana***, standards for Buddhist living: *metta, karuna, muditha, upeksha* (compassion, kindness, joy in others' prosperity, equanimity). The **vertical stripes** of **green** and **saffron** stand for the minority communities of Muslims and Tamils respectively.

AREA: 65,610sq km (25,332sq mi)
POPULATION: 16,864,544
CAPITAL (POPULATION): Colombo (642,020)
GOVERNMENT: Multi-party republic
ETHNIC GROUPS: Sinhalese 74%, Tamil 18%, Moor (Yonaka) 7%
LANGUAGES: Sinhala and Tamil (both official)
RELIGIONS: Theravada Buddhist 69%, Hindu 15%, Christian 8%, Muslim 7%
NATIONAL ANTHEM (DATE): "*Sri Lanka Matha*" "Mother Sri Lanka" (1952)

HISTORY

Sinhalese settlers made the island a centre of **Theravada Buddhism**. In the 14th century **Tamils** formed a **Hindu** kingdom in north-east Sri Lanka. The **Portuguese** landed in 1505. In 1658 Portuguese lands passed to the **Dutch East India Company**. In 1815 Britain captured the kingdom of **Kandy**, completing its control of the island. In 1948 Ceylon gained independence. **Don Senanayake** was the first prime minister. In 1959 Prime Minister **Solomon Bandaranaike** was assassinated and his widow, **Sirimavo**, became the world's first woman prime minister. Their daughter, **Chandrika Kumaratunga**, became president in 1993. In 1972 Ceylon became the republic of Sri Lanka ('Resplendent Island'). In 1983 the **Tamil Tigers** began a **civil war** that has claimed more than 40,000 lives.

Galle, south-west Sri Lanka, is a centre of lacemaking, a craft introduced by the Dutch.

SUDAN

FLAG RATIO: 1:2 USE: National/Civil DATE ADOPTED: 1970 LAST MODIFIED: 1970

Sudan's flag uses the red, white, black and green colours of the **Pan-Arab** movement. The **red stripe** symbolizes the blood shed in the struggle for freedom. The **white stripe** represents Islam, Sudan's dominant religion. The **black stripe** stands for the Mahdist revolution that briefly freed Sudan from colonial rule in the late 19th century. The **green triangle** at the hoist denotes prosperity. The **presidential flag** has the **coat of arms** in the middle of the white stripe. The arms feature a **secretary bird** with a **shield** on its breast. Above the bird is a **scroll** bearing the **national motto**.

HISTORY

Sudan is Africa's largest country by area. From the 11th century BC to *c*.AD 350, it formed part of the Kingdom of **Kush**. **Christianity** was introduced in the 6th century. In the 13th century, northern Sudan came under Muslim control. In 1821 **Muhammed Ali**'s Egyptian forces occupied northern Sudan. In 1881 **Muhammad Ahmad** declared himself the **Mahdi** and led a Muslim rising against colonial rule. In 1898 British **General Kitchener** defeated the Mahdists at **Omdurman**. The colony of **Anglo-Egyptian Sudan** emerged in 1899. In 1956 Sudan gained **independence**. Civil war broke out between the government, dominated by northern Muslims, and the mainly Christian south. **Gaafar Nimeiri** ruled from 1969 to 1985. In 1989 **Omar al-Bashir** came to power in a military coup. The US imposed **sanctions** on al-Bashir's regime in 1997.

AREA: 2,505,810sq km (967,493 sq mi)
POPULATION: 36,841,500
CAPITAL (POPULATION): Khartoum (1,244,500)
GOVERNMENT: Military regime
ETHNIC GROUPS: Sudanese Arab 49%, Dinka 12%, Nuba 8%, Beja 6%, Nuer 5%, Azande 3%
LANGUAGES: Arabic (official)
RELIGIONS: Sunni Muslim 73%, traditional beliefs 17%, Roman Catholic 4%, Protestant 2%
NATIONAL MOTTO: "*Al Nadr Nila*"
"Victory is Ours"
NATIONAL ANTHEM: "*Nahnu Djundullah*"
"We Are God's Army"

Sudan belongs to the Common Market for Eastern and Southern Africa (COMESA).

SURINAME

FLAG RATIO: 2:3   **USE:** National/Civil   **LAST MODIFIED:** 1975   **COAT OF ARMS:** 1975

Suriname's consists of **five coloured bands** and a **yellow, five-pointed star** at the centre of the middle band. The star symbolizes national unity – each point represents one of Suriname's five main ethnic groups. **Yellow** denotes Suriname's golden future. The **red stripe** stands for progress and the struggle for a better life. The **two green stripes** signify hope and fertility. The **two white stripes** symbolize freedom and justice. The presidential flag replaces the star with the **coat of arms** and **national motto**.

HISTORY

In 1499 Spanish explorer Alfonso de Ojeda reached Suriname's coast, but the **British** founded the first colony in 1651. In 1667 Britain ceded it to **Holland** in exchange for New Amsterdam (now New York City). It became known as **Dutch Guiana**. Most of the population are either descendants from **African slaves** brought over in the 17th and 18th centuries, or descendants of **Indian** and **Indonesian indentured labourers** who arrived in the 19th century. Suriname became autonomous in 1954, and gained full **independence** in 1975. In 1980 the **army** seized control and Suriname plunged into **civil war**. Civilian rule returned in 1991. **Ronald Venetiaan** served as president from 1991 to 1996. He was re-elected in 2000.

AREA: 163,270sq km (63,069 sq mi)
POPULATION: 434,000
CAPITAL (POPULATION): Paramaribo (200,970)
GOVERNMENT: Multi-party republic
ETHNIC GROUPS: Indian 37%, Creole, 31%, Indonesian 14%, Black 9%, Native American 3%, Chinese 3%, Dutch 1%
LANGUAGES: Dutch (official), Sranan
RELIGIONS: Hindu 27%, Roman Catholic 23%, Javanese Muslim 20%, Protestant 19%
NATIONAL MOTTO: "*Justitia, Pietas, Fides*" "Justice, Faith, Loyalty"
NATIONAL ANTHEM (DATE): "*God zij met ons Suriname*" "God Bless Our Suriname" (1959)

In 2000 Suriname issued this stamp to mark 25 years of independence.

SWAZILAND

FLAG RATIO: 2:3 USE: National/Civil DATE ADOPTED: 1968 LAST MODIFIED: 1968

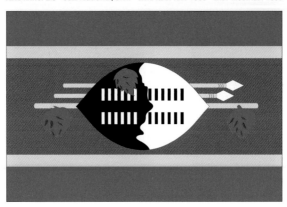

In 1941 King Sobhuza II gave a flag to the Emasotsha Regiment, a Swazi pioneer corps that fought in World War II. Swaziland's present flag is identical to that flag, except for the absence of a lion. It consists of **five horizontal stripes** and a central stylized depiction of a native oxhide **shield** with **two spears** and a **fighting staff**. From the staff and the shield hang tassels, symbols of the Swazi monarchy. The shield, staff and spear represent the defence of Swaziland. The **black and white** shield symbolizes racial harmony. The **blue stripes** denote peace. The **yellow stripes** stand for the nation's mineral wealth. The **red stripe** symbolizes the blood shed in past struggles.

HISTORY

In the 1840s, under attack from the **Zulu**, the Swazi sought **British** protection. In 1894 the British and **Boers** put Swaziland under the authority of the **Transvaal**. Britain took control at the end of the second **South African War** (1899–1902). In 1968 Swaziland gained **independence** with **King Sobhuza II** as head of state. In 1973 Sobhuza II assumed supreme power. He banned all political parties in 1978. In 1982 Sobhuza II died. His son, Makhosetive, became **King Mswati III** in 1986. Economically, Swaziland is heavily dependent on **South Africa**.

Ligcebesha *is a traditional Swazi costume worn by men.*

AREA: 17,360sq km (6703 sq mi)
POPULATION: 965,859
CAPITAL (POPULATION): Mbabane (67,200)
GOVERNMENT: Absolute monarchy
ETHNIC GROUPS: Swazi 84%, Zulu 10%, Tsonga 2%
LANGUAGES: Siswati, English (both official)
RELIGIONS: Protestant 37%, African churches 29%, traditional African beliefs 21%, Roman Catholic 11%
NATIONAL MOTTO: "*Siyinquaba*" "We are a Fortress"
NATIONAL ANTHEM (DATE): "Oh God, Bestower of the Blessings of the Swazi" (1968)

179

SWEDEN

FLAG RATIO: 5:8 USE: National/Civil DATE ADOPTED: 1906 LAST MODIFIED: 1906

The exact age of the Swedish flag is unknown but records date back to the reign (1523–60) of **Gustaf I**. Its 'Scandinavian cross' design probably derives from the Danish flag, while the **blue** and **gold** colours possibly come from Sweden's Lesser **coat of arms**. Sweden has two coat of arms: the Greater (*c*.1440) and the more frequently used Lesser (*c*.1336). The Lesser is **blue** with three **gold crowns**. In the 17th century Sweden flew a **triple-tailed flag**. Today, the royal family use this flag. The King and Queen's flag has the greater coat of arms in the centre of the cross.

HISTORY

Swedes were probably among the **Vikings** who plundered Europe between the 9th and 11th centuries. In 1319 **Magnus VII** joined Sweden and Norway.

Sweden united with Denmark and Norway under Danish leadership in the **Kalmar Union** of 1389. In 1520 **Gustaf Vasa** led a rebellion and later was crowned King **Gustaf I** of independent Sweden. Gustaf made **Lutheranism** the state religion. **Gustaf II** swept through central **Germany** in the **Thirty Years' War** (1618–48). **Karl X**'s efforts to capture the **Baltic** led to the **First Northern War** (1655–60). **Karl XII** lost the **Great Northern War** (1700–21) with **Russia**. In 1809 Sweden lost **Finland** to Russia, but acquired Norway from Denmark in 1814. In 1905 the union between Sweden and Norway dissolved. Under **Gustaf V**, Sweden remained **neutral** in both World Wars. **Tage Fritiof Erlander** was prime minister from 1946 to 1969. **Karl XVI Gustaf** succeeded **Gustaf VI Adolf** as King in 1973. In 1995 Sweden joined the European Union (EU).

AREA: 449,960sq km (173,730sq mi)
POPULATION: 8,909,128
CAPITAL (POPULATION): Stockholm (754,948)
GOVERNMENT: Constitutional monarchy
ETHNIC GROUPS: Swedish 91%, Finnish 3%
LANGUAGES: Swedish (official), Finnish
RELIGIONS: Lutheran 89%, Roman Catholic 2%
NATIONAL ANTHEM (DATE): "Du gamla, du fria"
"Thou ancient, thou freeborn" (1880s)

Face of King Karl XII's watch. Karl XII ruled Sweden from 1697 to 1718.

SWITZERLAND

FLAG RATIO: 1:1   **USE:** National/Civil   **DATE ADOPTED:** 1848   **LAST MODIFIED:** 1889

The Swiss flag derives from Christian iconography, symbolizing the blood shed by Christian martyrs. The flag of the Holy Roman Empire was a **white cross** extending to the edges of a **red field**, and represented the Emperor's role as the protector of Christianity. In the 14th century, all the cantons of the Swiss Confederation placed a white cross on their battle flags. In 1815 the Confederation designed a state seal with a short white cross on a red field. In 1817 General Henri-Guillaume Dufour proposed a federal flag consisting of a stocky white cross made of five equal sized squares on a red field. In 1848 the Swiss Federation officially adopted this flag. In 1889 the Federal Assembly amended the flag, making the arms of the cross one-sixth longer than they were wide. The flag of the **International Red Cross**, based in Geneva, is the reverse of the Swiss flag: a red cross on white field.

HELVETIA 180

Reutigen, Bern, with the Niesen and Eiger, Monch and Jungfrau mountains behind.

HISTORY

In the 11th century, Switzerland unified as part of the **Holy Roman Empire**. In 1291 the **cantons** of **Schwyz**, **Uri**, and **Unterwalden** formed a league, which defeated the **Habsburgs** in 1315. In the mid-14th century, **Lucerne**, **Bern** and **Zürich** joined the **Swiss Confederation**. In 1815 the Confederation re-established. In 1848, after the **Sonderbund War**, Switzerland became a federal state. In 2002 Switzerland voted to join the UN.

AREA: 41,290sq km (15,942sq mi)
POPULATION: 7,258,500
CAPITAL (POPULATION): Bern (122,484)
GOVERNMENT: Federal multi-party republic
ETHNIC GROUPS: German 64%, French 19%, Italian 8%, Yugoslav 3%, Spanish 2%, Romansch 1%
LANGUAGES: French, German, Italian, Romansch (all official)
RELIGIONS: Roman Catholic 46%, Protestant 40%
MOTTO: "*Honor et Fidelitas*" "Honour and Fidelity"
NATIONAL ANTHEM (DATE): "*Schweizer Psalm*" (German) "*Cantique Suisse*" (French) "*Salmo Svizzero*" (Italian) "*Psalm Svizzer*" (Romansch) "The Swiss Anthem" (1961)

SYRIA

FLAG RATIO: 2:3 USE: National/Civil DATE ADOPTED: 1958 REINTRODUCED: 1980

Like many other Arab nations, Syria's flag derives from the banner raised by Hussein ibn Ali during the Arab Revolt (1916) against Ottoman rule. Red, white, black and green are **Pan-Arab** colours. **Black** represented the Abbasid dynasty from Baghdad. **White** stood for the Umayyad dynasty from Damascus. **Green** denoted the Fatimid dynasty from Morocco, and **red** was the colour of the Hashemite dynasty. In 1932 Syria adopted a green-white-black horizontal tricolour with three red five-pointed stars, representing Damascus, Aleppo, and Dayr az-Zawr. In 1958 Syria and Egypt joined to form the United Arab Republic (UAR), adopting a **red-white-black horizontal tricolour** with **two green stars**. In 1961 Syria reverted to the 1946 flag. In 1963 the Ba'ath Party seized power, and added a green star to the flag. In 1972 Syria, Egypt and Libya united to form the Federation of Arab Republics, replacing the stars with the hawk of Quraish. In 1980 Syria reverted to the UAR flag.

HISTORY

In 637 **Arabs** conquered Syria, introducing **Islam**. From 661 to 750 **Damascus** was the capital of the **Umayyad dynasty**. In 1516 Syria became part of the **Ottoman Empire.** In 1920 it was mandated to **France**. In 1941 Syria gained **independence**. **Union** with other Arab nations failed in 1961 and 1972. In 1967 Syria lost the **Golan Heights** to Israel. **Hafez al-Assad** seized power in 1970. In 2000 Assad died and was succeeded as President by his son, **Bashar al-Assad.**

AREA: 185,180sq km (71,498sq mi)
POPULATION: 17,826,000
CAPITAL (POPULATION): Damascus (1,394,322)
GOVERNMENT: Multi-party republic
ETHNIC GROUPS: Arab 89%, Kurd 6%
LANGUAGES: Arabic (official)
RELIGIONS: Sunni Muslim 80%,
Alawite Muslim 10%, Eastern Orthodox 5%,
Druze 3%, Roman Catholic 3%
NATIONAL ANTHEM (DATE): "*Homat el Diyar*"
"Guardians of the Homeland" (1936)

Altusi (1201–74) was a great Islamic astronomer and pioneer of trigonometry.

TAIWAN

FLAG RATIO: 1:2 USE: National/Civil DATE ADOPTED: 1928 LAST MODIFIED: 1928

In 1895 Lu Hao-Tung designed the 'white sun in a blue sky' on the canton of Taiwan's national flag as the emblem of the Hsing-chung Hui (Society for Regenerating China), founded by Sun Yat Sen. Shortly before the overthrow of the Qing dynasty in 1911, the Society added a crimson field to its flag. In 1912 the Society was renamed the Kuomintang. In 1928 the Kuomintang's flag became the flag of the Republic of China. The flag's colours represent Sun Yat Sen's "Three Principles of the People": crimson stands for nationalism, blue for democracy, and white for prosperity. The 12 points of the white sun represent the two 12-hour periods of the day, symbolizing unceasing progress. In 1949 Chinese communists defeated the nationalist Kuomintang, which founded a government-in-exile on the island of Taiwan. The Kuomintang flag became the national flag of Taiwan.

HISTORY

In 1590 the Portuguese landed on the island, which they named **Formosa** ('Beautiful'). The **Dutch** established the first European settlements in 1625. In 1685 the **Qing** dynasty of **China** captured Taiwan. **Japan** governed Taiwan from 1895 to 1945. In 1949 China became a communist republic and **Chiang Kai-shek**, leader of the Kuomintang, fled to Taiwan, where he formed the **Republic of China**. In 1975 Chiang Kai-shek's son, **Chiang Ching-kuo** became president. In 2000 **Chen Shui-ban** led the first non-Kuomintang government for 50 years.

AREA: 35,760sq km (13,800sq mi)
POPULATION: 22,167,159
CAPITAL (POPULATION): Taipei (2,639,939)
GOVERNMENT: Multi-party republic
ETHNIC GROUPS: Han Chinese 98%, indigenous tribal peoples 2%
LANGUAGES: Mandarin (official)
RELIGIONS: Chinese traditional religion (blend of Buddhism, Taoism, Confucianism) 90%, Roman Catholic 2%, Presbyterian 1%
NATIONAL ANTHEM (DATE): "*San Min Chu I*" "The Rights of the People" (1930)

中華民國郵票
REPUBLIC OF CHINA 5.00

***Spirit Way**, a stone ramp between two staircases, is a feature of Taiwan's architecture.*

TAJIKISTAN

FLAG RATIO: 1:2 **USE:** National/Civil **DATE ADOPTED:** 1992 **LAST MODIFIED:** 1992

In 1992 Tajikistan adopted a **tricolour** flag of red, white and green **horizontal stripes** to celebrate its newly won independence. Iran's flag has the same colours, indicating the strong historical links between the two nations. **Red** stands for the land and also recalls Tajikistan's communist past. **White** symbolizes cotton, Tajikistan's main agricultural export. **Green** represents agriculture, the nation's chief economic activity. At the centre of the flag is a **gold crown** under an arc of **seven gold stars**. From 1953 to 1992, under Soviet rule, the Tajik flag had four horizontal bands (red, white, green, red) and the hammer and sickle on the hoist.

HISTORY

Tajiks are descendants of **Iranians**, who settled in the area *c*.2500 years ago. In the 4th century BC, **Alexander the Great** conquered the region. Arabs captured Tajikistan in the 7th century AD, introducing **Islam**. The Tajik cities of **Bukhara** and **Samarkand** were vital centres of trade and Muslim learning. In the 9th century, Tajikistan fell to the **Iranian Empire**. **Tamerlane** made Samarkand his capital in the 14th century. From the 16th to the 19th century, Uzbeks ruled the area as the **Khanate of Bukhara**. **Russia** conquered the Khanate in 1868. After the Russian Revolution of 1917, Tajikistan became part of the **Soviet Union**. In 1991 Tajikistan gained **independence**. **Civil war** ensued, lasting five years and killing more than 20,000 people. **Emomali Rakhmonov** served as President from 1992 to date. Tajikistan belongs to the **Commonwealth of Independent States**.

AREA: 143,100sq km (55,520sq mi)
POPULATION: 6,331,500
CAPITAL (POPULATION): Dushanbe (580,800)
GOVERNMENT: Multi-party republic
ETHNIC GROUPS: Tajik 62%, Uzbek 24%, Russian 8%, Tatar 1%, Kyrgyz 1%
LANGUAGES: Tajik (official)
RELIGIONS: Sunni Muslim 80%, Shi'a Muslim 5%
NATIONAL ANTHEM (DATE): Untitled

Tajikistan is famous for its fine geometric carpets, such as this 19th-century example.

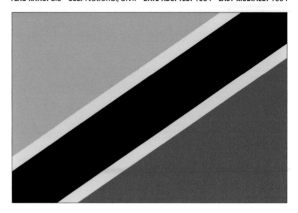

Tanzania's flag combines elements from the flags of the once separate lands of Tanganyika and Zanzibar. The **green triangle** came from the flag of Tanganyika. It symbolizes **agriculture**, the main economic activity. The **blue triangle** came from the flag of Zanzibar and represents the Indian Ocean. The **gold diagonal stripes** stand for the nation's mineral resources, principally diamonds. The central **black diagonal stripe** denotes Tanzania's people.

HISTORY

In 1498 **Vasco da Gama** became the first European to reach Tanzania. For the next 200 years, **Portugal** controlled coastal trade. In the 18th century, the island of **Zanzibar** was the main centre of the East African **ivory** and **slave trade**. In 1887 mainland Tanganyika became part of **German East Africa**.

Vanilla *is a climbing orchid. It flourishes on the 'spice island' of Zanzibar.*

Zanzibar became a **British Protectorate** in 1890. In 1919 the League of Nations mandated Tanganyika to Britain. In 1961 Tanganyika won **independence**. Julius **Nyerere** was the first President. Zanzibar gained independence in 1963. In 1964 Tanganyika and Zanzibar **unified** to form Tanzania. Nyerere issued the **Arusha Declaration** (1964). Tanzania helped Ugandan rebels topple Idi Amin in 1979. In 1985 **Ali Hassan Mwinyi** succeeded Nyerere as President. **Benjamin Mkapa** became president in 1995 elections.

AREA: 945,090sq km (364,899sq mi)
POPULATION: 33,917,600
CAPITAL (POPULATION): Dodoma (157,300)
GOVERNMENT: Multi-party republic
ETHNIC GROUPS: Sukuma 13%, Swahili 9%, Nyamwezi 4%, Haya 4%, Gogo 4%, Makonde 3%, Tumbuka 3%, Ha 2%, Hehe 2%, Nyaturu 2%, Ruguru 2%
LANGUAGES: Swahili, English (both official)
RELIGIONS: Muslim 35% (99% in Zanzibar), Roman Catholic 31%, Protestant 19%, traditional African beliefs 12%
MOTTO: "*Uhuru na Umoja*" "Peace and Unity"
NATIONAL ANTHEM (DATE): "*Mungu ibariki Afrika*" "God Bless Africa" (1961)

THAILAND

FLAG RATIO: 2:3   **USE:** National/Civil   **DATE ADOPTED:** 1917   **LAST MODIFIED:** 1917

Thailand's flag of **horizontal red, white** and **blue stripes** is called the *trairanga* (**tricolour**). From the mid-17th century, Thailand's flag was a plain red banner. During the reign (1851–68) of Rama IV, a white elephant was placed at the centre of the flag. In 1916 white stripes were introduced at the top and bottom of the flag. King Rama VI designed the current flag in 1917. The elephant was replaced by a central **blue band**, a symbol of solidarity with the Allies in World War 1. The colours represent the three pillars of the nation. The outer red stripes represent the land. Blue stands for the monarchy, and white symbolizes the purity of Buddhism, the national religion.

HISTORY

In *c*.1238 **Bang Klang Hao** overthrew **Khmer** rule and established the Thai Kingdom of **Sukhothai**. In 1350 **Ramathibodi** made **Ayutthaya** the capital of **Siam**. Thailand was the only Southeast Asian nation to escape European colonization. In 1767 **Burma** sacked Ayutthaya. In 1782 General Chakri became King **Rama I**, founding the **Chakri dynasty** that has ruled ever since. Rama I founded a new capital at **Bangkok**. In 1931 Siam became a constitutional monarchy. Premier **Phibun Songkhram** changed the country's name to Thailand in 1939. In 1950 Bhumbibol Adulyadej acceded as **Rama IX**.

AREA: 513,120sq km (198,116sq mi)
POPULATION: 60,606,947
CAPITAL (POPULATION): Bangkok (6,320,174)
GOVERNMENT: Constitutional monarchy
ETHNIC GROUPS: Thai 80%, Chinese 12%, Malay 4%, Khmer 3%
LANGUAGES: Thai (official)
RELIGIONS: Theravada Buddhist 94%, Muslim 4%, Christian 1%
NATIONAL ANTHEM (DATE): "*Phleng Chat*" "National Anthem" (1939)

Thotsakan*, King of the Demons, guards Wat Arun (Temple of Dawn), Bangkok.*

FLAG RATIO: 3:5 USE: National/Civil DATE ADOPTED: 1960 LAST MODIFIED: 1960

Togo adopted its present flag upon gaining independence. It has **five horizontal stripes** (three green and two yellow) and a **white five-pointed star** on a **red canton**. The **five** stripes represent action as well as the five regions of Togo. The **alternate** colours stand for unity in diversity. **Red** represents the blood shed in the struggle for independence. The **star** in the canton symbolizes life, liberty, and labour. **Green** represents hope and agriculture, the major economic activity. **Yellow** stands for Togo's mineral wealth.

HISTORY

The historic region of **Togoland** comprised what is now the Republic of Togo and western **Ghana**. From the 17th to the 19th century, the **Ashanti** raided Togoland, seizing the indigenous inhabi-

tants, the **Ewe**, and selling them to Europeans as **slaves**. In 1884 Togoland became a **German** protectorate. The Germans built the capital, **Lomé**. In 1914 Britain and France captured Togoland from Germany. In 1922 the League of Nations created the mandated territories of **British Togoland** and **French Togoland**. In 1957 British Togoland became part of Ghana. In 1960 French Togoland gained **independence** as the Republic of Togo. **Sylvanus Olympio** was the first premier. In 1963 Olympio was assassinated and **Nicolas Grunitzky** became premier. In 1967 **Gnassingbe Eyadema** overthrew Grunitzky.

AREA: 56,790sq km (21,927sq mi)
POPULATION: 4,951,400
CAPITAL (POPULATION): Lomé (658,100)
GOVERNMENT: Multi-party republic
ETHNIC GROUPS: Ewe 20%, Kabye 16%, Waci-Gbe 8%, Mina (Gen) 5%, Tem (Kotokoli) 5%
LANGUAGES: French (official), Ewe, Kabye
RELIGIONS: African traditional beliefs 59%, Roman Catholic 22%, Protestant 7%, Sunni Muslim 15%
MOTTO: "*Travail, Liberté, Patrie*" "Work, Liberty, Motherland"
NATIONAL ANTHEM (DATE): (1979)

Mocker swallowtail butterfly mimics other species of butterfly.

TONGA

FLAG RATIO: 1:2 **USE:** National/Civil **DATE ADOPTED:** 1875 **LAST MODIFIED:** 1875

Tonga's flag with its **red cross** in the **white canton** and a monochrome **red field** is full of Christian symbolism. The original design was white with a red cross but was changed to avoid confusion with the flag of the International Red Cross. The red cross represents Jesus Christ. The red field symbolizes the blood Jesus shed to save the world.

HISTORY

Tonga is a **South Pacific** island with the last remaining **Polynesian** monarchy. The archipelago consists of *c.*170 islands, only 36 of which are inhabited. The three main groups of islands are Tongatapu, Ha'apai, and Vava'u. **Captain James Cook** visited Tonga three times between 1773 and 1777. He named Tonga the '**Friendly Islands**' because of the warm welcome he received from the islanders. In 1849 King **George Tupou I** united the kingdom, ending more than 50 years of **civil war**. In the 19th century, **Wesleyan missionaries** converted the indigenous population to **Christianity**. In 1900 Tonga became a **British protectorate**. Queen **Salote Tupou III** reigned from 1918 to 1969, when **Tupou IV** acceded as King. In 1970 Tonga won **independence**.

AREA: 748sq km (289sq mi)
POPULATION: 97,446
CAPITAL (POPULATION): Nuku'alofa (24,300)
GOVERNMENT: Constitutional monarchy
ETHNIC GROUPS: Tongan 98%, other Polynesian and European 2%
LANGUAGES: English, Tongan (both official)
RELIGIONS: Wesleyan 41%, Church of Tonga 10%, Roman Catholic 16%, Mormon 14%, Baha'i 3%, Assemblies of God 2%
MOTTO: "*Koe 'Otua mo Tonga ko hoku Tofi'a*" "God and Tonga are my Inheritance"
NATIONAL ANTHEM (DATE): "*Koe Fasi Oe Tu'i Oe Otu Tonga*" "National Anthem of Tonga" (1874)

Tau'olunga *is a traditional ceremonial dance performed by Tongan women.*

TRINIDAD AND TOBAGO

FLAG RATIO: 3:5 **USE:** National/Civil **DATE ADOPTED:** 1962 **LAST MODIFIED:** 1962

An Independence Committee designed Trinidad and Tobago's flag in 1962. The colours represent the elements of earth, water, and fire. The broad **black diagonal stripe** stands for the republic's abundant resources of oil and gas. It also denotes the unity and determination of the people. The **two white diagonal stripes** symbolizes the Caribbean Sea, as well as purity and equality. The **red field** represents the warmth of the Caribbean sun. It also recalls the courage and vitality of the republic's people.

HISTORY

Christopher Columbus landed on the island of **Trinidad** in 1498. **Spain** built the first settlement in 1532. They enslaved the indigenous **Caribs** and **Arawaks**. In 1797 **Britain** captured Trinidad. English Captain **Robert Dudley** visited the island of **Tobago** in 1596, but no colonies appeared until 1632. In 1802 Tobago became a **British** possession. Britain and Spain brought **slaves** from Africa to work on the **sugarcane** plantations. In 1845 **Indians** arrived as **indentured labour**. In 1889 Trinidad and Tobago **united**. The islands gained **independence** in 1972, and became a republic in 1976. **Eric Williams** was Prime Minister from 1956 to 1981.

AREA: 5128sq km (1980sq mi)
POPULATION: 1,484,000
CAPITAL (POPULATION): Port-of-Spain (52,000)
GOVERNMENT: Multi-party republic
ETHNIC GROUPS: African 40%, East Indian 40%, mixed race 18%
LANGUAGES: English (official), Hindi, French, Spanish, Chinese
RELIGIONS: Roman Catholic 30%, Hindu 24%, Anglican 11%, Muslim 6%, Presbyterian 3%
MOTTO: "Together We Aspire, Together We Achieve"
NATIONAL ANTHEM (DATE): "Forged From The Love of Liberty" (1962)

Trinidadian artist Sybil Atteck (1911–75) painted this expressionist 'Fishermen'.

189

TUNISIA

FLAG RATIO: 2:3 USE: National/Civil DATE ADOPTED: 1959 LAST MODIFIED: 1959

Tunisia's flag is similar to Turkey's and originated in *c*.1831, when the country was under the rule of Hassine, eighth *bey* (governor) of the Turkish Husseinite Dynasty. The **red five-pointed star** and **Osmanli (Turkish) crescent** are traditional **Islamic** symbols. The **white disc** is a stylized depiction of the sun. It symbolizes unity. The **red field** represents the blood shed in the struggle for independence. The constitution confirmed the design of the national flag in 1959.

HISTORY

In 814 BC, **Phoenician Queen Dido** founded **Carthage**. Despite **Hannibal**'s dramatic advance over the Alps, **Rome** defeated Carthage in the **Punic Wars** (249–146 BC). In 46 BC, Carthage became part of the Roman province of **Tripolitania**. In AD 640, the **Arabs** invaded. The **Berbers** converted to **Islam** and adopted **Arabic** as the main language. In 670 **Oqba Ibn Nafaa** founded **Kairouan**, a centre of Islamic study. The **Hafsids** ruled from 1230 to 1574, when Spain's capture of **Tunis** led to the intervention of the **Ottoman Empire**. Turkish *beys* governed from 1612 to 1957. The **Husseinite dynasty** reigned from 1705 to 1881. Pirate attacks led to the **Tripolitan War** (1801–05) with the United States. In 1881 **France** invaded and Tunisia became a French **protectorate** (1883). It was a major battleground in **World War II**. In 1956 Tunisia gained **independence**. The following year, Tunisia became a republic. **Habib Bourguiba** was president from 1957 to 1987. **Zine el Abidine Ben Ali** succeeded him.

AREA: 163,610sq km (63,170sq mi)
POPULATION: 9,924,000
CAPITAL (POPULATION): Tunis (674,100)
GOVERNMENT: Multi-party republic
ETHNIC GROUPS: Arab 98%, Berber 1%
LANGUAGES: Arabic (official), French
RELIGIONS: Sunni Muslim 99%
MOTTO: "*Liberté, Ordre, Justice*"
"Freedom, Order, Justice"
NATIONAL ANTHEM (DATE): "*Himat Al Hima*"
"Defenders of the Homeland" (1987)

Tunisian *artisanal design marking the National Day of Sahara Tourism.*

TURKEY

FLAG RATIO: 2:3   USE: National/Civil   DATE ADOPTED: 1936   LAST MODIFIED: 1936

Turkey's flag is nicknamed *Ay Yildiz* (Moon Star). The **crescent moon** and **five-pointed star** are traditional **Islamic** symbols, but their association with Turkey may predate Islam. The moon was the symbol of Diana, the patron goddess of Byzantium (now Istanbul). In 330 Emperor Constantine renamed the city Constantinople, dedicating it to the Virgin Mary whose symbol is the star. In legend, Sultan Murad II adopted the symbols after seeing a reflection of the moon occulting a star in pools of blood at the Battle of Kosovo (1448), where the Ottomans Turks defeated the Christian forces. **Red** has been associated with the Ottomans since the birth of the Empire in the late 13th century. In 1793 Sultan Selim III adopted a red naval flag with a crescent and star. The five-pointed star dates from *c*.1844.

HISTORY

In 330 Emperor Constantine made **Constantinople** (now Istanbul) capital of the **Roman Empire**. In 398 it became capital of the **Byzantine Empire**. The **Seljuks** introduced **Islam** in the 11th century. In 1435 **Muhammad II** captured Constantinople, which became capital of the mighty **Ottoman Empire**. Defeat in **World War I** (1914–18) saw the overthrow of the Sultan by Mustafa Kemal (**Atatürk**). In 1923 Turkey became a **republic**. Atatürk created a **secular** state. **Ismet Inönü** was president from 1938 to 1950. A military **coup** created the second republic in 1960. In 1974 Turkey invaded **Northern Cyprus**. The army have fought against the **Kurds** in south-east Turkey since 1984.

AREA: 779,450sq km (300,946sq mi)
POPULATION: 62,610,252
CAPITAL (POPULATION): Ankara (3,693,390)
GOVERNMENT: Multi-party republic
ETHNIC GROUPS: Turkish 86%, Kurdish 11%, Arab 2%
LANGUAGES: Turkish (official)
RELIGIONS: Alawite Muslim 99%
NATIONAL ANTHEM (DATE): "*Istiklâl Marsi*" "March of Independence" (1921)

Floral motif on a Paçalik dress, worn by a bride on the day after her wedding.

TURKMENISTAN

FLAG RATIO: 1:2 USE: National/Civil DATE ADOPTED: 1992 LAST MODIFIED: 1997

Turkmenistan adopted its present flag upon gaining independence in 1992. The **white crescent moon** and **stars** are **Islamic** symbols. **Green** is the conventional colour of Islam. On the hoist of the flag is a **red vertical stripe** with **carpet designs** (*guls*) from each of the five regions of Turkmenistan. The crescent moon stands for hope and a clear future. **Five stars** represent the regions of Dashhowuz, Lebap, Balkan, Ahal, and Mary. In 1997 President Saparmurad Niyazov added **two olive branches** to the bottom of the vertical stripe to mark Turkmenistan's policy of permanent neutrality and to symbolize peace.

HISTORY

The **Kara Kum** desert covers almost 90% of Turkmenistan. In the 500s BC, it became part of the **Persian Empire**. **Arabs** invaded in the 8th century, introducing **Islam**. **Turkmens** migrated to the area in the 10th century. In the 11th century **Merv** became capital of the **Seljuk Tur**k lands. Part of the **Mongol** Empire of **Genghis Khan** in the 13th century, **Tamerlane** conquered it in the 14th century and founded the **Timurid dynasty**. The **Uzbeks** gained control in the 16th century. In 1881 **Russia** finally overcame fierce resistance. Turkmenistan became part of **Russian Turkistan** in 1899. In 1925 it became a republic of the **Soviet Union**. In 1991 Turkemenistan gained **independence**. **Saparmurad Niyazov** became President in 1990.

AREA: 488,100sq km (188,450 sq mi)
POPULATION: 4,585,000
CAPITAL (POPULATION): Ashgabat (536,000)
GOVERNMENT: Single-party republic
ETHNIC GROUPS: Turkmen 72%, Russian 10%, Uzbek 9%, Kazak 3%, Tatar 1%
LANGUAGES: Turkmen (official)
RELIGIONS: Sunni Muslim 89%
NATIONAL ANTHEM (DATE): "*Garashciiz Bitarap Turkmenistaniin Devlet Gimni*" "Independent, Neutral, Turkmenistan State Anthem" (1997)

The ram's horn (kotchak) *is a common and ancient motif of Turkmen nomads.*

FLAG RATIO: 1:2   **USE:** National/Civil   **DATE ADOPTED:** 1978   **LAST MODIFIED:** 1997

Tuvalu adopted a national flag upon gaining independence from Britain in 1978. The **Union Jack** recalls British colonial rule and the islands' membership of the Commonwealth. The **nine, five-pointed, yellow stars** roughly correspond with the position of the nine islands of the archipelago. The **light blue** field represents the surrounding Pacific Ocean. In 1995 Tuvalu introduced a new flag of red, white, and blue stripes with a chevron. It removed the Union Jack from the canton and reduced the number of stars from nine to eight. (In Tuvaluan, 'Tuvalu' means 'group of eight' – originally only eight coral atolls were inhabited.) In 1997, after nationwide protests, Tuvalu reverted to the original design.

HISTORY

Spanish navigator **Alvaro de Mendaña** sighted the island of **Nui** in 1568, and the island of **Niulakita** on a return voyage in 1595. In 1819 British Captain **Arent De Peyster** discovered **Nukufetau** and **Funafuti**, which he named **Ellice Island** after the owner of his ship. Between 1850 and 1880, the population fell from *c*.20,000 to 3000 mainly because Europeans abducted workers for other Pacific plantations. In 1892 **Britain** assumed control, and Tuvalu was subsequently administered with the nearby Gilbert Islands (now **Kiribati**). In 1978 Tuvalu gained **independence**. It faces demands to become a republic.

AREA: 24sq km (10sq mi)
POPULATION: 11,000
CAPITAL (POPULATION): Funafuti (5100)
GOVERNMENT: Constitutional monarchy
ETHNIC GROUPS: Polynesian 97%
LANGUAGES: Tuvaluan, English
RELIGIONS: Church of Tuvalu (Congregationalist) 97%, Seventh-Day Adventist 1%, Baha'i 1%
NATIONAL MOTTO: "*Maaka te atua, karinea te vea; matakusi te atua, fakamamalu ki te tupu*" "Honour all men, love the brotherhood, fear God, honour the king"
NATIONAL ANTHEM (DATE): "*Tuvalu mo te Atua*" "Tuvalu for the Almighty" (1912)

Fatele *is the national dance of Tuvalu. Women dance to a* pokih *drum rhythm.*

UGANDA

FLAG RATIO: 2:3 USE: National/Civil DATE ADOPTED: 1962 LAST MODIFIED: 1962

Uganda's flag consists of **six horizontal stripes** of black, yellow and red, the original colours of the Ugandan People's Congress. **Black** represents the African people. **Yellow** stands for the abundant sunshine, and **red** represents brotherhood. At the centre of the flag is a **white disc** with a **crested crane**. The crested crane, Uganda's national bird, faces the hoist and stands on one leg, symbolizing Uganda's progress. Its plumage includes the national colours.

HISTORY

In *c*.1500, the **Lwo** formed the Kingdoms of **Buganda** and **Bunyoro** in south-west Uganda. In 1862 British explorer **John Speke** became the first European to reach Buganda. **Sir Henry Stanley** soon followed. In 1894 Uganda became a **British Protectorate**. Britain encouraged **Asian** settlers. Uganda gained **independence** in 1962. **Milton Obote** of the Ugandan People's Congress (UPC) was the first prime minister. In 1966 King **Mutesa II** fled into exile. In 1971 **Idi Amin** led a military coup. Amin's **dictatorship** murdered more than 250,000 Ugandans. In 1979 Tanzania helped overthrow Amin, and Obote returned to power. Another military **coup** toppled Obote in 1985, and **Yoweri Museveni** became president in 1986. **AIDS** is a major problem.

AREA: 235,880sq km (91,073sq mi)
POPULATION: 23,453,300
CAPITAL (POPULATION): Kampala (953,400)
GOVERNMENT: Multi-party republic
ETHNIC GROUPS: Ganda 18%, Banyoro 14%,
Teso 9%, Banyan 8%, Basoga 8%, Bagisu 7%,
Bachiga 7%, Lango 6%, Acholi 5%
LANGUAGES: English, Swahili (both official)
RELIGIONS: Roman Catholic 40%, Protestant
29%, African traditional beliefs 18%,
Muslim 7%
MOTTO: "For God and My Country"
NATIONAL ANTHEM (DATE): "Pearl of Africa"
(1962)

The Karamojong live in the Karamoja
region, north-east Uganda.

Ukraine's flag consists of **two broad horizontal stripes** of **azure** and **yellow**. Apparently, azure and yellow were the colours of Kievan Rus, the first **Slavic** state founded in 882. The **azure** symbolizes the sky, mountains, and streams of Ukraine. **Yellow** represents the nation's golden fields. In 1848 the Ruthenian Council adopted a flag with a golden lion rampant on a blue field. In 1918, Ukraine declared independence and adopted the present flag. From 1949 to 1990, Ukraine's flag featured bands of red and blue with the Soviet hammer and sickle symbol. In 1991 Ukraine reintroduced the 1918 flag.

HISTORY

Ukraine was the heart of the medieval state of **Kievan Rus**. In 1240 the Mongols destroyed **Kiev**. In 1569 Ukraine became part of **Poland-Lithuania**. In 1648 the **Cossacks** overthrew Polish rule, but submitted to **Russia** in 1654. In the first two partitions of Poland (1772, 1793), Russia gained eastern Ukraine and Austria acquired the west. Ukraine was briefly **independent** after World War I, but in 1922 eastern Ukraine became part of the **Soviet Union**. In 1923 **Galicia**, western Ukraine, fell to Poland. In 1939 the Soviet Union held all Ukraine. In 1954 **Crimea** became part of Ukraine. The **Chernobyl** nuclear disaster in 1986 contaminated much of Ukraine. In 1991 Ukraine declared **independence**. **Leonid Kravchuk** was the first President.

AREA: 603,700sq km (233,100sq mi)
POPULATION: 48,860,000
CAPITAL (POPULATION): Kiev (2,619,000)
GOVERNMENT: Multi-party republic
ETHNIC GROUPS: Ukrainian 73%, Russian 22%, Jewish 1%, Belarussian 1%
LANGUAGES: Ukrainian (official)
RELIGIONS: Ukrainian Orthodox 80%, Ukrainian Catholic 10%, Protestant 3%
NATIONAL ANTHEM (DATE): "*Shche ne vmerla Ukraina*" "Ukraine Has Not Yet Perished" (1917)

Trio of musicians in national dress from Chernihivshchyna region, northern Ukraine.

UNITED ARAB EMIRATES

FLAG RATIO: 1:2 **USE:** National **DATE ADOPTED:** 1971 **LAST MODIFIED:** 1971

The flag of the United Arab Emirates (UAE) has **green, white** and **black** horizontal stripes and a **red vertical stripe** at the hoist. Six of the seven members of the federation have their own **state flag** – all of which are red and white. Fujairah uses the UAE flag as its state flag. Until the 19th century, the Gulf Emirates had **monochrome red** flags. In 1820 the Emirates signed the General Maritime Treaty with Britain, placing a white stripe on their flags to differentiate them from pirate ships on the Arabian Gulf. The UAE's flag has **Pan-Arab** colours. Green represents the fertility of its land. Black stands for its abundance of oil, and white represents neutrality.

HISTORY

In the Middle Ages, much of the UAE was part of the Kingdom of **Hormuz**. Portugal dominated the region from 1498 to 1633. The **Qawasim** tribe fought against **British** colonialism until 1820, when a truce gave Britain control of the defence and foreign policy of nine sheikhdoms (the **Trucial States**). The **Bani Yas Bedouins** dominated the Trucial interior. In 1971 British troops left the Gulf and the six sheikhdoms of **Abu Dhabi, Dubai, Ajman, Fujairah, Sharjah**, and **Umm Al-Qaiwain** federated to form the United Arab Emirates (UAE). **Sheikh Zayed bin Sultan Al Nahyan** became President. **Ras al-Khaimah** joined the UAE in 1972.

AREA: 83,600sq km (32,278 sq mi)
POPULATION: 2,800,000
CAPITAL (POPULATION): Abu Dhabi (942,463)
GOVERNMENT: Federation of Sheikhdoms
ETHNIC GROUPS: Expatriate workers 80% (South Asian 50%, other Arab and Iranian 23%, Euopean 7%), Emirati 20%
LANGUAGES: Arabic (official), English, Hindi, Urdu, Farsi (Persian)
RELIGIONS: Sunni Muslim 76%, Shi'a Muslim 12%, Hindi 8%, Christian 4%
NATIONAL ANTHEM (DATE): (1971)

In 1996 Sheikh Zayed celebrated 30 years as ruler of Abu Dhabi.

UNITED KINGDOM

FLAG RATIO: 1:2   USE: National/Civil   DATE ADOPTED: 1606   LAST MODIFIED: 1801

Officially called the 'Union Flag', but commonly known as the 'Union Jack', the flag of the United Kingdom consists of the **three crosses** of the patron saints. **Saint Andrew**, patron saint of Scotland, has a **white diagonal cross** set on a **blue background**. **Saint George**, patron saint of England, has a **red cross** on a **white field**. **Saint Patrick**, patron saint of Ireland, has a **red diagonal cross** on a **white background**. Soon after James VI of Scotland became King of England in 1601, the flag of Great Britain joined the crosses of Saint George and Saint Andrew. In 1801 Ireland became part of the United Kingdom and the red diagonal cross was added to the flag.

HISTORY

Britain emerged from the **Seven Years' War** (1756–63) as the world's leading imperial power, but soon lost the **United States** in the **American Revolution** (1775–83). Britain was the birthplace of the **Industrial Revolution**. The reign of **Victoria** saw the resurgence of the **British Empire**. **World War I** (1914–18) cost more than 750,000 British lives. In 1922 southern Ireland gained independence, and the UK became known as the United Kingdom of Great Britain and **Northern Ireland**. **Winston Churchill** led Britain through **World War II** (1939–45), which claimed more than 420,000 British lives. In 1947 **India** gained independence and the British Empire gradually dismantled. In 1952 **Elizabeth II** succeeded **George VI**.

AREA: 243,368sq km (94,202sq mi)
POPULATION: 58,789,194
CAPITAL (POPULATION): London (6,966,800)
GOVERNMENT: Constitutional monarchy
ETHNIC GROUPS: White 94%, Indian 1%, Pakistani 1%, West Indian 1%
LANGUAGES: English (official)
RELIGIONS: Anglican 57%, Roman Catholic 13%, Presbyterian 7%, Methodist 4%, Baptist 1%, Muslim 1%
NATIONAL ANTHEM (DATE): "God Save the Queen" (1745)

The Great Exhibition, London, displayed the world's first double-decker bus in 1851.

UNITED STATES OF AMERICA

FLAG RATIO: 10:19 USE: National/Civil DATE ADOPTED: 1771 LAST MODIFIED: 1960

In legend, **Betsy Ross** designed the 'Stars and Stripes' flag of the United States in 1776. In fact, it was probably designed by **Francis Hopkinson**. In 1777 the Continental Congress passed a Flag Act, which stated that the flag have "13 stripes, alternate red and white; that the union be 13 stars, white in a blue field." The stars and stripes represented the original 13 Colonies. In 1795, after Vermont and Kentucky joined the Union, the flag acquired 15 stripes and 15 stars. This flag is known as the 'Star-Spangled Banner'. In 1818 a new act provided for **13 stripes** and one star for each state, to be added to the flag on the Fourth of July following the admission of each new state. To date, there have been 27 amendments to the flag as new stars have been added. The last was in 1960, when Hawaii joined the union, making a total of **50 stars**.

HISTORY

In 1492 **Christopher Columbus** discovered the Americas. **Spain** built the first European settlement at **St Augustine**, Florida, in 1565. In 1607 the **British** founded **Jamestown**, Virginia. **Puritans** founded **Plymouth Colony** in 1620. In 1681 **William Penn** added Pennsylvania. The **American Revolution** (1775–83) ended British rule. **George Washington** was the first president. **Abraham Lincoln** guided the Union to victory in the **Civil War** (1861–65). **Franklin D. Roosevelt** led the US into World War II.

AREA: 9,372,610sq km (3,618,765sq mi)
POPULATION: 281,421,906
CAPITAL (POPULATION): Washington, D.C. (572,059)
GOVERNMENT: Federal multi-party republic
ETHNIC GROUPS: White 77%, African-American 12%, Asian 4%, Native American 1%
LANGUAGES: English (official), Spanish
RELIGIONS: Protestant 53%, Roman Catholic 26%, other Christian 8%, Muslim 2%, Jew 2%
NATIONAL MOTTO: "In God We Trust"
NATIONAL ANTHEM (DATE): "The Star Spangled Banner" (1931)

Firemen raise the flag at 'Ground Zero', after the terrorist attacks on September 11, 2001.

Uruguay's flag has **nine horizontal stripes** alternately **white** (top and bottom) and **blue**. On a white square on the upper hoist is a **yellow sun** bearing a **human face** with **16 rays** alternately straight and wavy. Like many other nations in South America, Uruguay adopted blue and white colours in homage to **Argentina**, the first South American nation to gain independence. The pattern recalls the design of the United States' flag. The nine stripes represent the original nine provinces of Uruguay. The sun symbol also appears on Argentina's flag. It is called the "**Sun of May**" in honour of the sun shining through the clouds above Buenos Aires on May 25, 1810, when Argentine rebels overthrew the Spanish Viceroy. It is an ancient **Inca** symbol.

HISTORY

In 1516 Spanish explorer **Juan Díaz de Solís** reached Uruguay. The native **Charrúa** resisted Spanish settlement until 1624. In 1726 they founded **Montevideo**. In 1777 Uruguay became part of the Spanish Viceroyalty of **Río de la Plata**. **José Gervais Artigas** led the **revolt** that overthrew the Spanish in 1814. In 1821 **Brazil** annexed Uruguay. Uruguay achieved **independence** in 1828. The **Blancos** and the **Colorados** fought a **civil war** from 1836 to 1872. Uruguay joined Brazil and Argentina in the **War of the Triple Alliance** (1865–70) against Paraguay. **José Batlle** was president from 1903 to 1907 and from 1911 to 1915.

AREA: 177,410sq km (68.498sq mi)
POPULATION: 3,322,141
CAPITAL (POPULATION): Montevideo (1,380,962)
GOVERNMENT: Multi-party republic
ETHNIC GROUPS: White 86%, Mestizo 8%, Mulatto or Black 6%
LANGUAGES: Spanish (official)
RELIGIONS: Roman Catholic 66%, Protestant 2%, Jew 1%
NATIONAL ANTHEM (DATE): "*Orientales, la Patria o la tumba!*" "Uruguayans, the Fatherland or Death! (1845)

The Spanish founded the neighbourhood of Cordon, Montevideo, south Uruguay, in 1750.

UZBEKISTAN

FLAG RATIO: 1:2 **USE:** National/Civil **DATE ADOPTED:** 1991 **LAST MODIFIED:** 1991

Uzbekistan's national flag consists of three **horizontal bands** of **blue**, **white** and **green**, and **two** thin **horizontal red stripes** either side of the middle white band. The **white crescent-moon** in the upper hoist is a traditional symbol of Islam and represents the rebirth of the nation. The **12 white stars** next to the moon recall the 12 signs of the zodiac. Blue stands for water and the eternal sky. Red represents life. White symbolizes peace, and green denotes nature.

HISTORY

Uzbekistan lies on the ancient **Silk Road**. In the 7th and 8th centuries the Arab Caliphate conquered Central Asia and introduced **Islam**. In the 10th century, **Ismail Samani** made **Bukhara** capital of the **Samanid dynasty**. In 1220 **Mongol** Emperor **Genghis Khan** laid waste to the region. In the 14th century **Tamelane** ruled a great empire from **Samarkand**. **Turkic Uzbek** people conquered the **Timurid** lands in the 16th century. In the 19th century the khanates of Bukhara, **Khiva** and **Kokand** joined the **Russian Empire**. Uzbekistan became a leading producer of **cotton** and a large **railway** network developed. Communists came to power after the Russian Revolution (1917) and Uzbekistan became a republic of the **Soviet Union** in 1924. In 1966 an earthquake hit the capital, **Tashkent**. In 1991 Uzbekistan gained **independence**. **Islam Karimov** was the first President. Uzbekistan is a leading member of the **Commonwealth of Independent States**.

AREA: 447,400sq km (172,740sq mi)
POPULATION: 24,449,000
CAPITAL (POPULATION): Tashkent (2,117,500)
GOVERNMENT: Presidential republic
ETHNIC GROUPS: Uzbek 71%, Russian 8%, Tajik 5%, Kazak 4%, Tatar 2%, Kara-Kalpak 2%
LANGUAGES: Uzbek (official), Russian, Tajik
RELIGIONS: Muslim 88% (mostly Sunni), Eastern Orthodox 9%
NATIONAL ANTHEM (DATE): Untitled (1992)

Uzbekistan's *state emblem has the 'Humo bird' of happiness at its centre.*

200

VANUATU

FLAG RATIO: 3:5 USE: National/Civil DATE ADOPTED: 1980 LAST MODIFIED: 1980

The **yellow 'Y'** design at the centre of the national flag is a stylized representation of the geographical distribution of the islands of Vanuatu. The **pig's tusk** and **crossed namele fern leaves** in the **black triangle** are traditional Vanuatan symbols. They symbolize prosperity and peace respectively. The **red band** symbolizes unity through blood. The **green band** represents Vanuatu's fertile agricultural land. Black stands for the Melanesian people, and yellow denotes sunshine and the Christian faith of Vanuatu's people. Prime Minister Walter Lini added black and yellow **fimbriations** to Malon Kalontas' design to emphasize the black triangle.

HISTORY

The earliest-known settlement was on **Malo Island**, where **Melanesian** pottery at least 4000 years old has been unearthed. Portuguese explorer **Pedro Fernandez de Queiros** landed on **Espiritu Santo** in 1606. **Louis de Bougainville** rediscovered the islands in 1768, and **James Cook** mapped them in 1774, naming them **New Hebrides**. **England** and **France** settled the islands in the early 1800s. Europeans brought disease, violence and slave running, which devastated the native population. Governed jointly by France and Britain from 1906, Vanuatu became a **independent republic** in 1980. Father **Walter Mini** was Prime Minister from 1981 to 1990.

Vanuatu's *Pacific waters are rich in fish such as marlin, tuna, mahi mahi, and wahoo.*

AREA: 12,190sq km (4707sq mi)
POPULATION: 206,000
CAPITAL (POPULATION): Port Vila (33,900)
GOVERNMENT: Multi-party republic
ETHNIC GROUPS: Melanesian 92%
LANGUAGES: English, French (both official), pidgin (Bislama or Bichelama)
RELIGIONS: Presbyterian 37%, Roman Catholic 15%, Anglican 15%, Seventh-Day Adventist 6%
NATIONAL ANTHEM (DATE): *"Yumi, Yumi, Yumi"* "We, We, We" (1980)

VATICAN CITY

FLAG RATIO: 1:1 USE: Civil DATE ADOPTED: 1929 LAST MODIFIED: 1929

Vatican City and Switzerland are the only nations with **square** flags. The Vatican's flag is **bicolour** with **vertical yellow** and **white stripes**. On the white stripe is the 14th-century **coat of arms**. The arms include the **crossed papal keys**. The **golden key** alludes to the power in the kingdom of the heavens, the **silver key** represents the spiritual authority of the papacy on Earth. The mechanisms are turned towards the heavens and the grips toward the Earth. The cord that binds the keys symbolizes the bond between the two powers. They are crowned by the **papal tiara**, formed by three crowns representing the triple power of the pope: father of kings, governor of the world, and vicar of Christ.

HISTORY

Vatican City is the smallest independent sovereign state, existing as a walled enclave within the city of **Rome**. It is the official home of the papacy and an independent base for the **Holy See**, the governing body of the **Roman Catholic Church**. According to tradition, **Saint Peter** was the first Bishop of Rome and the first church was built on the site of his tomb in 326. Popes ruled much of the Italian peninsula until the 19th century, when the newly united **Kingdom of Italy** seized many of the **Papal States**. In 1870 Italy annexed the city of Rome. Italy confirmed the Vatican's independence in the **Lateran Treaty** (1929). Saint Peter's Basilica includes the **Sistine Chapel**.

AREA: 0.44sq km (0.17sq mi)
POPULATION: 1000
CAPITAL (POPULATION): Vatican City (1000)
GOVERNMENT: Ecclesiastical pontificate
ETHNIC GROUPS: Italians, Swiss, other
LANGUAGES: Latin (official), Italian, French
RELIGIONS: Roman Catholic 100%
NATIONAL ANTHEM (DATE):
"*Inno e Marcia Pontificale*"
"Hymn and Pontifical March" (1950)

The crossed keys are the symbol of Saint Peter, keeper of the keys to heaven.

VENEZUELA

FLAG RATIO: 2:3 **USE:** National **DATE ADOPTED:** 1930 **LAST MODIFIED:** 1954

In 1806 revolutionary Francisco de Miranda hoisted a flag of **yellow, blue** and **red horizontal stripes**. Ecuador and Colombia have the same tricolour, but Venezuela's stripes are of **equal width**. The **eight white stars** were added in 1817 to represent the eight provinces that had declared themselves independent from Spanish rule: Caracas, Cumana, Barinas, Barcelona, Margarita, Merida, and Tujillo. In 1930 the stars were arranged in an **arc**. In 1954 the **state flag** added the **coat of arms** to the upper hoist. Yellow represents the wealth of the land. Blue stands for the sea seperating Venezuela from Spain, and red symbolizes the blood shed in the struggle for independence.

Christopher Columbus became the first European to sight Venezuela. Venezuela became part of the Spanish administrative area of **New Granada**. In the late 18th century, **Francisco de Miranda** led uprisings against Spanish rule. In 1821 **Simón Bolívar** liberated Venezuela and it became part of **Greater Colombia**. In 1830 Venezuela gained **independence**. Dictator **Antonio Guzmán Blanco** ruled from 1870 to 1888. **Juan Vicente Gómez** was President from 1908 to 1935. **Oil** was discovered in 1918. From 1945 to 1948 **Rómulo Betancourt** led a military junta, and he served as a civilian President from 1959 to 1964. In 1999 Venezuela became a **Bolivarian Republic**.

HISTORY

The indigenous inhabitants of Venezuela were the **Arawak** and **Carib**. In 1498

Women *from Macoa, north-east Venezuela, grinding maize.*

AREA: 912,050sq km (352,143sq mi)
POPULATION: 23,611,400
CAPITAL (POPULATION): Caracas (1,763,100)
GOVERNMENT: Federal multi-party republic
ETHNIC GROUPS: Mestizo 67%, White 21%, Black 10%, Native American 2%
LANGUAGES: Spanish (official), numerous indigenous dialects
RELIGIONS: Roman Catholic 70%, Protestant 29%
NATIONAL ANTHEM (DATE): "*Gloria al Bravo Pueblo*" "Glory to the Brave People" (1881)

VIETNAM

FLAG RATIO: 2:3 USE: National DATE ADOPTED: 1955 LAST MODIFIED: 1955

Resistance groups first adopted Vietnam's flag in the liberation struggle against Japan in World War II. The **star** can be seen as the star of communism, with the **five points** representing the groups who helped build socialism in Vietnam: farmers, workers, intellectuals, youths, and soldiers. Alternatively, it can be seen as a representation of the North Star. **Red** is the colour of communism, luck, and happiness.

HISTORY

In 111 BC China seized Vietnam, naming it **Annam**. In AD 939 it gained independence. In 1558 the north broke away as **Tonkin**. In 1802 **Nguyen** Emperor **Gia Long** reunited it as the Empire of Vietnam. In 1887 Vietnam became part of **French Indochina**. Japan conquered it during **World War II**. In 1954 France withdrew, and Vietnam split into **North Vietnam** (led by **Ho Chi Minh**) and **South Vietnam** (under **Bao Dai**). In 1955 Bao Dai was disposed and **Ngo Dinh Diem** was elected. The **United States** became embroiled in the **Vietnam War** (1954–75), which claimed about 1.5 million Vietnamese and *c*.50,000 US lives. In 1976 the reunited Vietnam became a socialist republic under **Pham Van Dong**. In 1979 Vietnam helped defeat the **Khmer Rouge** in Cambodia.

AREA: 331,689sq km (128,065sq mi)
POPULATION: 80,305,200
CAPITAL (POPULATION): Hanoi (1,372,800)
GOVERNMENT: Socialist republic
ETHNIC GROUPS: Vietnamese 85%, Chinese 2%, Hmong 1%, Tai 1%
LANGUAGES: Vietnamese (official), English, French, Chinese, Khmer
RELIGIONS: Buddhist (amalgam of Mahayana Buddhism, Taoism, Confucianism) 50%, Roman Catholic 8%, Cao Dai 2%, Hoa Hao 2%, Protestant 1%
NATIONAL ANTHEM (DATE): "*Tien quan ca*"
"March to the Front" (1976)

Vietnamese women sometimes wear beautiful, traditional long velvet dresses.

FLAG RATIO: 2:3 **USE:** National/Civil **DATE ADOPTED:** 1990 **LAST MODIFIED:** 1990

Yemen adopted its present **tricolour** flag of **red, white** and **black** horizontal stripes in 1990, when North Yemen united with South Yemen. The colours derive from the **Pan-Arab** revolt by Hussein ibn Ali in 1916. The flag of North Yemen had a green star on the middle stripe, while South Yemen had a red star on a blue triangle on the hoist. **Black** represents Yemen's colonial past. **White** symbolizes its bright future, and **red** stands for the blood shed in the struggle for liberation.

HISTORY

From 759 to 100 BC, the kingdom of **Sheba** flouished in southern Yemen. **Islam** arrived in AD 628, and the **Rassite dynasty** of the **Zaidi sect** established a theocratic state that lasted until 1962. In 1517 Yemen became part of the **Ottoman Empire**. It remained under Turkish control until 1918. In 1839 the British captured **Aden**. In 1937 Britain formed the **Aden Protectorate**. From 1958 to 1961 Yemen was part of the **United Arab Republic** (with Egypt and Syria). In 1962 a military coup overthrew the monarchy and created the **Yemen Arab Republic**. **Civil war ensued.** In 1967 the National Liberation Front forced the British to withdraw from Aden and founded the **People's Republic of South Yemen**. In 1970 Marxists won the war in South Yemen and renamed it the **People's Democratic Republic of Yemen**. In 1990 the two Yemens merged. **Ali Abdullah Saleh** became President.

AREA: 527,970sq km (203,849sq mi)
POPULATION: 18,078,035
CAPITAL (POPULATION): San'a (1,410,000)
GOVERNMENT: Multi-party republic
ETHNIC GROUPS: Arab 96%
LANGUAGES: Arabic (official)
RELIGIONS: Sunni Muslim (Shaf'i order) 65%, Shi'a Muslim 35% (Zaidi order)
NATIONAL ANTHEM (DATE):
"United Republic" (1990)

Bronze statue of Maadi Karib (800 BC) from the Awwam Temple in Marib, central Yemen.

205

YUGOSLAVIA

FLAG RATIO: 1:2 **USE:** National/Civil **DATE ADOPTED:** 1992 **LAST MODIFIED:** 1992

Yugoslavia's **tricolour** flag of horizontal stripes uses the **Pan-Slavic** colours of **blue**, **white** and **red**. The colours derive from the 19th-century flag of **Russia**. The present flag was the flag of the Kingdom of Serbs, Croats and Slovenes (1918–29) and of Yugoslavia (1929–45). In 1945 Yugoslavia became a socialist republic and placed the 'Partisan red star' at the centre of the flag. In 1992 the plain tricolour became the flag of the new Federal Republic of Yugoslavia.

HISTORY

Yugoslavia now consists of **Serbia** and **Montenegro**. In 1918 the Kingdom of Serbs, Croats, and Slovenes formed under **Peter I** of Serbia. **Alexander I** succeeded as King in 1921. In 1929 he renamed the country Yugoslavia. In 1941 **Germany** occupied Yugoslavia. **Tito**'s communist partisans and Royalist **chetniks** resisted the Nazis. In 1945 **Tito** formed a socialist republic in Yugoslavia. In 1989 **Slobodan Milosĕvić** became President of Serbia. In 1991 **Slovenia** and **Croatia** seceded from the Serb-dominated federation. In 1992 **Bosnia-Herzegovina** declared independence. Serbia helped Bosnian Serbs in the civil war. In 1992 a new Yugoslav federation emerged. In 1997 Milosĕvić became President of Yugoslavia. In 1999, after the forced expulsion of Albanians from the Serbian province of **Kosovo**, NATO launched air attacks against Yugoslavia. **Vojislav Kostunica** defeated Milosĕvić in 2000 elections.

AREA: 102,173sq km (39,449sq mi)
POPULATION: 10,617,000
CAPITAL (POPULATION): Belgrade (1,168,454)
GOVERNMENT: Federal multi-party republic
ETHNIC GROUPS: Serb 63%, Kosovar-Albanian 18%, Montenegrin 5%, Hungarian 3%, Croat 2%
LANGUAGES: Serbian 95%, Albanian 5% (both official)
RELIGIONS: Serbian Orthodox 80%, Muslim 10%, Roman Catholic 6%, Protestant 1%
NATIONAL ANTHEM (DATE): *"Hej Slaveni"* "O Slavs" (1945)

Traditional dress of Bunjevci Croats from Bačka, Vojvodina, northern Yugoslavia.

Zambia's flag consists of a **green field** with a **flying eagle** on the **top fly** and a **tricolour** of **red**, **black** and **orange vertical stripes** on the **bottom fly**. The colours appear to derive from the United Nationalist Independence Party (UNIP), which led the struggle against British colonialism. Red represents the blood shed in the struggle for freedom. Black stands for Zambia's people. Orange symbolizes Zambia's mineral wealth, and green denotes its natural resources. The eagle represents freedom.

HISTORY

In *c*.800 **Bantu speakers** migrated to Zambia. In 1855 **David Livingstone** became the first European to see **Victoria Falls**. In 1890 the British South Africa Company, managed by **Cecil Rhodes**, made treaties with local chiefs. The area divided into North-West and North-East **Rhodesia**. In 1911 the two regions joined to form **Northern Rhodesia**. In 1953 Britain established the Federation of **Rhodesia** (including present-day Zambia and **Zimbabwe**) and Nyasaland (now **Malawi**). In 1963, after a nationwide campaign of civil disobedience, the federation was dissolved. In 1964, Northern Rhodesia gained **independence** as the republic of **Zambia**. **Kenneth Kaunda** was Prime Minister from 1964 to 1990.

Zambian *traditional tribal hunter with shield and staff.*

AREA: 752,614sq km (290,586 sq mi)
POPULATION: 10,865,700
CAPITAL (POPULATION): Lusaka (1,218,200)
GOVERNMENT: Multi-party republic
ETHNIC GROUPS: Bemba 36%,
Maravi (Nyanja) 18%, Tonga 15%
LANGUAGES: English (official), Bemba, Kaonda,
Lozi, Lunda, Luvale, Nyanja, Tonga
RELIGIONS: Protestant 34%, Roman Catholic
26%, African traditional beliefs 29%, Muslim 1%
NATIONAL MOTTO: "One Zambia, One Nation"
NATIONAL ANTHEM (DATE): "*Lumbanyeni Zambia*"
"Stand and Sing of Zambia, Proud and Free"
(1961)

ZIMBABWE

FLAG RATIO: 1:2 USE: National/Civil DATE ADOPTED: 1980 LAST MODIFIED: 1980

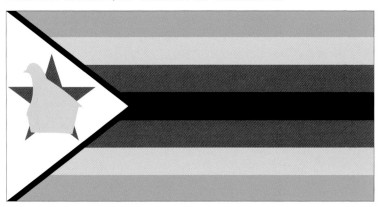

Zimbabwe's flag derives from the colours of the ruling Zimbabwe African National Union-Patriotic Front (ZANU-PF). It has **seven horizontal** stripes: **two tribands** of the **Pan-African** colours of **green**, **yellow** and **red** are separated by a **black stripe**. Green represents Zimbabwe's fertile land. Yellow stands for its mineral wealth. Red symbolizes the blood shed in the colonial struggle, and black represents its majority population. On the hoist is a **white triangle** symbolizing peace and progress. The triangle contains a stylized depiction of a **soapstone bird** (found at Great Zimbabwe) against a **red star**. The star represents internationalism and the socialist origins of ZANU-PF.

HISTORY

By 1200 the **Shona** formed a kingdom based around **Great Zimbabwe**. In 1889 the British South Africa Company, under **Cecil Rhodes**, began to exploit Zimbabwe's mineral wealth. In 1896 the area became **Southern Rhodesia**. In 1953 it federated with Northern Rhodesia (now **Zambia**) and Nyasaland (**Malawi**). In 1965 Ian Smith unilaterally declared independence from **Britain**. In 1980, after a long struggle against the white-minority regime, **Robert Mugabe** became prime minister.

AREA: 390,579sq km (150,873sq mi)
POPULATION: 13,899,500
CAPITAL (POPULATION): Harare (1,864,400)
GOVERNMENT: Multi-party republic
ETHNIC GROUPS: Shona 71%, Ndebele 16%, other Bantu-speaking Africans 11%, Europeans 2%
LANGUAGES: English (official), Shona, Sindebele (Ndebele), tribal dialects
RELIGIONS: Protestant 35%, African traditional beliefs 29%, Roman Catholic 12%, Muslim 1%
NATIONAL MOTTO: "Unity, Freedom, Work"
NATIONAL ANTHEM (DATE): "*Kalibusiswe Ilizwe leZimbabwe*" "Blessed Be the Land of Zimbabwe" (1994)

The chipendani is a plucked single-stringed mouth bow of the Shona people.

ENGLAND
RATIO : 3:5
FLAG NAME : Saint George's Cross

SCOTLAND
RATIO : 3:5
FLAG NAME : Saint Andrew's Saltire

WALES
RATIO : 3:5
FLAG NAME : *Y Ddraig Goch* (The Red Dragon)

ALDERNEY
RATIO : 3:5
DATE ADOPTED : 1906

GUERNSEY
RATIO : 2:3
DATE ADOPTED : 1985

ISLE OF MAN
RATIO : 1:2
DATE ADOPTED : 1971

JERSEY
RATIO : 3:5
DATE ADOPTED : 1981

SARK
RATIO : 3:5
DATE ADOPTED : 1938

STATE FLAGS OF THE UNITED STATES

ALABAMA

STATEHOOD :   December 14, 1819
NICKNAME :   The Heart of Dixie
STATE MOTTO : We dare defend our rights

ALASKA

STATEHOOD :   January 3, 1959
NICKNAME :   The Last Frontier
STATE MOTTO : North to the future

ARIZONA

STATEHOOD :   February 14, 1912
NICKNAME :   The Grand Canyon State
STATE MOTTO : God enriches

ARKANSAS

STATEHOOD :   June 15, 1836
NICKNAME :   The Land of Opportunity
STATE MOTTO : The people rule

CALIFORNIA

STATEHOOD :   September 9, 1850
NICKNAME :   The Golden State
STATE MOTTO : *Eureka*!

COLORADO

STATEHOOD :   August 1, 1876
NICKNAME :   The Centennial State
STATE MOTTO : Nothing without providence

CONNECTICUT

STATEHOOD :   January 9, 1788
NICKNAME :   Constitution State
STATE MOTTO : He who transplanted still sustains

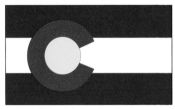

DELAWARE

STATEHOOD :   December 7, 1787
NICKNAME :   The First State
STATE MOTTO : Liberty and independence

STATE FLAGS OF THE UNITED STATES

FLORIDA

Statehood: March 3, 1845
Nickname: Sunshine State
State motto: In God we trust

GEORGIA

Statehood: January 2, 1788
Nickname: Empire state of the South
State motto: Wisdom, justice and moderation

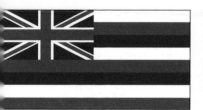

HAWAII

Statehood: August 21, 1959
Nickname: Aloha state
State motto: The life of the land is perpetuated in righteousness

IDAHO

Statehood: July 3, 1890
Nickname: Gem state
State motto: It is forever

ILLINOIS

Statehood: December 3, 1818
Nickname: Prairie state
State motto: State sovereignty, national union

INDIANA

Statehood: December 11, 1816
Nickname: Hoosier state
State motto: Crossroads of America

IOWA

Statehood: December 28, 1846
Nickname: Hawkeye state
State motto: Our liberties we prize and our rights we will maintain

KANSAS

Statehood: January 29, 1861
Nickname: Sunflower state
State motto: To the stars through difficulties

STATE FLAGS OF THE UNITED STATES

KENTUCKY

STATEHOOD : June 1, 1792
NICKNAME : Bluegrass state
STATE MOTTO : United we stand, divided we fall

LOUISIANA

STATEHOOD : April 30, 1812
NICKNAME : Pelican State
STATE MOTTO : Union, Justice and Confidence

MAINE

STATEHOOD : March 15, 1820
NICKNAME : Pine Tree State
STATE MOTTO : I direct

MARYLAND

STATEHOOD : April 28, 1788
NICKNAME : Old Line State, Free State
STATE MOTTO : Manly deeds, womanly words

MASSACHUSETTS

STATEHOOD : February 6, 1788
NICKNAME : Bay State
STATE MOTTO : By the sword we seek peace, but peace only under liberty

MICHIGAN

STATEHOOD : January 26, 1837
NICKNAME : Wolverine State
STATE MOTTO : If you seek a pleasant peninsula, look around you

MINNESOTA

STATEHOOD : May 11, 1858
NICKNAME : Gopher State
STATE MOTTO : Star of the North

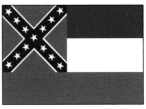

MISSISSIPPI

STATEHOOD : December 10, 1817
NICKNAME : Magnolia State
STATE MOTTO : By valour and arms

STATE FLAGS OF THE UNITED STATES

MISSOURI

STATEHOOD : August 10, 1821
NICKNAME : 'Show me' State
STATE MOTTO : The welfare of the people shall be the supreme law

MONTANA

STATEHOOD : November 8, 1889
NICKNAME : Treasure State
STATE MOTTO : Gold and silver

NEBRASKA

STATEHOOD : March 1, 1867
NICKNAME : The Cornhusker State
STATE MOTTO : Equality before the law

NEVADA

STATEHOOD : October 31, 1864
NICKNAME : The Silver State
STATE MOTTO : All for our country

NEW HAMPSHIRE

STATEHOOD : June 21, 1788
NICKNAME : The Granite State
STATE MOTTO : Live free or die

NEW JERSEY

STATEHOOD : December 18, 1787
NICKNAME : The Garden State
STATE MOTTO : Liberty and prosperity

NEW MEXICO

STATEHOOD : January 16, 1912
NICKNAME : The Land of Enchantment
STATE MOTTO : It grows as it goes

NEW YORK

STATEHOOD : July 26, 1788
NICKNAME : The Empire State
STATE MOTTO : Ever upward

STATE FLAGS OF THE UNITED STATES

NORTH CAROLINA
STATEHOOD : November 21, 1789
NICKNAME : The Tar Heel State
STATE MOTTO : To be, rather than to seem

NORTH DAKOTA
STATEHOOD : November 2, 1889
NICKNAME : The Flickertail State
STATE MOTTO : Liberty and union, now and forever, one and inseparable

OHIO
STATEHOOD : March 1, 1803
NICKNAME : The Buckeye State
STATE MOTTO : With God, all things are possible

OKLAHOMA
STATEHOOD : November 16, 1907
NICKNAME : The Sooner State
STATE MOTTO : Labour conquers all things

OREGON
STATEHOOD : February 14, 1859
NICKNAME : The Beaver State
STATE MOTTO : She flies with her own wings

PENNSYLVANIA
STATEHOOD : December 12, 1787
NICKNAME : The Keystone State
STATE MOTTO : Virtue, liberty and independence

RHODE ISLAND
STATEHOOD : May 29, 1790
NICKNAME : Ocean State
STATE MOTTO : Hope

SOUTH CAROLINA
STATEHOOD : May 23, 1788
NICKNAME : The Palmetto State
STATE MOTTO : Prepared in mind and resources

STATE FLAGS OF THE UNITED STATES

SOUTH DAKOTA
STATEHOOD : November 2, 1889
NICKNAME : The Sunshine State
STATE MOTTO : Under God the people rule

TENNESSEE
STATEHOOD : June 1, 1796
NICKNAME : The Volunteer State
STATE MOTTO : Agriculture and commerce

TEXAS
STATEHOOD : December 29, 1845
NICKNAME : The Lone Star State
STATE MOTTO : Friendship

UTAH
STATEHOOD : January 4, 1896
NICKNAME : The Beehive State
STATE MOTTO : Industry

VERMONT
STATEHOOD : March 4, 1791
NICKNAME : The Green Mountain State
STATE MOTTO : Freedom and unity

VIRGINIA
STATEHOOD : June 25, 1788
NICKNAME : Old Dominion
STATE MOTTO : Thus always to tyrants

WEST VIRGINIA
STATEHOOD : June 20, 1863
NICKNAME : The Mountain State
STATE MOTTO : Mountaineers are always free

WASHINGTON
STATEHOOD : November 11, 1889
NICKNAME : The Evergreen State
STATE MOTTO : *Alki* (Native American for 'by and by')

STATE FLAGS OF THE UNITED STATES

WISCONSIN

STATEHOOD : May 29, 1848
NICKNAME : The Badger State
STATE MOTTO : Forward

WYOMING

STATEHOOD : July 10, 1890
NICKNAME : The Equality State
STATE MOTTO : Equal rights

PROVINCE FLAGS OF CANADA

ALBERTA

RATIO : 1:2
DATE ADOPTED : 1968

BRITISH COLUMBIA

RATIO : 3:5
DATE ADOPTED : 1960

MANITOBA

RATIO : 1:2
DATE ADOPTED : 1966

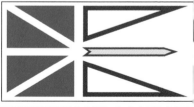

NEW BRUNSWICK

RATIO : 5:8
DATE ADOPTED : 1965

NEWFOUNDLAND & LABRADO

RATIO : 1:2
DATE ADOPTED : 1980

PROVINCE FLAGS OF CANADA

NORTHWEST TERRITORIES
RATIO : 1:2
DATE ADOPTED : 1969

NOVA SCOTIA
RATIO : 3:4
DATE ADOPTED : 1929

NUNAVUT
RATIO : 9:16
DATE ADOPTED : 1999

ONTARIO
RATIO : 1:2
DATE ADOPTED : 1965

PRINCE EDWARD ISLAND
RATIO : 2:3
DATE ADOPTED : 1964

QUÉBEC
RATIO : 2:3
DATE ADOPTED : 1948

SASKATCHEWAN
RATIO : 1:2
DATE ADOPTED : 1964

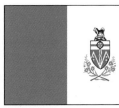

YUKON
RATIO : 1:2
DATE ADOPTED : 1967

STATE FLAGS OF AUSTRALIA

AUSTRALIA CAPITAL TERRITORY
RATIO :   1:2
DATE ADOPTED : 1993

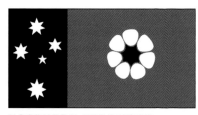

NORTHERN TERRITORY
RATIO :   1:2
DATE ADOPTED : 1978

NEW SOUTH WALES
RATIO :   1:2
DATE ADOPTED : 1876

QUEENSLAND
RATIO :   1:2
DATE ADOPTED : 1876
LAST AMENDED : 1953

SOUTH AUSTRALIA
RATIO :   1:2
DATE ADOPTED : 1904

TASMANIA
RATIO :   1:2
DATE ADOPTED : 1875
LAST AMENDED : 1975

VICTORIA
RATIO :   1:2
DATE ADOPTED : 1870
LAST AMENDED : 1953

WESTERN AUSTRALIA
RATIO :   1:2
DATE ADOPTED : 1953

INTERNATIONAL ORGANIZATION FLAGS

ARAB LEAGUE
Ratio : 1:2
Date Adopted : 1955

ASEAN
Full Name : Association of South-East Asian Nations
Ratio : 1:2
Date Adopted : 1955

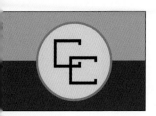

CARICOM
Full Name : Caribbean Community
Ratio : 2:3
Date Adopted : 1983

CIS
Full Name : Commonwealth of Independent States
Ratio : 1:2
Date Adopted : 1996

COMMONWEALTH OF NATIONS
Ratio : 1:2
Date Adopted : 1976

EU
Full Name : European Union
Ratio : 2:3
Date Adopted : 1955 (by the Council of Europe)

NATO
Full Name : North Atlantic Treaty Organization
Ratio : 3:4
Date Adopted : 1953

OAS
Full Name : Organization of American States
Ratio : 2:3
Date Adopted : 1961 (last amended 1991)

INTERNATIONAL ORGANIZATION FLAGS

OPEC
Full Name : Organization of Petroleum Exporting Countries
Ratio : 3:5
Date Adopted : 1970

AU
Full Name : African Union
Ratio : 2:3
Date Adopted : 1970 (by Organization of African Unity)

OLYMPIC MOVEMENT
Full Name : International Olympic Committee (IOC)
Ratio : 2:3
Date Adopted : 1913

RED CRESCENT
Ratio : 1:1
Date Adopted : 1876

RED CROSS
Ratio : 1:1
Date Adopted : 1864

PACIFIC COMMUNITY
Full Name : Secretariat of the Pacific Community (SPC)
Ratio : 7:10
Date Adopted : 1999

UN
Full Name : United Nations
Ratio : 2:3
Date Adopted : 1947

WEU
Full Name : Western European Union
Ratio : 2:3
Date Adopted : 1993

A - *ALPHA*
diver below (when stationary);
I am undergoing a speed trial

B - *BRAVO*
I am taking on or discharging
explosives

C - *CHARLIE*
Yes (affirmative)

D - *DELTA*
Keep clear, manoeuvring with
difficulty

E - *ECHO*
Altering course to starboard

F - *FOXTROT*
Disabled, communicate
with me

G - *GOLF*
I require a pilot

H - *HOTEL*
I have a pilot on board

I - *INDIA*
I am altering my course to
port

J - *JULIETT*
I am going to send a message
by semaphore

K - *KILO*
You should stop your vessel
instantly

L - *LIMA*
Stop, I have something
important to communicate

M - *MIKE*
I have a doctor on board

N - *NOVEMBER*
No (negative)

O - *OSCAR*
Man overboard

P - *PAPA* (*BLUE PETER*)
All aboard, ship is about to sail.
(At sea) Your lights are out

Q - *QUEBEC*
My vessel is healthy and I
request free pratique

R - *ROMEO*
The way is off my ship. You
may feel your way past me

S - *SIERRA*
My engines are going astern

T - *TANGO*
Do not pass ahead of me

U - *UNIFORM*
You are running into danger

V - *VICTOR*
I require assistance
(not distress)

W - *WHISKY*
I require medical assistance

X - *X-RAY*
Stop your intentions, watch
for my signals

Y - *YANKEE*
I am dragging anchor

Z - *ZULU*
I require a tug

A+E I must abandon vessel
C+J Do you require assistance?
C+N Unable to give assistance
J+I Are you aground?
J+L Risk of going aground
J+W I have sprung a leak
K+N I cannot take you in tow
K+N+1 I cannot take you in tow,
but will report you and ask for
immediate assistance

L+N Light (name follows) has
been extinguished
L+O Not in my correct position
L+R Bar is not dangerous
L+S Bar is dangerous
M+F Course to reach me is ...
M+G You should steer course...
N+C I am in distress
N+F You are running into danger
N+G You are in dangerous position

SIGNAL FLAGS *NUMERALS*

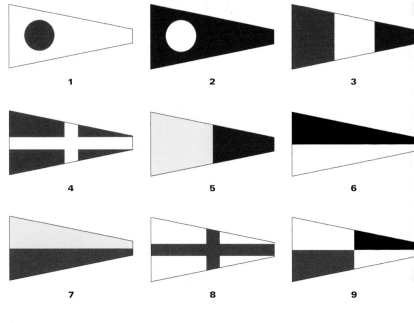

1

2

3

4

5

6

7

8

9

0

NUMERIC PENNANTS

A numeral is added to general messages to provide variation in meaning, to ask or answer a question, or to supplement the basic message.

FIRST REPEATER
Repeats the upper flag or pennant of a hoist.

SECOND REPEATER
Repeats the second flag or pennant of a hoist.

THIRD REPEATER
Repeats the third flag or pennant of a hoist.

ANSWERING PENNANT

ANSWERING PENNANT

The answering pennant is used as a decimal point when sending numeric data. Close up (top of mast), the receiving vessel indicates she understands the hoist.
At the end of the signal, it indicates that the message is complete.

At dip (half-mast), hoisted by receiving vessel as each hoist of the transmitting ship is seen.

USEFUL INFORMATION

Red, Gold, Green
Benin
Burkina Faso
Cameroon
Central African Republic
Congo
Eritrea
Ethiopia
Ghana
Grenada
Guinea
Guinea-Bissau
Guyana
Mali
Mozambique
São Tome and Príncipe
Senegal
Togo

FLAG NAMES

Canada	Maple Leaf Flag
Croatia	*Trobojnica/ Crven-Bijeli-Plavi/ S'ahovnica*
Cuba	*La Estrella Solitaria*
Denmark	*Dannebrog*
France	*Tricolore*
Germany	*Schwarz-Rot-Gold*
Greece	*Galanolefki*
Guyana	Golden Arrow
Indonesia	*Sang Saka/ Merah Putih*
Italy	*Tricolore*
Japan	*Hinomaru*
Netherlands	*Prinsenvlag*
Portugal	*Verde e Rubra*
South Korea	*Tae-Gheuk-Ghi*
Spain	*Rojigualda*
St. Vincent	The Gems
Switzerland	Federal Cross
Thailand	*Trairong*
Turkey	*Ayyildiz*
UK	Union Jack
USA	The Stars and Stripes, Star Spangled Banner *(eight red and seven white stripes, 15 stars)*, Old Glory *(seven red and six white stripes, 24 stars)*

PAN ARAB

Red, White, Black and Green
Afghanistan
Iraq
Jordan
Kuwait
Sudan
Syria
United Arab Emirates

Red, White, Black
Egypt
Yemen

USEFUL ADDRESSES

www.flags.net
www.fotw.ca/flags
www.flaggenlexikon.de/index-e.htm

Fédération internationale des associations vexillologiques (FIAV)
Clos de la Pasture, 6
1340 Ottignies-Louvain-La-Neuve
Belgium

The Flag Institute (FI)
9 Laurel Grove
Chester
CH2 3HU
United Kingdom

The Canadian Flag Association (CFA)
L'Association canadienne de vexillologie
c/o Kevin Harrington
50 Heathfield Drive
Scarborough ON
M1M 3B1
Canada

The Flag Research Center (FRC)
c/o Whitney Smith
P.O. Box 580
Winchester MA 01890-0880
USA

Flag Society of Australia Inc. (FSA)
P.O. Box 4142
Burwood
East Victoria 3151
Australia

NATIONAL FLAG DAYS (FIXED)

* = official national flag day
§ = independence day

Afghanistan   Apr 27
Albania   Jan 11, Apr 7*, Nov 29
Algeria   Jul 5§, Nov 1
Andorra   Sep 8
Angola   Nov 11§
Antigua and Barbuda
  Feb 27*, Nov 1
Argentina   Apr 2, May 25,
Jun 20*, Jul 9§, Jul 25*, Aug 17,
Oct 12
Armenia   Apr 7, Apr 24, May
28, Sep 20§
Australia   Jan 26, Apr 25,
May 22*, Aug 20, Sep 3*
Austria   May 1*, Oct 26§
Azerbaijan   May 28, Aug 30§
Bahamas   Jul 9§, Oct 12
Bahrain   Dec 16
Bangladesh   Feb 25*, Mar 26§,
Dec 16§
Barbados   Nov 30
Belarus   Jul 27§
Belgium   Jan 23* Jul 21§,
Oct 4§, Nov 11, Nov 15
Belize   Mar 9, Sep 10, Sep
20§, Nov 19
Benin   Aug 1§, Nov 16*, Nov 30
Bhutan   Nov 11
Bolivia   Jul 16, Aug 6§, Nov 30*
Bosnia and Herzegovina
  Apr 5§, May 4*
Botswana   Jul 20, Sep 30§
Brazil   Apr 21, Apr 22, Sep
7§, Nov 15, Nov 19*
Brunei   Feb 23§, May 31, Jul 16
Bulgaria   Feb 6, Mar 3§, May
24, Sep 9, Nov 7
Burkina Faso   Aug 4§
Burma   Jan 4§, Feb 12,
Mar 2, Mar 27, Jul 19
Burundi   Jul 1§
Cambodia   Apr 17§, Nov 9§
Cameroon   Jan 1§, Feb 11,
May 20, Aug 12
Canada   Feb 15*, Apr 17,
Jul 1, Oct 18, Nov 11
Cape Verde   Jan 20, Jul 5§, Sep
12, Sep 25*
Central African Republic
  Aug 13§, Dec 1
Chad   Jun 7, Aug 11§, Nov 6*,
Nov 26
Chile   May 21, Sep 18§,
Oct 12, Oct 18*
China   May 4, Jun 1, Oct 1
Colombia   Jul 20§, Aug 7, Oct
12, Nov 11, Nov 26*
Comoros   May 13, Jul 6§
Congo   Jul 31, Aug 14§
Congo, Democratic Republic of
  Jun 24, Jun 30§, Nov 17, Nov
21*
Costa Rica   Apr 11, Sep 15§,
Oct 12, Oct 21*
Côte d'Ivoire   Aug 7§
Croatia   Jan 6, May 9, May
30, Jun 22, Aug 5, Aug 15, Nov 1
Cuba   Jan 1, May 20§, Oct 27
Cyprus   Mar 25, Apr 1, Oct 1§
Czech Republic   May 8, Jun 5,
Jul 6, Oct 28
Denmark   Mar 28, Apr 9, Apr
16, Apr 27, Apr 29, May 5, May
26, Jun 5, Jun 7, Jun 11, Jun 15

Djibouti   Jun 27§
Dominica   Nov 3§, Nov 9*
Dominican Republic
  Feb 27§, Aug 16, Nov 6*
East Timor   May 20§
Ecuador   May 24, Jul 24, Aug 10§,
Oct 9, Oct 12, Nov 3
Egypt   Feb 28§, Apr 25, May 2,
Jun 18, Jul 23, Oct 24
El Salvador   Sep 15§, Oct 6, Oct
12, Nov 5
Equatorial Guinea   Mar 5, Jul 7,
Oct 12§
Eritrea   May 24§, Jun 20
Estonia   Feb 24§, May 12, Jun 14,
Jun 23, Aug 20§, Nov 16
Ethiopia   Apr 6, May 28, Sep 12
Fiji   Jul 25, Oct 10
Finland   Feb 5, Feb 28, Apr 9,
Apr 27, May 29*, Nov 6, Dec 6§
France   May 8, Jul 14, Nov 11
Gabon   Mar 12, Aug 9, Aug 17§
Gambia   Feb 18§, Apr 24
Georgia   Mar 31§, May 26§
Germany   May 3, May 5,
May 9*, May 23, Oct 3, Nov 16
Ghana   Mar 6§, Jul 1
Greece   Mar 25§, Oct 28
Grenada   Feb 7§, Mar 13, Oct 25
Guatemala   Jun 30, Sep 15§,
Oct 12, Oct 20
Guinea   Apr 3, Nov 10*
Guinea-Bissau   Sep 10§, Sep 12
Guyana   Feb 23, May 26§
Haiti   Jan 1§, May 18*, Nov 11
Honduras   Jan 18*, Feb 1§,
Sep 15§, Oct 12, Oct 16, Oct 21,
Oct 23
Hungary   Mar 15, Apr 4, Jun
16, Aug 20
Iceland   Jun 7, Jun 17, Oct 9
India   Jan 26, Aug 15§,
Aug 31*, Oct 2
Indonesia   Jan 27*, Aug 17§,
Sep 9
Iran   Feb 11, Apr 1
Iraq   Jul 14, Jul 17, Oct 3
Ireland   Mar 17, Oct 6
Israel   Apr 24§
Jamaica   May 23, Aug 5§
Japan   Jan 14, Feb 11, Apr 29,
May 3, May 5, Aug 6*, Sep 15,
Nov 3, Nov 23
Jordan   May 25§, Jun 10,
Aug 11
Kazakstan   Oct 25
Kenya   Jun 1, Oct 20, Dec 12§
Kiribati   Jul 12§
Korea, North   Feb 16, Mar 1, Apr
15, Sep 9
Korea, South   Jan 25*, Mar 1,
Jun 6, Jul 17, Aug 15, Oct 1, Oct
3
Kuwait   Feb 26*Sep 7*
Kyrgyzstan   Mar 3*, Aug 31§
Laos   Jan 6, Jan 20, Jun 1, Jul
19§, Aug 23
Latvia   May 12, Nov 18
Lebanon   Nov 22§
Lesotho   Jan 20, Mar 12, Jul
17, Oct 4§
Liberia   Feb 11, Apr 7, May
14, Jul 26§, Aug 27*, Nov 29
Libya   Sep 1, Dec 24§
Liechtenstein   Feb 14, Aug 16,
Sep 26, Oct 5

Lithuania   May 5, Jul 6
Luxembourg   Jun 12*, Jun 23,
Sep 19
Macedonia, Former Yugoslav Rep
  Jan 2§, Aug 2, Nov 16
Madagascar   Mar 29, Jun 26§,
Oct 14*
Malawi   Mar 3, May 14, Jul 6§
Malaysia   Aug 31§
Maldives   Jul 26§, Nov 11
Mali   Feb 10, Mar 1*,
Sep 22§, Nov 19
Malta   Mar 31§, Jun 7, Jun 29
Marshall Islands   May 1, Oct 21§
Mauritania   Apr 1*, Nov 28§
Mauritius   Mar 12§
Mexico   Feb 5, Feb 19, Feb
24*, Mar 21, May 5, Jun 1, Sep
16§, Oct 12, Oct 23, Nov 20
Micronesia, Federated States of
  May 10, Nov 3§
Moldova   Aug 27§
Monaco   Jan 27, Apr 4*, Nov 19
Mongolia   Jul 11
Morocco   Mar 2§, Mar 3,
May 23, Jul 9, Aug 14, Nov 6,
Nov 17*, Nov 18§
Mozambique   Feb 3, Jun 1, Jun
24§, Sep 5*, Sep 25
Namibia   Mar 21§, Aug 26, Oct 7
Nauru   Jan 31§
Nepal   Jan 11, Feb 18, Nov 7
Netherlands   Jan 19, Jan 31, Feb
19*, Apr 27, Apr 30, May 4, May
5, Jun 29, Sep 6, Dec 15
New Zealand   Feb 6, Apr 25, Jun
12*
Nicaragua   Jul 19, Sep 14, Oct
12
Niger   May 18, Aug 3§, Nov 23*,
Dec 18
Nigeria   Oct 1§
Norway   Feb 21, May 8,
May 17, Jun 7, Jul 4, Jul 17*, Jul
20, Jul 29, Sep 22, Dec 10
Oman   Nov 18
Pakistan   Mar 23, Aug 14§,
Sep 6, Sep 11
Palau   Mar 15, May 5, Jun
1, Jun 13*, Jul 9, Oct 1§, Oct 24
Panama   Jan 1, Jun 4*, Oct
11, Oct 12, Nov 1, Nov 3§, Nov
28§
Papua New Guinea   Sep 16§
Paraguay   May 14§, Jun 12,
Aug 15, Aug 25, Nov 27*
Peru   Feb 25*, Jun 24, Jun 29,
Aug 30, Oct 8
Philippines   May 6, May 28§, Jun
9, Jun 12§, Jul 4, Nov 30, Dec 30
Poland   May 3, Jul 22§, Nov 11§
Portugal   Apr 25, Jul 10, Jun
30*, Oct 5, Dec 1§
Qatar   Sep 3§
Romania   Aug 23
Russia   Feb 23, May 9, Jun
12, Nov 7
Rwanda   Jan 28, Apr 7, Jul
1§, Jul 5, Sep 25
Saint Kitts and Nevis   Sep 19§
Saint Lucia   Jan 22, Feb 22§,
Mar 1*
Saint Vincent and the Grenadines
  Jan 22, Oct 27§
Samoa   Jan 1§, Sep 5
San Marino   Feb 5§, Sep 4

São Tome and Príncipe
  Jul 12§, Sep 6
Saudi Arabia   Sep 23
Senegal   Apr 4§, Jul 14
Seychelles   Jun 5, Jun 29§
Sierra Leone   Apr 19
Singapore   Aug 9§
Slovak Republic   Aug 29, Sep 1
Slovenia   Feb 8, Apr 27, Jun
24§, Oct 29, Dec 26§
Solomon Islands   Jul 7§, Nov 18*
Somalia   Jun 26§, Jul 1§, Oct 21
South Africa   Mar 21, Apr 27,
May 10, May 31§, Jun 16, Aug 9,
Sep 24
Spain   Apr 22, Jul 25, Aug
29*, Oct 12, Oct 15
Sri Lanka   Feb 4§, May 22
Sudan   Jan 1§, Apr 6, May
20*, Jun 30
Suriname   Jul 1, Jul 22, Nov 25§
Swaziland   Apr 19, Apr 25*,
Aug 1, Sep 6§
Sweden   Jan 28, Mar 12, Apr 30,
May 18, Jun 6*, Jul 14,
Aug 8, Nov 6, Dec 10, Dec 23
Switzerland   Jan 2
Syria   Mar 8, Apr 17§
Taiwan   Mar 12, Mar 29, Sep 28,
Oct 10, Oct 25, Oct 28*,
Oct 29, Nov 12
Tajikistan   Sep 9§
Tanzania   Jan 12, Apr 26, Jun
30*, Jul 7
Thailand   Apr 6, May 5, Sep 28*
Togo   Jan 13, Apr 27§
Tonga   Apr 25, May 4, Jun 4,
Nov 4
Trinidad and Tobago
  May 24, Jun 19,
Aug 5, Sep 24, Nov 16
Tunisia   Jan 18, Mar 20§, Mar 21,
Apr 9, Jul 25, Aug 31§,
Oct 15, Nov 7
Turkey   Apr 23§, May 19, Jun 5*,
Aug 30, Oct 29, Nov 10
Turkmenistan   Feb 19*, Oct 27§
Tuvalu   Oct 1§
Uganda   Apr 11, May 27,
Oct 9§
Ukraine   May 9, Aug 24§
United Arab Emirates   Dec 2§
United Kingdom   Feb 6, Feb 19,
Mar 10, Apr 21, Jun 2, Jun 10,
Aug 4, Aug 15, Aug 20, Nov 5,
Nov 11
United States of America
  Jan 15, Feb 12, May 22, Jun 14*,
Jul 4, Sep 17, Oct 21, Oct 27,
Nov 11
Uruguay   Apr 19, May 18, Jun 19,
Jul 18, Aug 25§, Oct 12
Uzbekistan   Sep 1§, Oct 11*
Vanuatu   Mar 5, Jul 30, Oct
5, Oct 25
Vatican   Feb 11§, May 18, Oct 22
Venezuela   Mar 12*, Apr 19
Jun 24, Jul 5§, Oct 12
Vietnam   Apr 30, May 19
Sep 2, Nov 30*
Yemen   May 22, Sep 26
Oct 14, Nov 30*
Yugoslavia   Apr 27, Jul 4, Nov 29
Zambia   Mar 19, Oct 24
Zimbabwe   Apr 18§, Aug 11